THE POETS AND THEIR CRITICS

THE POETS AND THEIR CRITICS

THE POETS
AND THEIR CRITICS

Blake to Browning

HUGH SYKES DAVIES

Fellow of St. John's College
Cambridge

HUTCHINSON OF LONDON

HUTCHINSON & CO. (*Publishers*) LTD
178–202 Great Portland Street, London, W.1

London Melbourne Sydney
Auckland Bombay Toronto
Johannesburg New York

★

First published June 1962
Second impression December 1963
Third impression February 1966

This book has been set in Times, printed in Great Britain
on Antique Wove paper by Anchor Press and
bound by Wm. Brendon, both of Tiptree, Essex

Contents

Acknowledgements

For permission to use copyright material, acknowledgements are gladly made to:

W. H. Auden and Phoenix House Ltd (*Tennyson, A Selection*)

The Bodley Head Ltd (J. M. Robertson, *New Essays towards a Critical Method*)

Bowes & Bowes Ltd (E. Butler, *Byron and Goethe*)

Jonathan Cape Ltd (*The Autobiography of Mark Rutherford;* John Middleton Murry, *William Blake;* A. Symons, *William Blake*)

Cassell & Co. Ltd ('Byron' in *From Anne to Victoria*, ed. Bonamy Dobrée)

Chatto & Windus Ltd (A. Herzen, *My Past and Thoughts*, trans. Constance Garnett; F. R. Leavis, *Revaluation*)

Constable & Co. Ltd (Don Salvator de Madariaga, *Shelley and Calderon and Other Essays on English and Spanish Poetry*: George Santayana, *Interpretation of Poetry and Religion*)

Gerald Duckworth & Co. Ltd (B. de Selincourt, *William Blake*)

T. S. Eliot and Faber & Faber Ltd ('Blake' in *Selected Essays 1920*; *The Use of Poetry and the Use of Criticism 1933*)

John Farquharson Ltd and the James Estate (Henry James, *English Hours, Notes on Novelists, The Middle Years*)

William Heinemann Ltd (Sir Herbert Read, *In Defence of Shelley*)

The Literary Trustees of Walter de la Mare, The Society of Authors and Victor Gollancz Ltd (Walter de la Mare, 'Epitaph for Blake' in *The Divine Vision* ed. V. de Sola Pinto)

7

Macmillan & Co. Ltd (A. C. Bradley, *A Miscellany; Collected Essays of W. P. Ker* ed. Charles Wibley)

Sir Harold Nicolson and Constable & Co. Ltd (*Tennyson*)

Quarterly Review and John Murray Ltd (Percy Lubbock's review of Robert Browning's poems in *The Quarterly Review*, October 1912)

Routledge & Kegan Paul Ltd ('Wordsworth' from *Collected Poems of Sidney Keyes*)

The Society of Authors (John Middleton Murry, *Studies in Keats New and Old*)

Mrs W. B. Yeats and Macmillan & Co. Ltd ('Ideas of Good and Evil' from *Essays* by W. B. Yeats)

Preface

Though the general plan of this volume is the same as that of the first, it has somehow produced a rather different result. A part of this difference is no doubt due to my own lengthening years, with their slight diminution of ignorance, and their disproportionate growth in consciousness of ignorance. It has been more painstakingly compiled than the first volume, but not on that account any better. Other differences, of much greater interest and importance, have resulted from the great differences between the materials on which the two volumes have been based.

The poets criticized are seven, and perhaps there will be no fierce quarrel over the inclusion of any of them. But the exclusion of Coleridge might well excite some tart comment. Is it implied that he is a lesser poet than Tennyson, or Browning, or Shelley? By no means. He has been omitted solely because the criticism written on his poetry seemed to be either uninstructive or incapable of being included in this particular collection. His quality was recognized at once, and described in terms which left little more to later critics than repetition with elegant variations, so that the strictly critical comment upon Coleridge lacks contour, those ups and downs which make for interest, with their air of a continuing discussion, of discoveries and rediscoveries. The really interesting work on Coleridge has been in the field of scholarship, rather than of criticism. Professor Lowes' study of the process of poetic creation, in *The Road to Xanadu*, was a notable achievement, and it has been followed by fascinating studies of the same kind. Such work has, of course, a critical effect, in the sense that it may change—even raise—our opinion of the poetry which it explores; but the means employed are not those of criticism. Moreover, they are so massive, involving such a

spacious deployment of sources and interpretations, that they
entirely fail to lend themselves to the cut-and-come-again
occasions of the anthologist.

The same reason must be pleaded in excuse and explanation
to those readers who feel surprised (as I did myself) at the
comparative lack of modern criticism on most of these poets.
It is not, of course, that criticism came to an end in about
1910. It did, however, direct the best of its energies elsewhere,
to the seventeenth and eighteenth centuries. The Romantics
concerned it less, either because Romantic poetry was somewhat out of fashion or because nearly everything possible had
been said about it already. Thus it was left chiefly to the
scholars and biographers: moreover, what criticism there has
been is still easily accessible, and in the hands of readers
without the aid of an anthology.

This situation, however, is something more than a helpful
source of excuse and explanation for my own shortcomings.
It is a natural, and in some ways instructive, result of the broad
differences between the two tracts of material on which these
two volumes of poets and their critics have been based. The
first, dealing with poetry from Chaucer to Gray, was selected
from the whole mass of English criticism from the fifteenth
century to the twentieth. This second volume, dealing only
with the Romantic and Victorian poets, is confined to the
writings of the last century and a half. This great difference
of scale has produced a very different kind of map. In the
first volume there were broad outlines to follow, such as the
revolutions of poetic practice and theory generally called the
'Augustan' and the 'Romantic'. Here we are faced by a more
confused and niggling picture, lacking major features, but rich
in minor eddies of fashion, delicate adjustments of taste, and
nice discriminations of emphasis.

Some such foreshortening would no doubt have resulted
from such an alteration of time-scale, to whatever period of
criticism it had been applied. But its effect is all the more
marked upon this particular period because of certain characteristics peculiar to itself. Its beginning is in the midst of one
revolution, the Romantic; and its end is in another revolution
not yet officially nomenclatured by literary historians, no doubt

because it is still slightly in progress, and for the time being the word 'modern' serves to describe it in a vague and provisional fashion. Between the beginning and the end, however, lies a dismal interim of nearly a century, when the Romantic impulse was ebbing away and the new tide had not made its direction felt. It was indeed a trying time for poets and their critics. There hung about them a dim sense that the poetry of the Victorian age was not yet quite worthy of an age of such obvious greatness, yet they could not very well see how to make it much better, though they cast about, with ant-like industry and confusion, to find an effective nostrum for it. They discussed, at very great length, the nature of poetry itself. Should it depend mainly upon sensation and emotion or upon thought and reflection? Or upon some intricate mixture of these apparent opposites? Should it come to grips remorselessly with the modern world or should it keep an imaginative distance from it? Had the true and promising line of poetic descent come down to them through Wordsworth, or Byron, or Keats and Shelley, or Keats, or Shelley?

From these large and on the whole praiseworthy discussions, which are illustrated in this volume, there emerged at least two positive achievements. The first belongs to criticism, and it consisted essentially of an effective differentiation between the four chief poets who had, by the chances of time, been made to look as though they were the leaders of one more or less coherent movement, the Romantic revolution. If it now seems almost incredible that any sensitive and intelligent reader should ever have spoken of Wordsworth, Byron, Keats, and Shelley in the same breath, this incredulity is largely the end-product of the passionate discussions conducted by the Victorians. And it is, after all, very unlikely that any future revolution of taste will substantially alter their final (but by no means unanimous) verdict that Wordsworth was a very great poet indeed, Keats a good, if small one, Byron and Shelley hardly poets at all, though no doubt rich in fascination of a different order.

The second achievement of these great and exhaustive Victorian discussions was exhaustion itself: the final exhaustion of the possibility that the way back to better poetry

lay somewhere among the paths trodden by the four great
Romantic predecessors. It was, no doubt, somewhat negative
in character, but there are moments in the development of
literature when a negative must be established before the
direction which leads to a new positive can become clear.
The fact that the Romantic models had been so thoroughly
explored, and found wanting no less thoroughly, made it
easier for the poets of the new revolution, in the present
century, to turn to quite different models, and to seek their
starting-point in the older tradition of pre-Romantic poetry.
It so happens, however, that the negative character of this
side of the Victorian achievement casts something of a shadow
over these collections of criticism. It would have made a
rousing conclusion to the various sections in it to have quoted
a notable tribute by a distinguished modern poet to some
Romantic or Victorian forerunner. But it has not been possible,
for distinguished modern poets do not have Romantic or
Victorian forerunners. That is a fact of literary history, as
unalterable as it is important. The Romantic impulse, after
its long ebb, has finally run dry among the grains of fine sand
sifted by scholars and critics. As for the poets, you would as
soon find one denying Wordsworth to be a great poet as one
writing directly under his influence. Thus Mr G. S. Fraser,
certainly one of those who has his finger on the pulse of modern
poetry, wrote in the essay which he contributed to the volume
celebrating the centenary of Wordsworth's death in 1950:
'He was a very great man and I do not begrudge him his
return to fashion; but there are dangers, and I have tried
to indicate them, in setting him up as a model of poetic
style.'

But if the Romantic movement ended rather in a whimper
than a bang it is the more necessary to recall, and with a more
solidly circumstantial realization than our usual perfunctory
recognition of historical facts, that its beginning was rever-
berantly explosive. The outrage felt by the literary and social
Establishment on the first appearance of the Romantic poets
is in itself strong evidence that a very real effort of spirit, of
imagination, and of courage was needed to be a Wordsworth, a
Keats, a Byron, or a Shelley. All of them achieved something

in their day, the intrinsic difficulty of which is largely concealed from their modern readers by their success in doing it. They have, by now, completed that task which Wordsworth described as being incumbent upon every great and *original* author, 'of *creating* the taste by which he is to be enjoyed'. But the magnitude and nature of their task can now be sensed at its true worth only if the original battlefield of the early reviews is, however slightly, reconstructed. Some pains have been taken to make each of the following sections begin with the materials for such a reconstruction.

Of this nearly forgotten battlefield, and of its general appearance in 1831, at the moment when the Victorians occupied the positions established by the Romantics, the following account seems to me specially illuminating. It was written by a young man of twenty, himself a poet and a friend of poets, who saw the picture, not as we see it in the faded aspect of a period print, but in the fresher light of contemporary concern. Its comment is not, perhaps, very profound, but it has clearness and a remarkable prescience. The distinction, for example, between the poetry of 'sensation' and the poetry of 'reflection' will be found constantly repeated, in not very different terms, by later critics: indeed it was echoed only two years later by John Stuart Mill in the essay from which extracts are given on pp. 71–3 and 162–3. And the argument that any poetic creation not predominantly motivated by 'the desire of beauty' is 'false in art' looks forward no less acutely to the doctrine of art for art's sake in the later years of the century. It was written by Hallam, and, wrong as Tennyson certainly was in many things, he may well have been right in regarding the death of his friend as a heavy loss, not only to himself but to literature:

. . . When Mr Wordsworth, in his celebrated Preface to the *Lyrical Ballads*, asserted that immediate or rapid popularity was not the test of poetry, great was the consternation and clamour among those formers of public favour, the established critics. Never had so audacious an attack been made upon their undoubted privileges and hereditary charter of oppression.

'What! *The Edinburgh Review* not infallible!' shrieked the amiable petulance of Mr Jeffrey.

'*The Gentleman's Magazine* incapable of decision!' faltered the feeble garrulity of Silvanus Urban.

And straightway the whole sciolist herd, men of rank, men of letters, men of wealth, men of business, all the 'mob of gentlemen who think with ease', and a terrible number of old ladies and boarding-school misses began to scream in chorus, and prolonged the notes of execration with which they overwhelmed the new doctrine, until their wits and their voices fairly gave in from exhaustion. Much, no doubt, they did, for much persons will do when they fight for their dear selves: but there was one thing they could not do, and unfortunately it was the only one of any importance. They could not put down Mr Wordsworth by clamour, or prevent his doctrine, once uttered, and enforced by his example, from awakening the minds of men, and giving a fresh impulse to art. It was the truth, and it prevailed; not only against the exasperation of that hydra, the Reading Public, whose vanity was hurt, and the blustering of its keepers, whose delusion was exposed, but even against the false glosses and narrow apprehensions of the Wordsworthians themselves. It is the madness of all who loosen some great principle, long buried under a snow-heap of custom and superstition, to imagine that they can restrain its operation, or circumscribe it by their purpose. But the right of private judgment was stronger than the will of Luther; and even the genius of Wordsworth cannot expand itself to the full periphery of poetic art.

It is not true, as his exclusive admirers would have it, that the highest species of poetry is the reflective; it is a gross fallacy that, because certain opinions are acute or profound, the expression of them by the imagination must be eminently beautiful. Whenever the mind of the artist suffers itself to be occupied, during its periods of creation, by any other predominant motive than the desire of beauty, the result is false in art.

Now there is undoubtedly no reason why he may not find beauty in those moods of emotion, which arise from the combinations of reflective thought; and it is possible that he may delineate these with fidelity, and not be led astray by any suggestions of an unpoetical mood. But though possible, it is hardly probable; for a man whose reveries take a reasoning turn, and who is accustomed to measure his ideas by their logical relations rather than the congruity of the sentiments to which they refer, will be apt to mistake the pleasure he has in knowing a thing to be true, for the pleasure he would have in knowing it to be beautiful, and so will pile his thoughts in a rhetorical battery, that they may convince, instead of letting them flow in a natural course of contemplation, that they may enrapture.

It would not be difficult to shew, by reference to the most admired poems of Wordsworth, that he is frequently chargeable with this error; and that much has been said by him which is good as philosophy, powerful as rhetoric, but false as poetry. Perhaps this very distortion of the truth did more in the peculiar juncture of our literary affairs to enlarge and liberalize the genius of our age than could have been effected by a less sectarian temper.

However this may be, a new school of reformers began to attract attention, who, professing the same independence of immediate favour, took their stand on a different region of Parnassus from that occupied by the Lakers, and one, in our opinion, much less liable to perturbing currents of air from ungenial climates. We shall not hesitate to express our conviction, that the cockney school (as it was termed in derision from a cursory view of its accidental circumstances) contained more genuine inspiration, and adhered more steadily to that portion of truth which it embraced, than any *form* of art that has existed in this country since the days of Milton. Their *caposetta* was Mr Leigh Hunt, who did little more than point the way, and was diverted from his aim by a thousand personal predilections and political habits of thought.

But he was followed by two men of very superior make; men who were born poets, lived poets, and went poets to their untimely graves. Shelley and Keats were indeed of opposite genius; that of the one was vast, impetuous and sublime, the other seemed to be 'fed with honey-dew', and to have 'drunk the milk of Paradise'. Even the softness of Shelley comes out in bold, rapid, comprehensive strokes; he has no patience for minute beauties, unless they can be massed into a general effect of grandeur. On the other hand, the tenderness of Keats cannot sustain a lofty flight; he does not generalize or allegorize Nature; his imagination works with few symbols, and reposes willingly on what is given freely.

Yet in this formal opposition of character there is, it seems to us, a groundwork of similarity sufficient for the purposes of classification, and constituting a remarkable point in the progress of literature. They are both poets of sensation rather than reflection. Susceptible of the slightest impulse from external nature, their fine organs trembled into emotion at colours, and sounds, and movements, unperceived or unregarded by duller temperaments. Rich and clear were their perceptions of visible forms; full and deep their feelings of music. So vivid was the delight attending the simple exertions of eye and ear, that it became mingled more and more with their trains of active thought, and tended to absorb their whole being into the energy of sense. Other poets *seek* for images to illustrate their conceptions; these men had no need to seek; they lived in a world of images; for the most important and extensive portion of their life consisted in those emotions which are immediately conversant with the sensation. Like the hero of Goethe's novel, they would hardly have been affected by what is called the pathetic parts of a book; but the *merely beautiful* passages, 'those from which the spirit of the author looks clearly and mildly forth', would have melted them to tears. Hence they are not descriptive, they are picturesque. They are not smooth and *negatively* harmonious; they are full of deep and varied melodies.

This powerful tendency of imagination to a life of immediate sympathy with the external universe, is not nearly so liable to false views of art as the opposite disposition of purely intellectual contemplation. For where beauty is constantly passing before 'that inward eye, which is the bliss of solitude'; where the soul seeks it as a perpetual and necessary refreshment to the sources of activity and intuition; where all the other sacred ideas of our nature, the idea of good, the idea of perfection, the idea of truth, are habitually contemplated through the medium of this predominant mood, so that they assume its colour, and are subject to its peculiar laws, there is little danger that the ruling passion of the whole mind will cease to direct its creative operations, or the energetic principle of love for the beautiful sink, even for a brief period, to the level of a mere notion in the understanding.

From a review of Tennyson's poems in *The Englishman's Magazine*, 1831.

Another passage is given on pp. 245-7.

Blake

The earlier history of Blake criticism presents, at first sight, a picture very like that of Wordsworth criticism, but even more extreme in its impression of blank neglect and incomprehension on the part of an age which had nearly lost the ability to read imaginative poetry. And the early admirers of Blake were, like those of Wordsworth, a chosen few—but even choicer and fewer.

A more careful second glance, however, suggests that this picture needs some substantial alterations. First, it must be remembered that Blake's writings were available to the reading public only in a very special and limited degree; they were hardly 'published' in the usual sense of the word. His early poems, Poetical Sketches, *were privately printed and seem not to have been offered for sale in the usual manner—nor to have been sent to the reviewers. His later and more characteristic works were all engraved and illustrated by Blake himself, and they were on sale at his own house, nowhere else. They were 'collectors' pieces' from the start, and the number of those who collected them was naturally small. Among them, however, it is clear that the poems (in the more ordinary sense of the word) were appreciated at something like their real value.*

The second kind of distortion in the early critical picture is that caused by Blake's simultaneous use of two means of expression, verbal and visual. To many of his contemporaries he was primarily an engraver, and only incidentally a writer. Later in the nineteenth century the emphasis shifted—Ruskin thought poorly of the illustrations, but highly of the poetry. Modern Blake criticism and scholarship often returns to the obviously fairer and sounder task of taking both together, as Blake intended them to be taken: examples of this type of criticism, however, can hardly be given in this book, for they require illustrations, and perhaps take us somewhat beyond the limits of literary criticism.

But the third alteration required in the first simple picture is much the most difficult. Only a small part of Blake's output was in the form of verse of a more or less traditional kind; much the greater part, that which forms the Prophetic Books and everything like them, was quite different in its literary texture. Are we justified in separating the more traditional verse from the rest? Clearly not, for though the literary form may be different, the thought and feeling is continuous. All modern expositors of Blake take his work as a whole, and they must be right to do so. Yet their example can hardly be followed in this anthology, and our extracts must deal, in the main, with what is more simply and obviously Blake's 'poetry', even though this choice leads to serious distortions. Something, however, may be said in defence of this amputation. Much of the poetry in Songs of Innocence, Songs of Experience, and the Rossetti MS is accessible to the ordinary reader, even if his access to it depends upon a rather blinkered vision of its content. The Prophetic Books, on the other hand, demand a very extra-ordinary reader indeed, one who feels at home in the modes of thought, feeling, and expression characteristic of mysticism. The first enthusiast for Blake's writing was just such an extra-ordinary reader, Dr Garth Wilkinson, editor of Swedenborg and author of mystical prose and verse. In 1839 he reprinted Blake's Songs of Innocence and Songs of Experience, with a preface which condemns the Prophetic Books on the ground that in them Blake had 'naturalized the spiritual instead of spiritual-izing the natural'. Yet his condemnation is not that of in-comprehension, or of the mere blindness which makes the ordinary reader call these works simply 'mad'; it is the view of a man who talks the same language but takes a different view of a similar mystical world. And most of Blake's more recent critics and commentators have been of the same temper. They have been not so much literary critics as religious prophets, or at least commentators upon a prophet.

It has been under the influence of this type of exegesis that Blake's reputation has so astoundingly advanced after that initial period of almost complete neglect. Surely no ordinary *critic, lacking in special prophetic insight, could have foreseen in 1861 that by 1961 Blake would have been placed very high among our poets and would have generated such a vast body of comment. This extraordinary, this exponential, increase of reputation is surely something of a portent, but of what? Perhaps of the growth of a truer vision of religion, of the relations between body and soul, reason and imagination. Perhaps of the growing prevalence in the modern world of that special temperament which is at home with spirit-rapping, Swedenborg, Behmen, Borley Rectory, the Ghosts of Versailles, Teilhard de Chardin; whose characteristic typographical mode of expression is to use capital letters for words which are not proper names (Middleton Murry for example writes: 'We insist that Blake . . . was a great man of Science') and whose theories of the world have a strong tendency to rely upon Vibrations. It is no doubt evidence of some kind of greatness in Blake that his study now raises, and so inevitably, such vast issues as the relation between the science of laboratories and the Science of Middleton Murry; between the religion of the various churches and the Religions that are now being so extensively made at home with Do-it-Yourself Gods.*

BLAKE

Allegory addressed to the Intellectual powers, while it is altogether hidden from the Corporeal Understanding, is My Definition of the Most Sublime Poetry; it is also somewhat in the same manner defin'd by Plato.

Letter to Butts   1803

If it were not for the Poetic or Prophetic character, the Philosophic & Experimental would soon be at the ratio of all things, & stand still, unable to do other than repeat the same dull round over again.

There is no Natural Religion

Principle 1st. That the Poetic Genius is the true Man, and that the body or outward form of Man is derived from the Poetic Genius. . . .

Principle 2d. As all men are alike in outward form, so (and with the same infinite variety) all are alike in the Poetic Genius.

Principle 3d. No man can think, write, or speak from his heart, but he must intend truth. Thus all sects of Philosophy are from the Poetic Genius adapted to the weaknesses of every individual.

All Religions are One

COLERIDGE

I have this morning been reading a strange publication—*viz.* Poems with very wild and interesting pictures as swathing, etched (I suppose) but it is said printed and painted by the author, W. Blake. He is a man of Genius—and I apprehend a Swedenborgian—certainly a mystic *emphatically*. You may perhaps smile at *my* calling another poet a *Mystic*; but verily I am in the very mire of common-place common-place compared with Mr Blake, apo- or rather—ana-calyptic Poet, and Painter!

Letter to the Rev. H. F. Cary 1818

HAZLITT

. . . . I showed Hazlitt Blake's *Young* (1). He saw no merit in them as designs. I read him some of the poems. He was much struck with them and expressed himself with his usual strength and singularity. 'They are beautiful,' he said, 'and only too deep for the vulgar. He has no sense of the ludicrous, and, as to God, a worm crawling in a privy is as worthy an object as any other, all being to him indifferent. So to Blake the Chimney Sweeper etc. He is ruined by vain struggles to get rid of what presses on his brain—he attempts impossibles.'

Crabb Robinson's *Diary* 1811

SOUTHEY

Southey had been with Blake, and admired both his designs and his poetic talents, at the same time that he held

(1) Figures in the text refer to Appendix, pp. 339-42.

him for a decided madman. Blake, he says, spoke of his visions with the diffidence that is usual with such people, and did not seem to expect that he should be believed. He showed Southey a perfectly mad poem called *Jerusalem*—Oxford Street is in Jerusalem.

Crabb Robinson's *Diary* 1811

WORDSWORTH

. . . . Wordsworth said after reading . . . the *Songs of Innocence and Experience* showing the two opposite sides of the human soul—'There is no doubt this poor man was mad, but there is something in the madness of this man which interests me more than the sanity of Lord Byron and Walter Scott.' (2)

Crabb Robinson's *Reminiscences* 1852

[The remark was probably made in 1812]

LAMB

His poems have been sold hitherto only in Manuscript. I never read them; but a friend at my desire produced the *Sweep Song*. There is one to a tiger, which I have heard recited, beginning (3)

Tiger, Tiger, burning bright,
Thro' the deserts of the night, (3)

which is glorious, but alas! I have not the book; for the man is flown, whither I know not—to Hades or a Madhouse. But I must look on him as one of the most extraordinary persons of the age.

Letter to Barton 1824

CRABB ROBINSON

I have mentioned Blake. I forget whether I ever mentioned to you this very interesting man, with whom I am now become

acquainted. . . . I gave your brother some poems in MS. by
him, and they interested him—as well they might, for there is
an affinity between them, as there is between the regulated
imagination of a wise poet and the incoherent dreams of a
poet. Blake is an engraver by trade, a painter and a poet also,
whose works have been subject of derision to men in general;
but he has a few admirers, and some of eminence have eulo-
gised his designs. He has lived in obscurity and poverty, to
which the constant hallucinations in which he lives have
doomed him. I do not mean to give you a detailed account of
him. A few words will suffice to inform you of what class he
is. He is not so much a disciple of Jacob Böhmen and Swedenborg as a fellow Visionary. He lives, as they did, in a world
of his own, enjoying constant intercourse with the world of
spirits. He receives visits from Shakespeare, Milton, Dante,
Voltaire, etc. etc. etc., and has given me repeatedly their very
words in their conversations. His paintings are copies of what
he saw in his Visions. His books (and his MSS. are immense
in quantity) are dictations from the spirits. He told me yesterday that when he writes it is for the spirits only; he sees the
words fly about the room the moment he has put them on
paper, and his book is then published. A man so favoured, of
course, has sources of wisdom peculiar to himself.

Letter to Dorothy Wordsworth 1826

WILKINSON

The present volume contains nearly all that is excellent in
Blake's poetry; and great, rare, and manifest is the excellence
that is here. The faults are equally conspicuous, and he who
runs may read them. They amount to an utter want of elaboration, and even, in many cases, to an inattention to the ordinary
rules of grammar. Yet the *Songs of Innocence*, at least, are
quite free from the dark becloudment which rolled and
billowed over Blake in his later days. He here transcended
Self, and escaped from the isolation which Self involves; and,
as it then ever is, his expanding affections embraced universal
man, and, without violating, beautified and hallowed even his
individual peculiarities. Accordingly, many of these delicious

lays belong to the Era as well as to the Author. They are
remarkable for the transparent depth of thought which constitutes true simplicity—they give us glimpses of all that is
holiest in the childhood of the world and the individual—
they abound with the sweetest touches of that pastoral life,
by which the Golden Age may be still visibly represented to
the Iron one—they delineate full-orbed age, ripe with the
seeds of a second infancy, which is 'the Kingdom of Heaven'.
The latter half of the volume, comprising the *Songs of Experience*, consists, it is true, of darker themes; but they, too,
are well and wonderfully sung, and ought to be preserved,
because, in contrastive connection with the *Songs of Innocence*,
they do convey a powerful impression of 'THE TWO CONTRARY
STATES OF THE HUMAN SOUL'.

Preface to Songs of Innocence and Experience   1839

SAMUEL PALMER

His poems were variously estimated. They tested rather
severely the imaginative capacity of their readers. Flaxman
said they were as grand as his designs, and Wordsworth
delighted in his *Songs of Innocence*. To the multitude they
were unintelligible. In many parts full of pastoral sweetness,
and often flashing with noble thoughts or terrible imagery, we
must regret that he should sometimes have suffered fancy to
trespass within sacred precincts.

Letter to Gilchrist   1855

GILCHRIST

First of the Poems let me speak, harsh as seems their
divorce from the Design which blends with them, forming
warp and woof in one texture. It is like pulling up a daisy
by the roots from the green sward out of which it springs. To
me many years ago, first reading these weird Songs in their
appropriate environment of equally spiritual form and hue,
the effect was that of an angelic voice singing to an oaten
pipe, such as Arcadians tell of; or, as if a spiritual magician
were summoning before human eyes and through a human

medium, images and scenes of divine loveliness; and in the pauses of the strain, we seem to catch the rustling of angelic wings. The Golden Age independent of Space or Time, object of vague sighs and dreams for many generations of struggling humanity—an Eden such as childhood sees, is brought nearer than ever poet brought it before. For this poet was in assured possession of the Golden Age, within the chambers of his own mind. As we read, fugitive glimpses open, clear as brief, of our buried childhood, of an unseen world present, past, to come; we are endowed with new spiritual sight, with unwonted intuitions, bright visitants from finer realms of thought, which ever elude us, ever hover near. We encounter familiar objects, in unfamiliar, transfigured aspects, simple expression and deep meanings, type and antitype. True, there are palpable irregularities, metrical licence, lapse of grammar and even of orthography; but often the sweetest melody, most daring eloquence of rhythm, and, what is more, appropriate rhythm. They are *unfinished* poems: yet would finish have bettered their bold and careless freedom? that visible spontaneity, so rare and great a charm, the eloquent attribute of our old English Ballads and of the early Songs of all nations. . . .

After the *Songs of Experience*, Blake never again sang to like angelic tunes; nor even with the same approach to technical accuracy. His poetry was the blossom of youth and early manhood.

Life of William Blake   1863

SWINBURNE

There are two points in the works of Blake which first claim notice and explanation; two points connected, but not inseparable; his mysticism and his mythology. This latter is in fact hardly more in its relation to the former, than the clothes to the body or the body to the soul. To make either comprehensible, it is requisite above all things to get sight of the man in whom they became incarnate and active as forces or opinions. Now, to those who regard mysticism with distaste or contempt, as essentially in itself a vain or noxious thing— a sealed bag or bladder that can only be full either of wind or of poison—the man, being above all and beyond all a mystic in the most subtle yet most literal sense, must remain obscure and contemptible. Such readers—if indeed such men should choose or care to become readers at all—will be (for one thing) unable to understand that one may think it worth while to follow out and track to its root the peculiar faith or fancy of a mystic without being ready to accept his deductions and his assertions as absolute and durable facts. Servility of extended hand or passive brain is the last quality that a mystic of the nobler kind will demand or desire in his auditors . . . And assuredly it is not to be expected that Blake's mystical creed, when once made legible and even partially coherent, should prove likely to win over proselytes. Nor can this be the wish or the object of a reasonable commentator, whose desire is merely to do art a good turn in some small way, by explaining the 'faith and works' of a great artist. It is true that whatever a good poet or a good painter has thought worth representing by verse or design must probably be worth considering before one deliver judgment on it. But the office of an apostle of some new faith and the business of a commentator on some new evangel are two sufficiently diverse things. The present critic has not (happily) to preach the gospel as delivered by Blake; he has merely, if possible, to make the text of that gospel a little more readable. And this must be worth doing, if it be worth while to touch on Blake's work at all. What is true of all poets and artists worth judging is especially true of him; that critics who attempt to judge him piecemeal do not in effect judge him at all, but some one quite different from him, and some one (to any serious student) probably more inexplicable than the real man. For what are we to make of a man whose work deserves crowning one day and hooting the next? If the *Songs* be so good, are not those who praise them bound to examine and try what merit may be latent in the 'Prophecies'?—bound at least to explain as best they may how the one comes to be worth so much and the other worth nothing? . . .

First then for the *Songs of Innocence and Experience*. These at first naming recall only that incomparable charm of form in which they first came out clothed, and hence vex the souls of men with regretful comparisons. For here by hard necessity we miss the lovely and luminous setting of designs, which makes the *Songs* precious and pleasurable to those who know or care for little else of the master's doing . . . Nevertheless this decorative work is after all the mere husk and shell of the *Songs*. These also, we may notice, have to some extent shared the comparative popularity of the designs which serve as framework to them. They have absolutely achieved the dignity of a reprint; have had a chance before now of swimming for life; whereas most of Blake's offspring have been thrown into Lethe bound hand and foot, without hope of striking out in one fair effort. Perhaps on some accounts this preference has been not unreasonable. What was written for children can hardly offend men; and the obscurities and audacities of the prophet would here have been clearly out of place. It is indeed some relief to a neophyte serving in the outer courts of such an intricate and cloudy temple, to come upon this little side-chapel set about with the simplest wreaths and smelling of the fields rather than incense, where all the singing is done by clear children's voices to the briefest and least complex tunes. Not at first without a sense of release does the human mind get quit for a little of the clouds of Urizen, the fires of Orc, and all the Titanic apparatus of prophecy. And these poems are really unequalled in their kind. Such verse was never written for children since verse-writing began. Only in a few of those faultless fragments of childish rhyme which float without name or form upon the memories of men shall we find such a pure clear cadence of verse, such rapid ring and flow of lyric laughter, such sweet and direct choice of the just word and figure, such an impeccable simplicity; nowhere but here such a tender wisdom of holiness, such a light and perfume of innocence. . . .

One cannot say, being so slight and seemingly wrong in metrical form, how they come to be so absolutely right; but right even in point of verses and words they assuredly are. . . .

Against all articulate authority we do however class several of the *Songs of Experience* higher for the great qualities of verse than anything in the earlier division of these poems. If the *Songs of Innocence* have the shape and smell of leaves or buds, these have in them the light and sound of fire or the sea. Entering among them, a fresher savour and a larger breath strikes one upon the lips and forehead. In the first part we are shown who they are who have or who deserve the gift of spiritual sight: in the second, what things there are for them to see when that gift has been given. Innocence, the quality of beasts and children, has the keenest eyes; and such eyes alone can discern and interpret the actual mysteries of experience. It is natural that this second part, dealing as it does with such things as underlie the outer forms of the first part, should rise higher and dive deeper in point of mere words. . . .

The inexhaustible equable gift of Blake for the writing of short sweet songs is perceptible at every turn we take in this labyrinth of lovely words, of strong and soft designs. Considering how wide is the range of date from the earliest of these songs to the latest, they seem more excellently remote than ever from the day's verse and the day's habit. They reach in point of time from the season of Mason to the season of Moore; and never in any interval of work by any chance influence do these poems at their weakest lapse into likeness or tolerance of the accepted models. From the era of plaster to the era of pinchbeck, Blake kept straight ahead of the times. To the pseudo-Hellenic casts of the one school or the pseudo-Hibernian tunes of the other he was admirably deaf and blind. While a grazing public straightened its bovine neck and steadied its flickering eyelids to look up between whiles, with the day's damp fodder drooping half-chewed from its relaxed jaw, at some dim sick planet of the Mason system, there was a poet, alive if obscure, who had eyes to behold

> the chambers of the East,
> The chambers of the sun, that now
> From ancient melody have ceased;

who had ears to hear and lips to reveal the music and the splendour and the secret of the high places of verse. Again, in a changed century, when the reading and warbling world was fain to drop its daily tear and stretch its daily throat at the bidding of some Irish melodist—when the 'female will' of 'Albion' thought fit to inhale with wide and thankful nostril

the rancid flavour of rotten dance-roses and mouldy muck, to
feed 'in a feminine delusion' upon the sodden offal of perfumed
dog's meat, and take it for the very eucharist of Apollo—
then too while this worship of ape or beetle went so noisily
on, the same poet could let fall from lavish hand or melodious
mouth such grains of solid gold and flakes of perfect honey as
this:

> Silent, silent night,
> Quench the holy light
> Of thy torches bright;
>
> For possessed of day,
> Thousand spirits stray,
> That sweet joys betray.
>
> Why should love be sweet,
> Used with deceit,
> Nor with sorrows meet?

Verse more nearly faultless and of a more difficult perfection
was never accomplished. The sweet facility of being right,
proper to great poets, was always an especial quality of Blake's.
To go the right way and do the right thing, was in the nature
of his metrical gift—a faculty mixed into the very flesh and
blood of his verse. . . .

Before entering upon any system of remark or comment
on the *Prophetic Books*, we may set down in as few and
distinct words as possible the reasons which make this a thing
seriously worth doing; nay, even, requisite to be done, if we
would know rather the actual facts of the man's nature, than
the circumstances and accidents of his life. Now, first of all,
we are to recollect that Blake himself regarded these works as
his greatest, and as containing the sum of his achieved
ambitions and fulfilled desires: as in effect, inspired matter, of
absolute imaginative truth and eternal import. We shall not
again pause to rebut the familiar cry of response, to the effect
that he was mad and not accountable for the uttermost madness of error. It must be enough to reply here that he was by
no means mad, in any sense that would authorize us in

rejecting his own judgment of his aims and powers on a plea
which would be held insufficient in another man's case. Let all
readers and all critics get rid of that notion for good—clear
their minds of it utterly and with all haste; let them know and
remember, having once been told it, that in these strangest of
all written books there is purpose as well as power, meaning
as well as mystery. Doubtless nothing quite like them was
ever pitched out headlong into the world as they were. The
confusion, the clamour, the jar of words that half suffice and
thoughts that half exist—all these and other more absolutely
offensive qualities—audacity, monotony, bombast, obscure
play of licence and tortuous growth of fancy—cannot quench
or even wholly conceal the living purport and the imperishable beauty which are here latent.

William Blake   1866

RUSKIN

You must have nearly all heard of, many must have seen,
the singular paintings—some also may have read the poems—
of William Blake. The impression that his drawings once made
is fast, and justly, fading away, though they are not without
noble merit. But his poems have much more than merit;
they are written with absolute sincerity, with infinite tenderness, and, though in the manner of them diseased and wild,
are in verity the words of a great and wise mind, disturbed,
but not deceived by its sickness; nay, partly exalted by it, and
sometimes giving forth in fiery aphorism some of the most
precious words of existing literature.

The Eagle's Nest, Lecture II   1872

WILLIAM ROSSETTI

The character of Blake's poetry bears, it need hardly be
said, a considerable affinity to that of his work in the art of
design; he himself, it is said, thought the former the finer of
the two. There is, however, no little difference between them,
when their main elements are considered proportionally. In
both, Blake almost totally ignores actual life and its evolution,

and the passions and interactions of men as elicited by the wear and tear of real society. True, individual instances might be cited where he has in view some topic of the day, or some incident of life, simple or harrowing, such as social or dramatic writers might take cognizance of. But these also he treats with a primitiveness of singularity which, if it does not remove the subjects from our sympathy—and a few cases of very highly sympathetic treatment are to be found—does at least leave them within the region of the ideal, or sometimes of the intangible. As a rule, Blake does not deal at all with the complicated practical interests of life, or the influence of these upon character; but he possesses the large range of primordial emotion, from the utter innocence and happy unconscious instinct of infancy, up to the fervours of the prophet, inspired to announce, to judge, and to reprobate.

This range of feeling and of faculty is, as we have just said, expressed equally in the designs and in the poetry of Blake, but not in the same proportions. In the designs, the energetic, the splendid, the majestic, the grand, the portentous, the terrific, play the larger part, and constitute the finer portion of the work; while the softer emotions, and the perception of what is gentle in its loveliness, are both less prominent in quantity, and realized with less mastery and sureness. In the poems these conditions are reversed. We find Blake expressing frequently and with the most limpid and final perfection—in some of its essential aspects, unsurpassed, or indeed unequalled —the innocent and simple impulses of human nature; the laughter and prattle of a baby, the vivid transforming fresh-ness of youthful love, the depth and self-devotion of parental affection, the trust in the Father whom the eye hath not seen. Very noble utterance is also given from time to time to some subject of discipline or of awe to the human soul, or even of terror: but generally it is not with these topics that Blake deals in his lyrical poems. He reserves them for his *Prophetic Books*, written in a style which, though poetical and rhapsodic, does not bring the works within the pale of verse, and barely allows them to obtain access to the human under-standing. It is in these scriptures, rather than in the poems properly so called, that we have to seek for the written counter-

part of that supernatural stress and that sense of the appalling
—now profound in its quietude, now almost bacchant in its
orgies—which tell upon us so potently in his designs; and
certainly the written form of all this is by no means equal to
the plastic one. Leaving these *Prophetic Books* for the present,
we may say of the other rhythmic poems that the spiritual
intuition of which we have already spoken as Blake's most
central faculty, and a lyric outflow the purest and most spontaneous, fashioning the composition in its general mould, and
directing aright each word and cadence, are the most observ-
able and precious qualities. This statement as to the wording
and cadences must of course be understood with limitation;
for Blake, exquisitely true to the mark as he can come in such
matters, is often also palpably faulty—transgressing even the
obvious laws of grammar and of metre. Power of thought is
likewise largely present in several cases; not of analytic or
reasoning thought, for which Blake had as little turn in his
poems as liking in his *dicta*, but broad and strong intellectual
perception, telling in aid of that still higher and primary
faculty of intuition.

Prefatory Memoir to The Poetical Works of William Blake
                                                            1874

JAMES THOMSON

[The writer, best known as the poet of *The City of Dreadful
Night*, wrote a short essay on Blake in 1864. It was not, he
says, published until 1866, just before Swinburne's much
longer study. Extracts have not been made from it, because
it seemed comparatively slight; but fifteen years later, Thomson
wrote an essay, *A Strange Book*, on a volume of poems published
by Garth Wilkinson, who had edited Blake's poems in 1839.
Some parts of this essay are much more instructive, both on
Thomson's maturer view of Blake, and on the kind of mind
to which Blake was specially full of meaning]

In order to make clear how strange is this book, I must cite
at considerable length from the Note which concludes it, but
really serves as a Preface:

'The history of this little volume may be told in a few words.

It is written by a new method, partly explained in the title, *Improvisations*.

Last autumn my attention was particularly directed to the phenomena of drawing, speaking, and writing by Impression; and I determined to make an experiment of the kind, in composition, myself. The following poems are the result. Let me now explain more precisely what is meant by Writing by Impression, so far as my own personal experience is concerned; for I cannot refer to any other.

A theme is chosen and written down. So soon as this is done, the first impression upon the mind which succeeds the act of writing the title is the beginning of the evolution of that theme, no matter how strange or alien the word or phrase may seem. That impression is written down: and then another, and another, until the piece is concluded. An Act of Faith is signalized in accepting the first mental movement, the first word that comes, as the response to the mind's desire for the unfolding of the subject. . . .

This little volume . . . is one man's earliest essay to receive with upstretched palms some of these long-travelling, most-unnoticed, and yet unchangeable and immortal rays. It was given just as the reader reads it—with no hesitation, without the correction of one word from beginning to end; and how much it differs from other similar collections in *process* it were difficult to convey to the reader; suffice it to say that every piece was produced without premeditation or preconception: had these processes stolen in, such production would have been impossible . . .'

We have seen that this volume fully deserves its title of 'Improvisations'; but what of the 'from the Spirit,' meaning 'from the Lord?' Some of these pieces, as shown by the quotations in Section I, were obtained in answer to direct invocation of the Lord. But in a large number of cases, it is not *the* Spirit of the Lord who dictates; it is not even the writer himself, who may be supposed but the medium of the

Spirit; the spirits of those whose names are the titles of the
poems, speak in the first person; and in these cases, so far as
I can see, Dr Wilkinson sinks to the level of the ordinary
mediums (save that we can absolutely confide in his sincerity,
however much he may be mistaken), who allege communica-
tions from the spirits of the departed. . . . it seems clear to me
that the volume ought to have been entitled 'Improvisations
from the Spirits,' or 'from *the* Spirit and certain human
spirits,' or in some such style marking variety of dictation.

And now, what of the poems themselves, thus strangely
produced? Perhaps the first thing that strikes one is what
struck Mr Rossetti, their remarkable resemblance to Blake's;
not in themes, not in doctrine, but in essence. None indeed
are quite so lovely as Blake's best lyrics; none so turbid and
turbulent as his Titanic wildest in the prophetic books; none
approach in depth and original daring the *Marriage of Heaven
and Hell*. But the more limpid are very like Blake's, in style
and cadence, in artlessness and occasional laxity, in primitive
simplicity, as of the historical or legendary childhood of our
race, though with Wilkinson the childlike sometimes becomes
childish. . . . There are strange alternations of grandeur and
littleness. The satire and invective also are closely akin to
Blake's in their uncouth strength, their furious, awkward
hard-hitting; though here again the younger poet never
equals some of the happy decisive strokes of the elder.

A Strange Book, Improvisations from the Spirit   1879

YEATS

This philosophy kept him more simply the poet than any
poet of his time, for it made him content to express every
beautiful feeling that came into his head without troubling
about its utility or chaining it to any utility. Sometimes one
feels even when one is reading poets of a better time—Tennyson
or Wordsworth, let us say—that they have troubled the energy
and simplicity of their imaginative passions by asking whether
they were for the helping or for the hindrance of the world,
instead of believing that all beautiful things have 'lain burningly
on the Divine hand.' But when one reads Blake, it is as though

B

the spray of an inexhaustible fountain of beauty was blown
into our faces, and not merely when one reads the *Songs of
Innocence*, or the lyrics he wished to call *The Ideas of Good and
Evil*, but when one reads those *Prophetic Works* in which he spoke
confusedly and obscurely because he spoke of things for whose
speaking he could find no models in the world about him. . . .

He cried again and again that everything that lives is holy,
and that nothing is unholy except things that do not live—
lethargies, and cruelties, and timidities, and that denial of the
imagination which is the root they grew from in old times.
Passions, because most living, are most holy—and this was a
scandalous paradox in his time—and man shall enter eternity
borne upon their wings.

Ideas of Good and Evil   1903

SYMONS

To define the poetry of Blake, one must find new definitions
for poetry; but, these definitions once found, he will seem to
be the only poet who is a poet in essence; the only poet who
could, in his own words, 'enter into Noah's rainbow, and make
a friend and companion of one of these images of wonder,
which always entreat him to leave mortal things'. In this verse
there is, if it is to be found in any verse, the 'lyrical cry'; and
yet, what voice is it that cries in this disembodied ecstasy?
The voice of desire is not in it, nor the voice of passion, nor
the cry of the heart, nor the cry of the sinner to God, nor of
the lover of nature to nature. It neither seeks nor aspires nor
laments nor questions. It is like the voice of wisdom in a
child, who has not yet forgotten the world out of which the
soul came. It is as spontaneous as the note of a bird, it is an
affirmation of life; in its song, which seems mere music, it is
the mind which sings; it is lyric thought. What is it that
transfixes one in any couplet such as this:

> If the sun and moon should doubt
> They'd immediately go out?

It is no more than a nursery statement, there is not even an
image in it, and yet it sings to the brain, it cuts into the very

flesh of the mind, as if there were a great weight behind it. Is it that it is an arrow, and that it comes from so far, and with an impetus gathered from its speed out of the sky? . . .

The poetry of Blake is a poetry of the mind abstract in substance, concrete in form; its passion is the passion of the imagination, its emotion is the emotion of thought, its beauty is the beauty of idea. When it is simplest, its simplicity is that of some 'infant joy' too young to have a name, or of some 'infant sorrow' brought aged out of the world of eternity into 'the dangerous world,' and there,

> Helpless, naked, piping loud,
> Like a fiend hid in a cloud.

There are no men and women in the world of Blake's poetry, only primal instincts and the energies of the imagination.

His work begins in the garden of Eden, or of the childhood of the world, and there is something in it of the naïveté of beasts: the lines gambol awkwardly like young lambs. His utterance of the state of innocence has in it something of the grotesqueness of babies, and enchants the grown man, as they do. Humour exists unconscious of itself, in a kind of awed and open-eyed solemnity. He stammers into a speech of angels, as if just awakening out of Paradise. It is the primal instincts that speak first, before riper years have added wisdom to intuition. It is the supreme quality of this wisdom that it has never let go of intuition. It is as if intuition itself ripened. . . .

Blake is the only poet who sees all temporal things under a form of eternity. To him reality is merely a symbol, and he catches at its terms, hastily and faultily, as he catches at the lines of the drawing-master, to represent, as in a faint image, the clear and shining outlines of what he sees with the imagination; through the eye, not with it, as he says. Where other poets use reality as a spring-board into space, he uses it as a foothold on his return from flight. Even Wordsworth seemed to him a kind of atheist, who mistook the changing signs of 'vegetable nature' for the unchanging realities of the imagination. 'Natural objects,' he wrote in a copy of Wordsworth, 'always did and now do weaken, deaden, and obliterate imagination in me. Wordsworth must know that what he writes valuable is not to be found in nature.' And so his poetry is the most abstract of all poetry, although in a sense the most concrete. It is everywhere in affirmation, the register of vision; never observation. To him observation was one of the daughters of memory, and he had no use for her among his Muses, which were all eternal, and the children of the imagination. 'Imagination,' he said, 'has nothing to do with memory.'

William Blake 1907

DE SELINCOURT

Yet the central word about Blake can never be a word of depreciation. It can never cease to be true of him that he embodied and proclaimed at its purest the impulse of which all art is the issue, and raising art, as all the greatest artists do, to a level with the noblest achievements of the human spirit, showed that in its essence the artistic principle is the very principle of life itself; and that all religion, all conduct, are barren and profitless except in so far as they express it. He is, of course, greatest both as a man and as an artist when circumstances allow him to exemplify rather than to uphold truth; and it was his life's misfortune that circumstances enabled him to exemplify it so seldom and forced him to waste so much of his energy in upholding it. He was driven, in the bulk of his work, to passionate vindication of the inmost principle of his being; he did not see that it ceased to show the qualities he claimed for it in proportion to the necessity he found of claiming them. But the work which puts Blake among the immortals is his *Songs of Innocence*. Innocence is his secret; as life becomes a problem to him, the problem presents itself simply as the search for a means to preserve innocence in all the freshness and purity of its youth:

> Youth of delight, come hither,
> And see the opening morn,
> Image of truth new-born.

And he is great, he is among the greatest, because although the secret is often obscured and buried in his art, he yet knew how to keep himself, as a man, in living touch with it, so that to the end of his life, in spite of the prejudices and arrogance of his egotism, and in the very hour of death itself, he was a child.

It is in the *Songs of Innocence*, then, and whatever other song, or fragment of song, whatever painting, drawing, or decorative design he may have conceived in the same spirit, it is in these that Blake's immortality is to be looked for, in these that he possesses, with the complete, the indefinable possession of the artist, that spring of life which most of his after years were spent in unavailing efforts to recover. The purity and rapture of his early vision were so little appreciated or understood that there can be small matter for wonder if Blake was ready to stray from the green pastures of delight into the wilderness of conflict and justification. . . .

For, as a matter of fact, the entire mystical mechanism of the *Prophetic Books*, with its gigantic *dramatis personae*, its geography that violates the laws of space, its history that neglects the passage of time, its unexampled fusion of violence and vagueness in almost every department of thought, is a mere fungus of the mind, owing, we must at once add, the luxuriance of its growth to the great vitality, exuberance, and creative power of the individual mind from which it sprang. Everything that Blake tasks this machinery to convey, he conveys more truly and far more incisively in occasional passages where he relapses into terms of common speech; and, in so far as he believed himself to be doing a poet's or an artist's work in allegorization of his ideas, the content of the *Prophetic Books* themselves is the reply to him. They show the man who, in his sense of lyric appropriateness of speech, ranks with the greatest in our literature, wading knee-deep in a morass of futile terminology, and wasting unique powers of imaginative design in representation of subjects, which, having no recognizable relation to life as men commonly understand and live it, can never carry the full significance of conception he aimed at giving them, can never, except to a small circle of disciples, make any other than the comparatively trivial aesthetic appeal.

William Blake 1909

ELIOT

If one follows Blake's mind through the several stages of his poetic development it is impossible to regard him as a naif, a wild man, a wild pet for the supercultivated. The strangeness is evaporated, the peculiarity is seen to be the peculiarity of all great poetry: something which is found (not everywhere) in Homer and Aeschylus and Dante and Villon, and profound and concealed in the work of Shakespeare— and also in another form in Montaigne and in Spinoza. It is merely a peculiar honesty, which, in a world too frightened to be honest, is peculiarly terrifying. It is an honesty against which the whole world conspires, because it is unpleasant. Blake's poetry has the unpleasantness of great poetry. Nothing that can be called morbid or abnormal or perverse, none of these things which exemplify the sickness of an epoch or a fashion, has this quality; only those things which, by some extraordinary labour of simplification, exhibit the essential sickness or strength of the human soul. And this honesty never exists without great technical accomplishment. The question about Blake the man is the question of the circum- stances that concurred to permit this honesty in his work, and what circumstances define its limitations. The favouring con- ditions probably include these two: that, being early appren- ticed to a manual occupation, he was not compelled to acquire any other education in literature than he wanted, or to acquire it for any other reason than that he wanted it; and that being a humble engraver, he had no journalistic-social career open to him. . . .

The *Songs of Innocence and Experience*, and the poems of the Rossetti manuscript, are the poems of a man with a pro- found interest in human emotions, and a profound knowledge of them. The emotions are presented in an extremely simplified, abstract form. This form is one illustration of the eternal struggle against education, of the literary artist against the continuous deterioration of language. . . .

Blake . . . knew what interested him, and he therefore presents only the essential, only, in fact, what can be presented, and need not be explained. And because he was not distracted, or frightened, or occupied in anything but exact statements, he understood. He was naked, and saw man naked, and from the centre of his own crystal. To him there was no more reason why Swedenborg should be absurd than Locke. He accepted Swedenborg, and eventually rejected him for reasons of his own. He approached everything with a mind unclouded by current opinions. There was nothing of the superior person about him. This makes him terrifying. . . .

But if there was nothing to distract him from sincerity there were, on the other hand, the dangers to which the naked man is exposed. His philosophy, like his visions, like his insight, like his technique, was his own. And accordingly he was inclined to attach more importance to it than an artist should; this is what makes him eccentric, and makes him inclined to formlessness. . . .

We have the same respect for Blake's philosophy (and perhaps for that of Samuel Butler) that we have for an ingenious piece of home-made furniture: we admire the man who has put it together out of the odds and ends about the house. England has produced a fair number of these resourceful Robinson Crusoes; but we are not really so remote from the Continent, or from our own past, as to be deprived of the advantages of culture if we wish them. . . .

. . . about Blake's supernatural territories, as about the supposed ideas that dwell there, we cannot help commenting on a certain meanness of culture. They illustrate the crankiness, the eccentricity, which frequently affects writers outside of the Latin traditions, and which such a critic as Arnold should certainly have rebuked. And they are not essential to Blake's inspiration.

Blake was endowed with a capacity for a considerable understanding of human nature, with a remarkable and original sense of language, and a gift of hallucinated vision. Had these been controlled by a respect for impersonal reason, for common sense, for the objectivity of science, it would have been better for him. What his genius required, and what it sadly lacked, was a framework of accepted and traditional ideas which would have prevented him from indulging in a philosophy of his own, and concentrated his attentions upon the problems of the poet.

William Blake 1920

MIDDLETON MURRY

Suddenly, in the midst of the queer, fantastic, disillusioned manuscript of *An Island in the Moon*, William Blake broke into the lovely song of the charity children in St Paul's, and followed it with the still more lovely:

> When the voices of children are heard on the green
>   And laughing is heard on the hill,
> My heart is at rest within my breast
>   And everything else is still.

There is the magic. One's heart sinks to rest; and everything else becomes still. Stillness within, stillness without. For those voices are not heard with the bodily ear; that laughter breaks no silence. They pipe to the spirit ditties of no tone. 'Imagination is Spiritual Sensation.'

Such was the beginning of the *Songs of Innocence*; from such a poised and silent vortex of spiritual sensation they took birth. And such a poise of silence, we know immediately, is an achievement. The clamour lapses into an eternal moment, and the world is born anew. The sentient soul is bathed in the waters of the spirit. The doors of perception are cleansed; and the world gleams forth with the bloom and brightness of a new creation.

We have known these moments. If we have not known them, there—in those four simple lines—one is offered to us. We have only to receive it. If we can receive it, how shall we express what we have received? Shall we not express it thus:

> Man's perceptions are not bounded by organs of perception; he perceives more than sense (tho' never so acute) can discover.

By what sense—the question will be asked by Oothoon—do we hear the voices of those children on the green, or their laughter on the hill? To what sense shall we assign this spiritual ear, for which sound is but the key to silence? The first of Blake's propositions in *There is no Natural Religion* becomes the utterance of a simple sanity.

The recognition of this sense beyond sense is fundamental to Blake, and to an understanding of Blake. . . . For this sense beyond sense we shall use the adjective 'spiritual'. It is the faculty of that Spiritual Sensation which, Blake said, is Imagination. . . .

The *Songs of Innocence* are the creative uprush which followed Blake's perception of the Infinite in all things. They are songs of 'innocence' because this entry into the world of Spiritual Sensation is the entry of a reborn soul into a new world. There is a total renewal of the being, which finds its most natural symbolic expression in the innocence of a child. 'Except ye be born again . . .' Hence the *Songs of Innocence* contain no trace of mawkishness. That which finds utterance in them is real innocence; not what we imagine to be the innocence of a child, which cannot be uttered, but the achieved innocence of a reborn man. . . .

There is pathos and tragedy in the three poems with which the manuscript of *Songs of Experience* begins . . . There cannot be much doubt about the story these three poems tell, or conceal. Blake had loved someone not his wife, and had straightway told his wife of his love; and the result had been disaster. To the simpler soul of his wife, Blake's doctrine that Love, being the mutual recognition of two Identities, was its own complete justification, was wickedness; or perhaps she persuaded herself that it was wickedness. Probably her reaction was the simple and elemental one of jealousy, which she clothed in the garments of righteousness.

It appears that this was one of the great disillusions of Blake's life. Whether it was a single and sudden happening, with prolonged repercussions, or whether it was a happening spread over months or even years, there are no means of knowing and it would be unprofitable to guess. The details are of singularly little importance. Traces of the old experience, or fresh realizations of it in new forms, haunt his work continually henceforward; and the shock of his awakening was so profound that the Female principle came to represent to him a resistance to the Divine Vision even more stubborn than that of the Selfhood itself. It became almost the supreme form of the Selfhood.

Blake's mystical certainty had come into direct conflict with the facts of existence. The *Songs of Experience* were the immediate outcome of this disillusion, as the *Songs of Innocence* were the immediate outcome of the mystical experience itself. . . .

It was Blake's destiny to precede, by a term of years substantial enough to make him a complete stranger to it, the period when Nature, imaginatively apprehended, was a veritable inspiration to Art and Science alike. Whereas the poetry of Keats and Wordsworth, the painting of Crome and Constable, have their natural place in a period which was reaching towards its scientific expression in the theory of evolution and historical growth, Blake does not belong to it at all. In this regard the comparison between Blake and Goethe which we have already suggested is significant. Although it is conceivable that Goethe's *Hymn to Nature* and his dithyramb on Granite would have sounded in Blake's ears like the voice of Satan, proclaiming the Atheistical Epicurean Philosophy, and denying Eternity; yet it is conceivable only with difficulty. It is impossible for one who comes one hundred and fifty years afterwards to believe that these two great spirits were essentially opposed: that there is any real difference between Goethe beholding the 'pure phenomenon', which filled him with awe, and beyond which (he warned them) men would never get, and Blake staring at the Minute Particulars of a knot in a piece of wood until he was terrified. Or between Blake's doctrine that Vision is of necessity minutely organized, and Goethe's teaching that the Universal *is* the Particular.

The difference is not between actual experience, but between the idiom of experience. Goethe was one to whom pre-human history was real; Blake's history began, and ended, with the adult human consciousness. We might say that Goethe was the man of Science, Blake the man of Art; but, since their

Science and their Art were imaginative, these pass into one
another. There is no dividing line between them. Blake's Art
is a veritable Science of the human soul. . . .

We insist that Blake, no less than Goethe, was a great man
of Science.

William Blake 1933

WALTER DE LA MARE

A Lifetime:

Epitaph for William Blake

I Lived; I toiled—day in, day out,
Endless labour, shafts of bliss,
For three score years and ten,
    And then;
I watched, with speechless joy and grief,
My last and loveliest spring
    Take wing.

Think you, I grudged the travailing?
I, who am come to this.

1956

[This poem was specially written for *The Divine Vision*, a
collection of essays on Blake made by Professor da Sola Pinto.
It was probably the last poem written by its author, who died
before it was published]

Wordsworth

That Wordsworth's poetic doctrine and example had 'awakened the minds of men and given a fresh impulse to art' was the belief of Hallam. But in his account of the victory over 'the sciolist herd' there are naturally simplifications, dramatizations, which must be resolved into somewhat more complex and less exciting terms if the real nature of Wordsworth's battle is to be understood. It had not been a battle against harsh and illiberal reviews, against The Quarterly, The Edinburgh, *and* Blackwood's; *it had next to nothing in common with the assault upon Keats. The burden which Wordsworth had to bear during the whole of the essentially creative decade of his life, from about 1797 to 1807, was not that of hostility and ridicule but the dull remorseless weight of sheer neglect. The reviewers took little notice of his work, the general reading public took none at all. The extracts given below fairly represent the quality and volume of public comment in this period, and it is not surprising that they should have produced in Wordsworth the frame of mind expressed in his letter to Lady Beaumont written in 1807: a frame of mind no less clearly implied in that great and centrally Wordsworthian poem,* Resolution and Independence, *written in the same year.*

In contrast with the deafness of the public, however, his poetry was already exercising that special power which it has always possessed, and still possesses in unique degree, to penetrate into the minds of a few individuals with all the force of a religious revelation. It was clearly the growth of its reputation with such individuals—Coleridge above all—that led to the long series of reproofs and attacks from The Edinburgh *and Francis Jeffrey. It was in 1807 that the first of Jeffrey's attacks appeared, and it was the first open recognition—though a hostile one— that Wordsworth's poetry had become a force in the world. It was a strange coincidence that at the very moment of this recognition the force itself should have reached the point of being almost spent, of losing the capacity to produce any more of the poetry which had embodied it. From this point onwards Wordsworth was almost a passive spectator of the growth of his reputation in the sense that he did no more, could do no more, to further it by creative writing. He was already well on the path to his later state of Grand Old Manliness.*

The fact that he was no longer in active competition with them as a poet perhaps made it easier for the younger Romantics both to see and to acknowledge the greatness of what he had done to open the way for them. It was, after all, easier to pay such tributes as Keats and Shelley paid, to a Grand and slightly awkward Old Man than to a writer actively and presently greater than themselves. They could afford to pay them the more generously because their own achievement, with Byron's, caught the public ear so much more completely than Wordsworth's had ever done, and left him, during the last twenty years of his long life, to those private disciples upon whom his special power has always been exercised: men such as Mill and Fitzgerald in the earlier Victorian period, Mark Rutherford in the later.

It was only some twenty years after his death that the final Victorian assessment was made, in the essays of Pater, Arnold, Stephen—and, I think, Swinburne. After them biography has made some advances in the understanding of the personal background of the poetry, but criticism has made but slight progress. The greatness of the poetry is not questioned, but it is not explored either. Indeed, there is some slight ground for misgiving about its future recognition in the fact that his influence is so completely absent from the most characteristic trends of feeling and expression in modern poetry.

It is, and has always been, subject to one other curious limitation: the complete inability of other than English readers to perceive that his poetry is of the same order of magnitude as Milton's, and only a little way below Shakespeare's, though very different in kind. Wordsworth has never enjoyed anything like the European reputation of Byron, to the English reader clearly a much—an almost ridiculously—lesser poet. The last extract given here is an attempt, by a critic not of British birth, to explain this curiosity of comparative literature.

SOUTHEY

Of these experimental poems, the most important is *The Idiot Boy*. . . . Upon this subject the author has written nearly 500 lines. . . . No tale less deserved the labour that appears to have been bestowed upon this. It resembles a Flemish picture in the worthlessness of its design and the excellence of its execution. . . . The other ballads are as bald in story, and are not so highly embellished in narration. With that which is entitled *The Thorn*, we were altogether displeased. The advertisement says, it is not told in the person of the author, but in that of some loquacious narrator. The author should have recollected that he who personates tiresome loquacity, becomes tiresome himself. . . . With pleasure we turn to the serious pieces, the better part of the volume . . . the author seems to discover still superior powers in the *Lines written near Tintern Abbey*. On reading this production, it is impossible not to lament that he should have condescended to write such pieces as *The Last of the Flock*, *The Convict*, and most of the ballads. In the whole range of English poetry, we scarcely recollect anything superior to a part of the following passage:

And so I dare to hope,
Though changed, no doubt, from what I was when first
I came among these hills . . .

The experiment, we think, has failed, not because the language of conversation is little adapted to 'the purposes of poetic pleasure', but because it has been tried upon uninteresting subjects. Yet every piece discovers genius; and, ill as the author has frequently employed his talents, they certainly rank him with the best of living poets.

Review of the first edition of
Lyrical Ballads: Monthly Magazine 1798

DR BURNEY

Though we have been extremely entertained with the fancy, the facility, and (in general) the sentiments, of these pieces, we cannot regard them as *poetry*, of a class to be cultivated at the expense of a higher species of versification, unknown in our language at the time when our elder writers, whom this author condescends to imitate, wrote their ballads. . . .

Anecdote for Fathers. Of this, the dialogue is ingenious and natural: but the object of the child's choice, and the inferences, are not quite obvious.

We are Seven—innocent and pretty infantine prattle. . . .

The Last of the Flock is more gloomy than the rest. . . . No oppression is pointed out; nor are any means suggested for his relief. If the author be a wealthy man, he ought not to have suffered this poor peasant to part with the last of his flock. . . .

Lines written near Tintern Abbey. The reflections of no common mind; poetical, beautiful, and philosophical: but somewhat tinctured with gloomy, narrow, and unsociable ideas of seclusion from the commerce of the world: as if men were born to live in woods and wilds, unconnected with each other. . . . So much genius and originality are discovered in this publication, that we wish to see another from the same hand, written on more elevated subjects, and in a more cheerful disposition.

The Monthly Review   1799

THE LYRICAL BALLADS:

WORDSWORTH

The principal object then which I proposed to myself in these Poems was to make the incidents of common life interesting, by tracing in them, truly though not ostentatiously, the primary laws of our nature: chiefly as far as regards the manner in which we associate ideas in a state of excitement. Low and rustic life was generally chosen because in that situation the essential passions of the heart find a better soil in which they can attain their maturity, are less under restraint, and speak a plainer and more emphatic language; because in that situation our elementary feelings exist in a state of greater simplicity and consequently may be more accurately contemplated and more forcibly communicated; because the manners of rural life germinate from those elementary feelings; and from the necessary character of rural occupations are more easily comprehended; and are more durable; and lastly, because in that situation the passions of men are incorporated with the beautiful and permanent forms of nature. The language too of these men is adopted (purified indeed from what appear to be its real defects, from all lasting and rational causes of dislike or disgust) because such men hourly communicate with the best objects from which the best part of language is originally derived; and because, from their rank in society and the sameness and narrow circle of their intercourse, being less under the action of social vanity they convey their feelings and notions in simple and unelaborated expressions. Accordingly such a language arising out of repeated experience and regular feelings is a more permanent and a far more philosophical language than that which is frequently substituted for it by Poets, who think that they are conferring honour upon themselves and their art in proportion as they separate themselves from the sympathies of men, and indulge in arbitrary and capricious habits of expression in order to furnish food for fickle tastes and fickle appetites of their own creation.

Preface to Lyrical Ballads   Second edition   1800

I am not a critic, and set little value upon the art. The *Preface* which I wrote long ago to my own Poems I was persuaded to write by the urgent entreaties of a friend, and I heartily regret I ever had anything to do with it; though I do not reckon the principles then advanced erroneous. . . . I do not think that great poems can be cast in a mould. Homer's, the greatest of all, certainly was not.

Letter to J. A. Heraud   1830

LAMB

. . . All the rest is eminently good, and your own. I will just add that it appears to me a fault in the *Beggar*, that the instructions conveyed in it are too direct, and like a lecture:

they don't slide into the mind of the reader while he is imagin-
ing no such matter. An intelligent reader finds a sort of insult
in being told, 'I will teach you how to think upon this subject.'
This fault, if I am right, is in a ten-thousandth worse degree
to be found in Sterne, and in many novelists and modern
poets, who put up a sign-post to show you where you are to
feel.

Letter to Wordsworth 1801

WRANGHAM [?]

Whatever may be thought of these poems, it is evident that
they are not to be confounded with the flood of poetry which
is poured forth in such profusion by the modern Bards of
Science, or their Brethren, the Bards of Insipidity. The author
has thought for himself; he has deeply studied human nature,
in the book of human action; and he has adopted his language
from the same source as his feelings. Aware that his Poems are
materially different from those upon which general approbation is at present bestowed, he has now defended them in a
Preface of some length; not with the foolish hope of reasoning
his readers into the approbation of these particular Poems,
but as a necessary justification of the species of poetry to
which they belong. . . .

Each separate Poem has, as its distinct *purpose*, the development of a feeling, which gives importance to the action and
situation, and not the action and situation to the feeling.
Whether the particular purpose is, in every case, *worthy* of a
Poet, will perhaps admit of some doubt. We have no hesitation
in saying, that it is generally interesting, often invaluable. . . .

Even where the feeling intended to be called forth is of a
rich and noble character, such as we may recur to, and feed
upon, it may yet be wrought up so gradually, including so
many preparatory circumstances of appropriate manners of
local description, of actual events, etc. that the subtle uniting
thread will be lost, without a persevering effort towards
attention on the part of the reader. Who that has studied
Shakespeare, must not be conscious how often the connection
of minute and trifling incidents with the main story has eluded

his observation, until after repeated perusals? Something of this kind will probably occur to the readers of the *Brothers*, the *Cumberland Beggar*, and more particularly of the Poem entitled *Michael*; yet these three are of the highest order of poems in the volume. . . .

British Critic 1801

[The writer was probably Francis Wrangham, a friend of Wordsworth's]

JEFFREY

The authors, of whom we are now speaking, have, among them, unquestionably, a very considerable portion of poetical talent, and have, consequently, been enabled to seduce many into an admiration of the false taste (as it appears to us) in which most of their productions are composed. They constitute, at present, the most formidable conspiracy that has lately been formed against sound judgment in matters poetical; and are entitled to a larger share of our censorial notice, than could be spared for an individual delinquent. . . .

Their most distinguishing symbol is, undoubtedly, an affectation of great simplicity and familiarity of language. . . . The followers of simplicity are at all times in danger of occasional degradation; but the simplicity of this new school seems intended to ensure it. *Their* simplicity does not consist, by any means, in the rejection of glaring or superfluous ornament—in the substitution of elegance to splendour, or in that refinement of art which seeks concealment in its own perfection. It consists, on the contrary, in the positive and *bona fide* rejection of art altogether, and in the bold use of those rude and negligent expressions, which would be banished by a little discrimination. One of their authors, indeed, has very ingenuously set forth (in a kind of manifesto that preceded one of their most flagrant acts of hostility), that it was their capital object 'to adapt to the uses of poetry, the ordinary language of conversation among the middling and lower orders of the people'. What advantages are to be gained by the success of this project, we confess ourselves unable to conjecture. . . .

. . . if we were in want of examples to illustrate the preceding observations, we should certainly look for them in the
effusions of that poet who commemorates, with so much
effect, the chattering of Harry Gibbs' teeth; tells the tale of
the one-eyed huntsman 'who had a cheek like a cherry'; and
beautifully warns his studious friend of the risk he ran of
'growing double'.

Review of Southey's Thalaba *in The Edinburgh Review* 1802

DE QUINCEY

On coming up to Oxford, I had taken up one position in
advance of my age by full thirty years: that appreciation of
Wordsworth, which it has taken full thirty years to establish
amongst the public, I had already made, and had made
operative to my own intellectual culture, in the same year
when I clandestinely quitted school. Already, in 1802, I had
addressed a letter of fervent admiration to Mr Wordsworth.
I did not send it until the spring of 1803; and, from mis-
direction, it did not come into his hands for some months.
But I had an answer from Mr Wordsworth before I was
eighteen; and that my letter was thought to express the homage
of an enlightened admirer may be inferred from the fact that
his answer was long and full. On this anecdote I do not mean
to dwell; but I cannot allow the reader to overlook the circumstances of the case. At this day [1835] it is true, no journal
can be taken up which does not habitually speak of Mr
Wordsworth as of *a* great, if not *the* great, poet of the age. . . .
Such is the opinion held of this great poet in 1835; but what
were those of 1805–15—nay, of 1825? For twenty years
after the date of that letter to Mr Wordsworth above referred
to, language was exhausted, ingenuity was put on the rack,
in the search after images and expressions vile enough, insolent enough, to convey the unutterable contempt avowed
for all that he had written by the fashionable critics. . . . In
short, up to 1820, the name of Wordsworth was trampled
under foot; from 1820 to 1830, it was militant; from 1830 to
1835, it has been triumphant. In 1803, when I entered at
Oxford, the name was absolutely unknown; and the finger of

scorn, pointed at it in 1802 by the first or second number of the *Edinburgh Review*, failed to reach its mark from absolute defect of knowledge in the public mind. Some fifty besides myself knew who was meant by 'that poet who had cautioned his friend against growing double', etc.; to all others it was a profound secret.

Autobiography   1835

JOHN WILSON (CHRISTOPHER NORTH)

[The only surviving piece of early Wordsworthian fan-mail is a letter from this boy of seventeen, later to become famous —and notorious—as a writer for *Blackwood's* and a Professor at Edinburgh. These extracts show the general tone of the praise bestowed. The immediate objects, which were to express a ponderous objection to *The Idiot Boy* and to extract an autograph letter from the poet, seem hardly worth remembering]

Professor Jardine's College, Glasgow
May 24th, 1802

My dear Sir,
          You may perhaps be surprised to see yourself addressed in this manner by one who never had the happiness of being in company with you, and whose knowledge of your character is drawn solely from the perusal of your poems. But, sir, though I am not personally acquainted with you, I may almost venture to affirm that the qualities of your soul are not unknown to me. In your poems I discovered such marks of delicate feeling, such benevolence of disposition, and such knowledge of human nature, as made an impression on my mind that nothing will ever efface; and while I felt my soul refined by the sentiments contained in them, and filled with those delightful emotions which it would be almost impossible to describe, I entertained for you an attachment made up of love and admiration. . . . To receive a letter from you would afford me more happiness than any occurrence in this world, save the happiness of my friends, and greatly enhance the

pleasure I receive from reading the *Lyrical Ballads*. . . . Your poems, sir, are of very great advantage to the world. . . . They point out the proper way to happiness. They show that such a thing as perfect misery does not exist. They flash on our souls convictions of immortality. Considered, therefore, in this view, the *Lyrical Ballads* is, to use your own words, the book which I value next to my Bible; and though I may, perhaps, never have the happiness of seeing you, yet I always consider you as a friend, who has, by his instructions, done me a service which it can never be in my power to repay.

[Whether Wordsworth replied to this letter seems not to be known. But six years later, the young man met him frequently, and familiarity with the object of his admiration did not breed contempt]

COLERIDGE

Wordsworth is a poet, a most original poet. He no more resembles Milton than Milton resembles Shakespeare—no more resembles Shakespeare than Shakespeare resembles Milton. He is himself, and, I dare affirm, that he will hereafter be admitted as the first and greatest philosophical poet, the only man who has effected a complete and constant synthesis of thought and feeling and combined them with poetic forms, with the music of pleasurable passion, and with Imagination or the *modifying* power in that highest sense of the word, in which I have ventured to oppose it to Fancy, or the *aggregating* power—in that sense in which it is a dim analogue of creation—not all that we can *believe*, but all that we *conceive* of creation. Wordsworth is a poet, and I feel myself a better poet, in knowing how to honour *him* than in all my own poetic compositions, all I have done or hope to do; and I prophesy immortality to his *Recluse* as the first and finest philosophical poem, if only it be (as undoubtedly it will be) a faithful transcript of his own habitual feelings and modes of seeing and hearing.

Letter to Richard Sharp   1804

SOUTHEY

Wordsworth will do better [than Coleridge], and leave behind him a name, unique in his way; he will rank among the very first poets, and probably possess a mass of merit superior to all except only Shakespeare.

Letter to J. Rickman   1804

JOSEPH COTTLE [first publisher of *Lyrical Ballads*]

As a curious literary fact, I might mention that the sale of the first edition of the *Lyrical Ballads* was so slow, and the severity of most of the reviews so great, that their progress to oblivion, notwithstanding the merits which I was quite sure they possessed, seemed ordained to be as rapid as it was certain. I had given thirty guineas for the copyright, as detailed in the preceding letters; but the heavy sale induced me at length, to part with, at a loss, the largest proportion of the impression of five hundred, to Mr Arch, a London bookseller.

Reminiscences

SOUTHEY

I went to Arch's, a pleasant place, for half an hour's book news: you know he purchased the edition of the *Lyrical Ballads*; he told me he believed he should lose by them, as they sold very heavily.

Letter to his wife   May, 1799

WORDSWORTH

It is impossible that any expectations can be lower than mine concerning the immediate effect of this little work upon what is called the public. I do not here take into consideration the envy and malevolence, and all the bad passions which always stand in the way of a work of any merit from a living poet; but merely think of the pure, absolute, honest ignorance

in which all worldlings of every rank and situation must be
enveloped, with respect to the thoughts, feelings, and images,
on which the life of my poems depends. The things which I
have taken, whether from within or without, what have they
to do with routs, dinners, morning calls, hurry from door to
door, from street to street, on foot or in carriage; with Mr Pitt
or Mr Fox, Mr Paul or Sir Francis Burdett, the Westminster
election or the borough of Honiton? In a word—for I cannot
stop to make my way through the hurry of images that present
themselves to me—what have they to do with endless talking
about things nobody cares anything for except as far as their
own vanity is concerned, and this with persons they care
nothing for but as their vanity or *selfishness* is concerned?—
what have they to do (to say all at once) with a life without
love? In such a life there can be no thought; for we have no
thought (save thoughts of pain) but as far as we have love and
admiration.

It is an awful truth, that there neither is, nor can be, any
genuine enjoyment of poetry among nineteen out of twenty
of those persons who live, or wish to live, in the broad light
of the world—among those who either are, or are striving to
make themselves, people of consideration in society. This is a
truth, and an awful one, because to be incapable of a feeling
of poetry, in my sense of the word, is to be without love of
human nature and reverence for God.

Upon this I shall insist elsewhere; at present let me confine
myself to my object, which is to make you, my dear friend, as
easy-hearted as myself with respect to these poems. Trouble
not yourself upon their present reception; of what moment
is that compared with what I trust is their destiny?—to console
the afflicted; to add sunshine to day-light, by making the
happy happier; to teach the young and the gracious of every
age to see, to think, and feel, and, therefore, to become more
actively and securely virtuous; this is their office, which I
trust they will faithfully perform, long after we (that is, all
that is mortal of us) are mouldered in our graves.

Letter to Lady Beaumont   1807

The *Lyrical Ballads* were unquestionably popular, and, we
have no hesitation in saying, deservedly popular; for in spite
of their occasional vulgarity, affectation, and silliness, they
were undoubtedly characterized by a strong spirit of originality,
of pathos, and natural feeling; and recommended to all good
minds by the clear impression which they bore of the amiable
dispositions and virtuous principles of the author. By the help
of these qualities, they were enabled, not only to recommend
themselves to the indulgence of many judicious readers, but
even to beget among a pretty numerous class of persons, a sort
of admiration of the very defects by which they were attended.
. . . It was precisely because the perversness and bad taste
of this new school was combined with a great deal of genius
and of laudable feeling, that we were afraid of their spreading
and gaining ground among us, and that we entered into the
discussion with a degree of zeal and animosity which some
might think unreasonable towards the authors, to whom so
much merit had been conceded.

The Edinburgh Review   1807

There is a set of writers from whose works those of Mr
Crabbe might receive all that elucidation which results from
contrast, and from an entire opposition in all points of taste
and opinion. We allude to the Wordsworths, and the Southeys,
and Coleridges, and all that misguided fraternity, that, with
good intentions and extraordinary talents, are labouring to
bring back our poetry to the fantastical oddity, and puling
childishness of Withers, Quarles, or Marvel. These gentlemen
write a great deal about rustic life, as well as Mr Crabbe; and
they even agree with him in dwelling much on its discomforts;
but nothing can be more opposite than the views they take of
the subject, or the manner in which they execute their representation of them.

Mr Crabbe exhibits the common people of England pretty
much as they are; at the same time he renders his sketches in a
very high degree interesting and beautiful. . . . The gentlemen

of the new school, on the other hand, scarcely ever condescend to take their subjects from any descriptions of persons
that are at all known to the common inhabitants of the world;
but invent for themselves certain whimsical and unheard of
beings, to whom they impute some fantastical combination
of feelings, and labour to excite our sympathy for them, either
by placing them in exaggerated moralization or a vague and
tragical description. . . . They introduce us to beings whose
existence was not previously suspected by the acutest observers
of nature, and excite an interest for them, more by an eloquent
and refined analysis of their own capricious feelings, than by
any obvious or very intelligible ground of sympathy in their
situation. . . . They have an idiosyncrasy, upon which all
common occurrences operate in a peculiar manner; and those
who are best acquainted with human nature, and with other
poetry, are at a loss to comprehend the new system of feeling
and of writing which is here introduced to their notice. Instead
of the men and women of ordinary humanity, we have certain
moody and capricious personages, made after the poet's own
heart and fancy—acting upon principles, and speaking in a
language of their own. . . .

A village schoolmaster, for instance, is a pretty common
poetical character. Goldsmith has drawn him inimitably; so
has Shenstone, with the slight change of sex; and Mr Crabbe,
in two passages, has followed their footsteps. Now, Mr
Wordsworth has a village schoolmaster also—a personage who
makes no small figure in three or four of his poems. But by
what traits is this worthy old gentleman delineated by the
new poet? No pedantry, no innocent vanity of learning, no
mixture of indulgence with the pride of power, and of poverty
with the consciousness of acquirements. Every feature which
belongs to the situation, or marks the character in common
apprehension, is scornfully discarded by Mr Wordsworth,
who represents this grey-haired rustic pedagogue as a sort of
half-crazy sentimental person, over-run with fine feelings,
constitutional merriment, and a most humourous melancholy.
Here are the two stanzas in which this consistent and intelligible
character is pourtrayed. The diction is at least as new as the
conception:

> The sighs which Mathew heard were sighs
> Of one tired out with fear and madness;
> The tears which came to Mathew's eyes
> Were tears of light—the oil of gladness.
>
> Yet sometimes, when the secret cup
> Of still and serious thought went round,
> He seemed as if he drank it up,
> He felt with spirit so profound, etc.

A frail damsel is a character common enough in all poems; and one upon which many fine and pathetic lines have been expended. Wordsworth has written more than three hundred lines on that subject; but instead of new images of tenderness, or delicate representation of intelligible feelings, he has contrived to tell us nothing whatever of the unfortunate fair one, but that her name is Martha Ray; and that she goes up to the top of a hill, in a red cloak, and cries, 'O Misery'. All the rest of the poem is filled with a description of an old thorn and a pond, and of the silly stories which the neighbouring old women told about them.

The sports of childhood and the untimely death of promising youth, is also a common topic of poetry. Mr Wordsworth has made some blank verse about it; but, instead of the delightful and picturesque sketches with which so many authors of moderate talents have presented us on this inviting subject, all that he is pleased to communicate of the rustic child, is, that he used to amuse himself with shouting to the owls, and hearing them answer. To make amends for this brevity, the process of his mimicry is most accurately described.

> With fingers interwoven, both hands
> Press'd closely, palm to palm, and to his mouth
> Uplifted, he, as though an instrument,
> Blew mimic hootings to the silent owls,
> That they might answer him.

This is all that we hear of him; and for the sake of this one accomplishment, we are told that the author has frequently stood mute, and gazed on his grave for half an hour together.

Love, and the fantasies of lovers, have afforded an ample theme to poets of all ages. Mr Wordsworth, however, has thought fit to compose a piece, illustrating this copious subject, by one single thought. A lover trots away to see his mistress one fine evening, staring all the way at the moon: when he comes to her door,

> O mercy, to myself I cried,
> If Lucy should be dead.

And there the poem ends.

The Edinburgh Review   1808

This [*The Excursion*] will never do. It bears no doubt the stamp of the author's heart and fancy: but unfortunately not half so visibly as that of his peculiar system. His former poems were intended to recommend that system, to bespeak favour for it by their individual merit; but this, we suspect, must be recommended by the system—and can only expect to succeed where it has been previously established. It is longer, weaker, and tamer, than any of Mr Wordsworth's other productions; with less boldness of originality, and less even of that extreme simplicity and lowliness of tone which wavered so prettily, in the *Lyrical Ballads*, between silliness and pathos. We have imitations of Cowper, and even of Milton here; engrafted on the natural drawl of the Lakers—and all diluted into harmony by that profuse and irrepressible worldliness which deluges all the blank verse of this school of poetry, and lubricates and weakens the whole structure of their style.

The Edinburgh Review   1814

HAZLITT

In describing human nature, Mr Wordsworth equally shuns the common vantage-grounds of popular story, of striking incident, or fatal catastrophe, as cheap and vulgar modes of producing an effect. He scans the human race as the naturalist measures the earth's zone, without attending to the picturesque points of view, the abrupt inequalities of surface. He contemplates the passions and habits of men, not in their extremes, but in their first elements; their follies and vices, not at their height, with all their embossed evils upon their heads, but as lurking in embryo, the seeds of the disorder inwoven with our very constitution. He only sympathizes with those simple forms of feeling which mingle at once with his own identity, or with the stream of general humanity. To him the great and the small are the same; the near and the remote; what appears, and what only is. The general and the permanent, like the Platonic ideas, are his only realities. All accidental varieties and individual contrasts are lost in an endless continuity of feeling, like drops of water in the ocean stream. An intense intellectual egotism swallows up everything. . . . The power of his mind preys upon itself. It is as if there were nothing but himself and the universe. He lives in the busy solitude of his own heart; in the deep silence of thought. His imagination lends life and feeling only to the 'bare trees and mountain bare', peoples the viewless tracts of air, and converses with the silent clouds.

Review of The Excursion   1814

Mr Wordsworth's genius is a pure emanation of the Spirit of the Age. Had he lived in any other period of the world, he would never have been heard of. As it is, he has some difficulty to contend with the hebetude of his intellect, and the meanness of his subject. With him 'lowliness is young ambition's ladder': but he finds it a toil to climb in this way the steep of Fame. His homely Muse can hardly raise her wing from the ground, nor spread her hidden glories to the sun. He has 'no figures nor no fantasies, which busy *passion* draws in the brains of men': neither the gorgeous machinery of mythologic lore, nor the splendid colours of poetic diction. His style is vernacular: he delivers household truths. He sees nothing loftier than human hopes; nothing deeper than the human heart. . . . He takes the simplest elements of nature and of the human mind, the mere abstract conditions inseparable from our being, and tries to compound a new system of poetry from them; and has perhaps succeeded as well as anyone could. '*Nihil humani a me alienum puto*'—is the motto of his works. He thinks nothing low or indifferent of which this can be affirmed: every thing that professes to be more than this, that is not an absolute essence of truth and feeling, he holds to be vitiated, false, and spurious. In a word, his poetry is founded on setting up an opposition (and pushing it to the utmost length) between the natural and the artificial; between the spirit of humanity, and the spirit of fashion and of the world!

It is one of the innovations of the time. It partakes of, and is carried along with, the revolutionary movement of our age: the political changes of the day were the model on which he formed and conducted his experiments. His Muse (it cannot be denied, and without this we cannot explain its character at all) is a levelling one. It proceeds on a principle of equality, and strives to reduce all things to the same standard. It is distinguished by a proud humility. It relies upon its own resources, and disdains external show and relief. It takes the commonest events and objects, as a test to prove that nature is always interesting from its inherent truth and beauty, without any of the ornaments of dress or pomp of circumstances to set it off. Hence the unaccountable mixture of seeming simplicity and real abstruseness in the *Lyrical Ballads*. Fools have laughed at, wise men scarcely understood them. He takes a subject or a story merely as pegs or loops to hang thought and feeling on; the incidents are trifling, in proportion to his contempt for imposing appearances; the reflections are profound, according to the gravity and the aspiring pretensions of his mind. . . .

The daisy looks up to him with sparkling eye as an old acquaintance: the cuckoo haunts him with sounds of early youth not to be expressed: a linnet's nest startles him with boyish delight: an old withered thorn is weighed down with a heap of recollections: a grey cloak, seen on some wild moor, torn by the wind, or drenched in the rain, afterwards becomes an object of imagination to him: even the lichens on the rock have a life and being in his thoughts. He has described all these objects in a way and with an intensity of feeling that no one else had done before him, and has given a new view or aspect of nature. He is in this sense the most original poet now living, and the one whose writings could least be spared: for they have no substitute elsewhere. The vulgar do not read them, the learned, who see all things through books, do not understand them: but the author has created himself an interest in the heart of the retired and lonely student of nature, which can never die.

The Spirit of the Age 1825

COLERIDGE

To . . . defects which . . . are only occasional, I may oppose, with far less fear of encountering the dissent of any candid and intelligent reader, the following (for the most part correspondent) excellences. First, an austere purity of language both grammatically and logically; in short a perfect appropriateness of the words to the meaning. Of how high value I deem this, and how particularly estimable I hold the example at the present day, has been already stated: and in part too the reasons on which I ground both the moral and intellectual importance of habituating ourselves to a strict accuracy of expression. . . .

The second characteristic excellence of Mr W.'s work is: a correspondent weight and sanity of Thoughts and Sentiments —won, not from books, but—from the poet's own meditative observation. . . .

Both in respect of this and of the former excellence, Mr Wordsworth strikingly resembles Samuel Daniel, one of the golden writers of our golden Elizabethan age, now most causelessly neglected: Samuel Daniel, whose diction bears no mark of time, no distinction of age, which has been, and as long as our language shall last, will be so far the language of the today and for ever, as that it is more intelligible to us, than the transitory fashions of our own particular age. A similar praise is due to his sentiments. No frequency of perusal can deprive them of their freshness. For though they are brought into the full daylight of every reader's comprehension: yet are they drawn up from depths which few in any age are priviledged to visit, into which few in any age have courage or inclination to descend. If Mr Wordsworth is not equally with Daniel alike intelligible to all readers of average understanding in all passages of his works, the comparative difficulty does not arise from the greater impurity of the ore, but from the nature and uses of the metal. A poem is not necessarily obscure, because it does not aim to be popular. It is enough, if a work be perspicuous to those for whom it is written, and

> Fit audience find, though few.

To the *Ode on the intimation of immortality from recollections of early childhood* the poet might have prefixed the lines which Dante addresses to one of his own *Canzoni*—

> *Canzon, io credo, che saranno radi*
> *Che tua ragione intendan bene,*
> *Tanto lor sei faticoso ad alto.*

> O lyric song, there will be few, think I,
> Who may thy import understand aright:
> Thou art for *them* so arduous and so high!

But the ode was intended for such readers only as had been accustomed to watch the flux and reflux of their inmost nature, to venture at times into the twilight realms of consciousness, and to feel a deep interest in modes of inmost being, to which they know that the attributes of time and space are inapplicable and alien, but which yet cannot be conveyed save in symbols of time and space. For such readers the sense is sufficiently plain. . . .

Third (and wherein he soars far above Daniel) the sinewy strength and originality of single lines and paragraphs: the frequent *curiosa felicitas* of his diction. . . . This beauty, and as eminently characteristic of Wordsworth's poetry, his rudest assailants have felt themselves compelled to acknowledge and admire.

Fourth: the perfect truth of nature in his images and descriptions, as taken immediately from nature, and proving a long and genial intimacy with the very spirit which gives the physiognomic expression to all the works of nature. Like a green field reflected in a calm and perfectly transparent lake, the image is distinguished from the reality only by its greater softness and lustre. . . .

Fifth: a meditative pathos, a union of deep and subtle thought with sensibility; a sympathy with man as man; the sympathy indeed of a contemplator, rather than a fellow-sufferer or co-mate (spectator, *haud particeps*) but of a contemplator from whose view no difference of rank conceals the sameness of the nature; no injuries of wind or weather, or toil, or even of ignorance, wholly disguise the human face divine. The superscription and the image of the Creator still remain legible to *him* under the dark lines with which guilt or calamity had cancelled or cross-barred it. Here the man and the poet lose and find themselves in each other, the one as glorified, the latter as substantiated. In this mild and philosophic pathos, Wordsworth appears to me without a compeer. Such he *is*: so he *writes*. . . .

Lastly, and pre-eminently, I challenge for this poet the gift of *Imagination* in the highest and strictest sense of the word. In the play of *Fancy*, Wordsworth, to my feelings, is not always graceful, and sometimes *recondite*. The *likeness* is occasionally too strange, or demands too peculiar a point of view, or is such as appears the creature of predetermined research, rather than spontaneous presentation. Indeed his fancy seldom displays itself as mere and unmodified fancy. But in imaginative power, he stands nearest of all modern writers to Shakspere and Milton; and yet in a kind perfectly unborrowed and his own. To employ his own words, which are at once an instance and an illustration, he does indeed to all thoughts and to all objects

> add the gleam,
> The light that never was, on sea or land,
> The consecration, and the poet's dream.

Elegiac Stanzas on a Picture of Peele Castle. . . .

The following analogy will, I am apprehensive, appear dim and fantastic, but in reading Bartram's 'Travels' I could not help transcribing the following lines as a sort of allegory, or connected simile and metaphor of Wordsworth's intellect and genius.—'The soil is a deep, rich, dark mould, on a deep stratum of tenacious clay; and that on a foundation of rocks, which often break through both strata, lifting their back above the surface. The trees which chiefly grow here are the gigantic black oak; *magnolia magniflora; fraxinus excelsior; platane;* and a few stately tulip trees.' What Mr Wordsworth will produce, it is not for me to prophesy: but I could pronounce with the liveliest convictions what he is capable of producing. It is the FIRST GENUINE PHILOSOPHIC POEM. . . .

His *fame* belongs to another age, and can neither be accelerated nor retarded. How small the proportion of the defects are to the beauties, I have repeatedly declared; and that no one of them originates in deficiency of poetic genius. Had they been more and greater, I should still, as a friend to his literary character in the present age, consider an analytic display of them as *pure gain*; if only it removed, as surely to all reflecting minds even the foregoing analysis must have removed, the strange mistake, so slightly grounded, yet so widely and industriously propagated, of Mr Wordsworth's turn for *simplicity*! I am not half so much irritated by hearing his enemies abuse him for vulgarity of style, subject, and conception; as I am disgusted with the gilded side of the same meaning, as displayed by some affected admirers with whom he is, forsooth, a *sweet, simple poet*! and *so* natural, that little master Charles, and his younter sister, are *so* charmed with them, that they play at 'Goody Blake', or at 'Johnny and Betty Foy'!

Biographia Literaria 1817

ANON

One of the causes which have prevented Mr Wordsworth's writings from becoming popular is that he does not confine himself, like most other poets, to the task of representing poetical objects, or of moving our sympathies, but, also, proposes and maintains a system of philosophical opinions. In most of his poems, and in *The Excursion*, especially, he

C

scarcely makes poetry for its own sake, but chiefly as a vehicle for his doctrines, and the spirit of these doctrines is, unfortunately for his success, at variance with the philosophy at present most fashionable in this country. Although possessed of the requisite genius, he does not seem to care for composing poems, adapted to the exclusive purpose of taking hold of the feelings of the people; and among the philosophers, he is rejected because he holds a different language from them. Besides, the habits of thought, in which he chiefly delights, are not calculated to produce that strength of vividness of diction, which must ever constitute one of the chief attractions of poetry. Imagination seems insufficient of itself to produce diction always nervous and poetical, without the aid of human passion and worldly observation. It is from there that the greatest poignancy of words must spring. . . .

Mr Wordsworth has been thought to have more affinity to Milton than any other poet. If this is the case, the affinity is rather in manner than in substance. One beauty cannot fail to strike the reader of his poetry; and that is, the perfect homogeneousness of its spirit. A systematic correspondence pervades the whole, so that the perusal of one piece frequently leads the reader's own mind into a tract of thought, which is afterwards found to be developed by the poet himself, in some other performance. The defects of his poetry originate in the same system of thought which produce its beauties. They are not the result of casual whims, or imperfections, of taste. Certain great convictions of sentiment have so completely pervaded his mind, as to produce a degree of consistency in all its emanations, that we vainly look for in works founded upon observation.

Blackwood's Magazine   1818

LEIGH HUNT

The downfall of the French school of poetry has of late been increasing in rapidity; and its cold and artificial compositions have given way, like so many fantastic figures of snow; and imagination breathes again in a more green and genial time. . . . This has undoubtedly been owing, in the first instance, to the political convulsions of the world, which shook up the minds of men, and rendered them too active and speculative to be satisfied with their commonplaces. A second cause was the revived inclination for our older and greater school of poetry, chiefly produced, I have no doubt, by the commentators on Shakespeare, though they were certainly not aware what fine countries they were laying open. The third, and not the least, was the accession of a new school of poetry itself, of which Wordsworth has justly the reputation of being the most prominent ornament, but whose inner priest of the temple was Coleridge—a man who has been the real ornament of the time in more than one respect, and who ought to have been the greatest visible person in it, instead of a hopeless and dreary sophist.

Preface to Foliage   1818

KEATS

It may be said that we ought to read our contemporaries: that Wordsworth, etc., ought to have their due from us. But for the sake of a few fine imaginative and domestic passages, are we to be bullied into a certain Philosophy engendered in the whims of an Egotist? Every man has his speculations, but every man does not brood and peacock over them. . . .

Letter to Reynolds   1818

[A more important comment on Wordsworth by Keats is given on pp. 200–1]

SHELLEY

He had a mind which was somehow
    At once circumference and centre
Of all he might or feel or know;
Nothing went ever out, although
    Something did ever enter.

He had as much imagination
　　As a pint-pot;—he never could
Fancy another situation,
From which to dart his contemplation
　　Than that wherein he stood.

Yet his was individual mind,
　　And new created all he saw
In a new manner, and refined
Those new creations, and combined
　　Them, by a master-spirit's law.

Thus—though unimaginative—
　　An apprehension clear, intense,
Of his mind's work, had made alive
The things it wrought on; I believe
　　Wakening a sort of soul in sense. . . .

For in his thought he visited
　　The spots in which, ere dead and damned,
He his wayward life had led;
Yet knew not whence his thoughts were fed
　　Which thus his fancy crammed.

And these obscure remembrances
　　Stirred such harmony in Peter,
That whensoever he should please,
He could speak of rocks and trees
　　In poetic metre.

For though it was without a sense
　　Of memory, yet he remembered well
Many a ditch and quick-set fence;
Of lakes he had intelligence,
　　He knew something of heath and fell.

He had also dim recollections
　　Of pedlars tramping on their rounds;
Milk-pans and pails; and odd collections
Of saws, and proverbs; and reflections
　　Old parsons make in burying-grounds.

But Peter's verse was clear, and came
   Announcing from the frozen hearth
Of a cold age, that none might tame
The soul of that diviner flame
   It augured to the Earth:

Like gentle rains, on the dry plains,
   Making that green which late was gray,
Or like the sudden moon, that stains
Some gloomy chamber's window-panes
   With a broad light like day.

For language was in Peter's hand
   Like clay while he was yet a potter;
And he made songs for all the land,
Sweet both to feel and understand,
   As pipkins late to mountain Cotter.

Peter Bell the Third 1819

JOHN STUART MILL

   This state of my thoughts and feelings made the fact of my reading Wordsworth for the first time [in the autumn of 1828], an important event in my life. I took up the collection of his poems from curiosity, with no expectation of mental relief from it, though I had before resorted to poetry with that hope. In the worst period of my depression, I had read through the whole of Byron (then new to me), to try whether a poet, whose peculiar department was supposed to be that of the intenser feelings, could rouse any feeling in me. As might be expected, I got no good from this reading, but the reverse. The poet's state of mind was too like my own. His was the lament of a man who had worn out all pleasures, and who seemed to think that life, to all who possess the good things of it, must necessarily be the vapid, uninteresting thing which I found it. . . . But while Byron was exactly what did not suit my condition, Wordsworth was exactly what did. I had looked into *The Excursion* two or three years before, and found little in it; and I should probably have found as little, had I read it at this time. But the miscellaneous poems, in the two-volume edition of 1815 (to which little of value was added in the latter part of the author's life), proved to be the precise thing for my mental wants at that particular juncture.

In the first place these poems addressed themselves powerfully to one of the strongest of my pleasurable susceptibilities, the love of rural objects and natural scenery; to which I had been indebted not only for much of the pleasure of my life, but quite recently for relief from one of my longest relapses into depression. In this power of rural beauty over me, there was a foundation laid for taking pleasure in Wordsworth's poetry; the more so, as his scenery lies mostly among mountains, which owing to my early Pyrenean excursion, were my ideal of natural beauty. But Wordsworth would never have had any great effect on me, if he had merely placed before me beautiful pictures of natural scenery. Scott does this still better than Wordsworth, and a very second-rate landscape does it more effectually than any poet. What made Wordsworth's poems a medicine for my state of mind, was that they expressed, not mere outward beauty, but states of feeling, and of thought coloured by feeling, under the excitement of beauty. They seemed to be the very culture of the feelings, which I was in quest of. In them I seemed to draw from a source of inward joy, of sympathetic and imaginative pleasure, which could be shared in by all human beings; which had no connection with struggle or imperfection, but would be made richer by every improvement in the physical or social condition of mankind. From them I seemed to learn what would be the perennial sources of happiness, when all the greater evils of life shall have been removed. And I felt myself at once better and happier as I came under their influence. There have certainly been, even in our own age, greater poets than Wordsworth; but poetry of deeper and loftier feeling could not have done for me at that time what his did. I needed to be made to feel that there was real, permanent happiness in tranquil contemplation. Wordsworth taught me this not only without turning away from, but with a greatly increased interest in the common feelings and common destiny of human beings. And the delight which these poems gave me, proved that with culture of this sort, there was nothing to dread

from the most confirmed habit of analysis. At the conclusion
of the *Poems* came the famous Ode, falsely called Platonic,
Intimations of Immortality in which, along with more than his
usual sweetness of melody and rhythm, and along with the
two passages of grand imagery but bad philosophy so often
quoted, I found that he too had had similar experience to
mine; that he also had felt that the first freshness of youthful
enjoyment of life was not lasting; but that he had sought for
compensation, and found it, in the way in which he was now
teaching me to find it. The result was that I gradually, but
completely, emerged from my habitual depression, and was
never again subject to it. I long continued to value Wordsworth less according to his intrinsic merits, than by the
measure of what he had done for me. Compared with the greatest
poets, he may be said to be the poet of unpoetical natures,
possessed of quiet and contemplative tastes. But unpoetical
natures are precisely those which require poetic cultivation.
This poetic cultivation Wordsworth is much more fitted to
give, than poets who are intrinsically far more poets than
he.

Autobiography 1873

The difference . . . between the poetry of a poet, and the
poetry of a cultivated but not naturally poetic mind, is, that
in the latter, with however bright a halo of feeling the thought
may be surrounded and glorified, the thought itself is still
the conspicuous object; while the poetry of a poet is Feeling
itself, employing Thought only as the medium of its utterance.
In the one, feeling waits upon thought; in the other, thought
upon feeling. The one writer has a distinct aim, common to
him with any other didactic author; he desires to convey the
thought, and he conveys it clothed in the feelings which it
excites in himself or which he deems most appropriate to it.
The other merely pours forth the overflowing of his feelings;
and all the thoughts which those feelings suggest are floated
promiscuously along the stream.

It may assist in rendering our meaning intelligible, if we
illustrate it by a parallel between the two English authors of
our own day who have produced the greatest quantity of

true and enduring poetry, Wordsworth and Shelley. Apter
instances could not be wished for; the one might be cited as
the type, the *exemplar*, of what the poetry of culture may
accomplish; the other as perhaps the most striking example
ever known of the poetic temperament. How different, accordingly, is the poetry of these two great writers. In Wordsworth, the poetry is almost always the mere setting of a
thought. The thought may be more valuable than the setting,
or it may be less valuable, but there can be no question as to
which was first in his mind: what he is impressed with, and
what he is anxious to impress, is some proposition, more or
less distinctly conceived; some truth, or something which he
deems such. He lets the thought dwell in his mind, till it
excites, as is the nature of thought, other thoughts, and also
such feelings as the measure of his sensibility is adequate to
supply. Among these thoughts and feelings, had he chosen a
different walk of authorship (and there are many in which he
might equally have excelled), he would probably have made a
different selection of media for enforcing the parent-thought;
his habits, however, being those of poetic composition, he
selects in preference the strongest feelings, and the thoughts
with which most of feeling is naturally or habitually connected.
His poetry, therefore, may be defined to be, his thoughts,
coloured by, and impressing themselves by means of, emotions.
Such poetry, Wordsworth has occupied a long life in producing.
And well and wisely has he so done. Criticisms, no doubt,
may be made occasionally both upon the thoughts themselves,
and upon the skill he has demonstrated in the choice of his
media: for, an affair of skill and study, in the most rigorous
sense, it evidently was. But he has not laboured in vain: he
has exercised, and continues to exercise, a powerful, and
mostly a highly beneficial influence over the formation and
growth of not a few of the most cultivated and vigorous of the
youthful minds of our time, over whose heads poetry of the
opposite description would have flown, for want of an original
organization, physical and mental, in sympathy with it.

On the other hand, Wordsworth's poetry is never bounding,
never ebullient: he has little even of the appearance of spon-
taneousness: the well is never so full that it overflows. There

is an air of calm deliberateness about all he writes, which is not characteristic of the poetic temperament: his poetry seems one thing, himself another; he seems to be poetical because he wills to be so, not because he cannot help it: did he will to dismiss poetry, he need never again, it might almost seem, have a poetical thought. He never seems *possessed* by any feeling; no emotion seems ever so strong as to have entire sway, for the time being, over the current of his thoughts. He never, even for the space of a few stanzas, appears entirely *given up* to exultation, or grief, or pity, or love, or admiration, or devotion, or even animal spirits. He now and then, though seldom, *attempts* to write as if he were; and never, we think, without leaving an impression of poverty: as the brook which on nearly level ground quite fills its banks, appears but a thread when running rapidly down a precipitous declivity. He has feeling enough to form a decent, graceful, even beautiful decoration to a thought which is in itself interesting and moving; but not so much as suffices to stir up the soul by mere sympathy with itself in its simplest manifestation, nor enough to summon up that array of 'thoughts of power' which in a richly stored mind always attends the call of really intense feeling. It is for this reason, doubtless, that the genius of Wordsworth is essentially unlyrical. Lyric poetry, as it was the earliest kind, is also, if the view we are now taking of poetry be correct, more eminently and peculiarly poetry than any other: it is the poetry most natural to a really poetic temperament, and least capable of being successfully imitated by one not so endowed by nature. (Wordsworth's attempts in that strain, if we may venture to say so much of a man whom we so exceedingly admire, appear to us cold and spiritless.)

The Two Kinds of Poetry   1833

FITZGERALD

I have been poring over Wordsworth lately: which has had much effect in bettering my Blue Devils: for his philosophy does not abjure melancholy, but puts a pleasant countenance upon it, and connects it with humanity. It is very well, if the sensibility that makes us fearful of ourselves is diverted to become a cause of sympathy and interest with Nature and mankind: and this I think Wordsworth tends to do.

Letter to John Allen   1832

DE QUINCEY

He was, upon the whole, not a well-made man. His legs were pointedly condemned by all female connoisseurs in legs; not that they were bad in any way which *would* force itself upon your notice—there was no absolute deformity about them; and undoubtedly they had been serviceable legs beyond the average standard of human requisition; for I calculate, upon good data, that with these identical legs Wordsworth must have traversed a distance of 175,000 to 180,000 English miles—a mode of exertion which, to him, stood in the stead of alcohol and all other stimulants whatsoever to the animal spirits; to which, indeed, he was indebted for a life of unclouded happiness, and we for much of what is most excellent in his writings.

Literary Reminiscences   1839

Not, therefore, in *The Excursion* must we look for that reversionary influence which awaits Wordsworth with posterity. It is the vulgar superstition in behalf of big books and sounding pretensions that must have prevailed upon Coleridge and others to undervalue, by comparison with the direct philosophic poetry of Wordsworth, those earlier poems which are all short, but generally scintillating with gems of far profounder truth. I speak of that truth which strengthens into solemnity an impression very feebly acknowledged previously, or truth which suddenly unveils a connexion between objects hitherto regarded as irrelate and independent. In astronomy, to gain the rank of discovery, it is not required that you should reveal a star absolutely new: find out with respect to an old star some new affection—as, for instance, that it has an ascertainable parallax—and immediately you bring it within the verge of human interest; or, with respect to some old familiar planet, that its satellites suffer periodical eclipses, and immediately you bring it within the verge of terrestrial uses. Gleams of steadier vision that brighten into certainty appearances else doubtful, or that unfold relations else unsuspected, are not less discoveries of truth than the downright revelations of the telescope, or the absolute conquests of the diving-bell. It is astonishing how large a harvest of new truths would be reaped simply through the accident of a man's feeling, or being made to feel, more *deeply* than other men. He sees the same objects, neither more nor fewer, but he sees them engraved in lines far stronger and more determinate: and the difference in the strength makes the whole difference between consciousness and subconsciousness. And in questions of the mere understanding we see the same fact illustrated. The author who wins notice the most is not he that perplexes men by truths drawn from fountains of absolute novelty—truths as yet unsunned, and from that cause obscure—but he that awakens into illuminated consciousness ancient lineaments of truth long slumbering in the mind, although too faint to have extorted attention. Wordsworth has brought many a truth into life, both for the eye and for the understanding, which previously had slumbered indistinctly for all men.

For instance, as respects the eye, who does not acknowledge instantaneously the magical strength of truth in his saying of a cataract seen from a station two miles off that it was 'frozen by distance'? In all nature there is not an object so essentially at war with the stiffening of frost as the headlong and desperate life of a cataract; and yet notoriously the effect of distance is to lock up this frenzy of motion into the most petrific column of stillness. This effect is perceived at once when pointed out; but how few are the eyes that ever *would* have perceived it for themselves! . . .

Another great field is amongst the pomps of nature which, if Wordsworth did not first notice, he certainly has noticed most circumstantially. I speak of cloud-scenery, or those pageants of sky-built architecture which sometimes in summer, at noonday, and in all seasons about sunset, arrest or appal the meditative; 'perplexing monarchs' with the spectacles of armies manœuvring, or deepening the solemnity of evening by towering edifices that mimic—but which also in mimicking mock—the transitory grandeurs of man. It is singular that these gorgeous phenomena . . . have been so little noticed by poets. . . . I remember one notice of it in Hesiod—a case where the clouds exhibited:

> The beauteous semblance of a flock at rest.

Another there is, a thousand years later, in Lucan . . . Up and down the next eight hundred years are scattered evanescent allusions to these vapoury appearances; in *Hamlet* and elsewhere occur gleams of such allusions; but I remember no distinct sketch of such an appearance before that in the *Antony and Cleopatra* of Shakspere, beginning:

> Sometimes we see a cloud that's dragonish.

Subsequently to Shakspere, these notices, as of all phenomena whatsoever that demanded a familiarity with nature in the spirit of love, became rarer and rarer. At length as the eighteenth century was winding up its accounts, forth stepped William Wordsworth; of whom, as a reader of all pages in nature, it may be said that, if we except Dampier, the admirable buccaneer, the gentle Filibuster, and some few professional naturalists, he first and he last looked at natural objects with the eye that neither will be dazzled from without nor cheated by preconceptions from within. Most men look at nature in the hurry of a confusion that distinguishes nothing; *their* error is from without. Pope, again, and many who live in towns, makes such blunders as that of supposing the moon to tip with silver the hills *behind* which she is rising, not by erroneous use of their eyes (for they use them not at all), but by inveterate preconceptions. Scarcely has there been a poet with what could be called a learned eye, or an eye *extensively* learned, before Wordsworth. Much affectation there has been of that sort since *his* rise, and at all times much counterfeit enthusiasm; but the sum of the matter is this—that Wordsworth had his passion for nature fixed in his blood; it was a necessity, like that of the mulberry-leaf to the silk-worm; and through his commerce with nature did he live and breathe. Hence it was— *viz* from the *truth* of his love—that his knowledge grew;

whilst most others, being merely hypocrites in their love, have turned out merely sciolosts in their knowledge. This chapter, therefore, of *sky*-scenery may be said to have been revivified amongst the resources of poetry by Wordsworth— re-kindled, if not absolutely kindled. The sublime scene indorsed upon the draperies of the storm in the fourth book of *The Excursion*—that scene again witnessed upon the passage of the Hamilton Hills in Yorkshire—the solemn 'sky prospect' from the fields of France—are unrivalled in that order of composition; and in one of these records Wordsworth has given first of all the true key-note of the sentiment belonging to these grand pageants. They are, says the poet, speaking in a case where the appearance had occurred towards night:

> Meek nature's evening comment on the shows
> And all the fuming vanities of earth. . . .

A volume might be filled with such glimpses of novelty as Wordsworth has first laid bare, even to the apprehension of the *senses*. For the *understanding* when moving in the same track of human sensibilities, he has done only not so much. How often (to give an instance or two) must the human heart have felt the case, and yearned for an expression of the case, when there are sorrows which descend far below the region in which tears gather; and yet who has ever given utterance to this feeling until Wordsworth came with his immortal line:

> Thoughts that do often lie too deep for tears?

This sentiment, and others that might be adduced (such as 'The child is father to the man'), have even passed into the popular heart, and are often quoted by those who know not *whom* they are quoting.

. . . in poetry of this class, which appeals to what lies deepest in man, in proportion to the native power of the poet, and his fitness for permanent life, is the strength of resistance in the public taste. Whatever is too original will be hated at the first. It must slowly mould a public for itself; and the resistance of the early thoughtless judgments must be overcome by a counter-resistance to itself in a better audience slowly mustering against the first. Forty and seven years it is since William Wordsworth first appeared as an author. Twenty of those years he was the scoff of the world, and his poetry a byword of scorn. Now, at this moment, whilst we are talking about him, he has entered upon his seventy-sixth year. For himself, according to the course of nature, he cannot be far from his setting; but his poetry is only now clearing the clouds that gathered about its rising. Meditative poetry is perhaps that province of literature which will ultimately maintain most power amongst the generations which are coming; but in this department, at least, there is little competition to be apprehended by Wordsworth from anything that has appeared since the death of Shakspere.

Tait's Magazine 1845

BAGEHOT

Now it came to pass in those days that William Wordsworth went up in to the hills. It has been attempted in recent years to establish that the object of his life was to teach Anglicanism. A whole life of him has been written by an official gentleman, with the apparent view of establishing that the great poet was a believer in rood-lofts, an idolator of piscinae. But this is not capable of rational demonstration. Wordsworth, like Coleridge, began life as a heretic, and as the shrewd Pope unfallaciously said, 'once a heretic, always a heretic'. Sound men are sound from the first; safe men are safe from the beginning; and Wordsworth began wrong. His real reason for going to live in mountains was certainly in part sacred, but it was not in the least Tractarian. . . .

A sense sublime
Of something far more deeply interfused,
Whose dwelling is the light of setting suns,
And the round ocean and the living air
And the blue sky, and in the mind of man.
A motion and a spirit that impels
All thinking things, all objects of all thought,
And rolls through all things.

The defect of this religion is, that it is too abstract for the practical, and too bare for the musing. What active men require is personality: the meditative require beauty. But Wordsworth gave us neither. The worship of sensuous beauty —the southern religion—is of all sentiments the one most deficient in his writings. His poetry hardly even gives the charm, the entire charm, of the scenery in which he lived. The lighter parts are little noticed: the rugged parts protrude. The bare waste, the folding hill, the rough lake, Helvellyn with a brooding mist, Ullswater on a grey day, these are his subjects. He took a personal interest in the corners of the universe. There is a print of Rembrandt said to represent a piece of the Campagna, a mere waste, with a stump and a man, and under is written *'Tacet et loquitur'*, and thousands will pass the old print-shop where it hangs, and yet have a taste for paintings, and colours, and oils: but some fanciful students, some lonely stragglers, some long-haired enthusiasts, by chance will come, one by one, and look, and look, and be hardly able to take their eyes from the fascination, so massive is the shade, so still the conception, so firm the execution. Thus is it with Wordsworth and his poetry. *Tacet et loquitur.* Fashion apart, the million won't read it. Why should they?— they could not understand it—don't put them out—let them buy, and sell, and die—but idle students, and enthusiastic wanderers, and solitary thinkers, will read, and read, and read, while their lives and their occupations hold. In truth, his works are the Scriptures of the intellectual life; for that same searching, and finding, and penetrating power which the real Scripture exercises on those engaged, as are the mass of men, in practical occupations and domestic ties, do his works exercise on the meditative, the solitary, and the young.

National Review 1864

PATER

An intimate consciousness of the expression of natural things, which weighs, listens, penetrates, where the earlier mind passed roughly by, is a large element in the complexion

of modern poetry. It has been marked as a fact in mental
history again and again. It reveals itself in many forms; but
is strongest and most attractive in what is strongest and most
attractive in modern literature . . . it has doubtless some latent
connexion with those pantheistic theories which locate an
intelligent soul in material things, and have largely exercised
men's minds in some modern systems of philosophy: it is
traceable even in the graver writings of historians: it makes
as much difference between ancient and modern landscape art
as there is between the rough masks of an early mosaic and a
portrait by Reynolds or Gainsborough. Of this new sense, the
writings of Wordsworth are the central and elementary
expression: he is more simply and entirely occupied with it
than any other poet, though there are fine expressions of
precisely the same thing in so different a poet as Shelley. . . .

    . . . this sense of a life in natural objects, which in most
poetry is but a rhetorical artifice, is with Wordsworth the
assertion of what for him is almost literal fact. To him every
natural object seemed to possess more or less of a moral or
spiritual life, to be capable of a companionship with man, full
of expression, of inexplicable affinities and delicacies of intercourse. An emanation, a particular spirit, belonged, not to
the moving leaves or water only, but to the distant peak of
the hills arising suddenly, by some change of perspective, above
the nearer horizon, to the passing space of light across the
plain, to the lichened Druidic stone even, for a certain weird
fellowship in it with the moods of men. It was like a 'survival',
in the peculiar intellectual temperament of a man of letters at
the end of the eighteenth century, of that primitive condition,
which some philosophers have traced in the general history of
human culture, wherein all outward objects alike, including
even the works of men's hands, were believed to be endowed
with animation, and the world was 'full of souls'—that mood
in which the old Greek gods were first begotten, and which
had many strange aftergrowths. . . .

    And it was through nature, thus ennobled by a semblance
of passion and thought, that he approached the spectacle of
human life. Human life, indeed, is for him, at first, only an
additional, accidental grace on the expressive landscape.

When he thought of man, it was of man as in the presence and under the influence of these effective natural objects, and linked to them by many associations. . . .

And, seeing man thus as a part of nature, elevated and solemnised in proportion as his daily life and occupations brought him into companionship with permanent natural objects, his very religion forming new links for him with the narrow limits of the valley, the low vaults of his church, the rough stones of his home, made intense for him now with profound sentiment, Wordsworth was able to appreciate passion in the lowly. He chooses to depict people from humble life, because, being nearer to nature than others, they are on the whole more impassioned, certainly more direct in their expression of passion than other men; it is for this direct expression of passion that he values their humble words. In much that he said in exaltation of rural life, he was pleading indirectly for that sincerity, that perfect fidelity to one's own inward presentations, to the precise features of the picture within, without which any profound poetry is impossible. It was not for their tameness, but for this passionate sincerity, that he chose incidents and situations from common life, 'related in a selection of language really used by men' . . . .

And so he has much for those who value highly the con- centrated presentment of passion, who appraise men and women by their susceptibility to it, and art and poetry as they afford the spectacle of it. Breaking from time to time into the pensive spectacle of their daily toil, their occupations near to nature, come those great elementary feelings, lifting and solemnizing their language and giving it a natural music. The great, distinguishing passion came to Michael by the sheepfold, to Ruth by the wayside, adding these humble children of the furrow to the true aristocracy of passionate souls. In this respect, Wordsworth's work resembles most that of George Sand, in those of her novels which depict country life. With a penetrative pathos, which puts him in the same rank with the masters of the sentiment of pity in literature, with Meinhold and Victor Hugo, he collects all the traces of vivid excitement which were to be found in that pastoral world. . . . A sort of biblical depth and solemnity hangs over

this strange, new, passionate, pastoral world, of which he first
raised the image, and the reflection of which some of our best
modern fiction has caught from him.

He pondered much over the philosophy of his poetry, and
reading deeply in the history of his own mind, seems at times
to have passed the borders of a world of strange speculations,
inconsistent enough, had he cared to note such inconsistencies,
with those traditional beliefs, which were otherwise the object
of his devout acceptance. Thinking of the high value he set
upon customariness, upon all that is habitual, local, rooted in
the ground, in matters of religious sentiment, you might sometimes regard him as one tethered down to a world, refined,
and peaceful indeed, but with no broad outlook, a world
protected, but somewhat narrowed, by the influence of
received ideas. But he is at times also something very different
from this. A chance expression is overheard, and placed in a
new connexion, the sudden memory of a thing long past
occurs to him, a distant object is relieved for a while by a
random gleam of light—accidents turning up for a moment
what lies below the surface of our immediate experience—
and he passes from the humble graves and lowly arches of
'the little rock-like pile' of a Westmoreland church, on bold
trains of speculative thought, and comes, from point to point,
into strange contact with thoughts which have visited, from
time to time, far more venturesome, perhaps errant, spirits.
He had pondered deeply, for instance, on those strange
reminiscences and forebodings, which seem to make our lives
stretch before and behind us, beyond where we can see or
touch anything, or trace the lines of connexion. . . .

And so he has something, also, for those who feel the
fascination of bold speculative ideas, who are really capable of
rising upon them to conditions of poetical thought. He uses
them, indeed, always with a very fine apprehension of the
limits within which alone philosophical imaginings have any
place in true poetry; and using them only for poetical purposes,
is not too careful even to make them consistent with each
other . . . it is the contact of these thoughts, the speculative
boldness in them, which constitutes, at least for some minds,
the secret attraction of much of his best poetry—the sudden

passage from lowly thoughts and places to the majestic forms
of philosophical imagination, the play of these forms over a
world so different, enlarging so strangely the bounds of its
humble churchyards, and breaking such a wild light on the
graves of christened children.

And these moods always brought with them faultless
expression. In regard to expression, as with feeling and
thought, the duality of the higher and lower moods was
absolute. It belonged to the higher, the imaginative mood, and
was the pledge of its reality, to bring the appropriate language
with it. In him, when the poetical motive worked at all, it
united, with absolute justice, the word and the idea; each, in
the imaginative flame, becoming inseparable one with the
other, by that fusion of matter and form, which is the characteristic of the highest poetical expression. His words are themselves thought and feeling; not eloquent, or musical words
merely, but that sort of creative language which carries the
reality of what it depicts, directly to the consciousness. . . .

That the end of life is not action but contemplation—*being*
as distinct from *doing*—a certain disposition of the mind: is,
in some shape or other, the principle of all the higher morality.
In poetry, in art, if you enter into their true spirit at all, you
touch this principle, in a measure: these, by their virtual
sterility, are a type of beholding for the mere joy of beholding.
To treat life in the spirit of art, is to make life a thing in which
means and ends are identified: to encourage such treatment,
the true moral significance of art and poetry. Wordsworth,
and other poets who have been like him in ancient or more
recent times, are the masters, the experts, in this art of impassioned contemplation. Their work is not to teach lessons,
or enforce rules, or even to stimulate us to noble ends; but
to withdraw the thoughts for a little while from the mere
machinery of life, to fix them, with appropriate emotions, on
the spectacle of those great facts in man's existence which no
machinery affects, 'on the great and universal passions of men,
the most general and interesting of their occupations, and the
entire world of nature',—on 'the operations of the elements
and the appearance of the visible universe, on storm and
sunshine, on the revolutions of the seasons, on cold and heat,

on the loss of friends and kindred, on injuries and resentments, on gratitude and hope, on fear and sorrow'.

To witness this spectacle with appropriate emotions is the aim of all culture; and of these emotions poetry like Wordsworth's is a great nourisher and stimulant. . . .

Such is the figure of the more powerful and original poet, hidden away, in part under those weaker elements in Wordsworth's poetry, which for some minds determine their entire character; a poet somewhat bolder and more passionate than might at first be supposed, but not too bold for true poetical taste; an impassioned writer, you might sometimes fancy, yet thinking the chief aim, in life and art alike, to be a certain deep emotion; seeking most often the great elementary passions in lowly places; having at least this condition of all impassioned work, that he aims always at an absolute sincerity of feeling and diction, so that he is the true forerunner of the deepest and most passionate poetry of our own day, yet going back also, with something of a protest against the conventional fervour of much of the poetry popular in his own time, to those older English poets, whose unconscious likeness often comes out in him.

Appreciations 1874

LESLIE STEPHEN

Under every poetry, it has been said, there lies a philosophy. Rather, it may almost be said, every poetry is a philosophy. The poet and the philosopher live in the same world and are interested in the same truths. What is the nature of man and the world in which he lives, and what, in consequence, should be our conduct? These are the great problems, the answers to which may take a religious, a poetical, a philosophical, or an artistic form. The difference is that the poet has intuitions, while the philosopher gives demonstrations; that the thought which in one mind is converted into emotion, is in the other resolved into logic; and that a symbolic representation of the idea is substituted for a direct expression. . . .

The task, indeed, of deducing the philosophy from the

poetry, of inferring what a man thinks from what he feels, may at times perplex the acutest critic. Nor, if it were satisfactorily accomplished, could we infer that the best philosopher is also the best poet. Absolute incapacity for poetical expression may be combined with the highest philosophical power. All that can safely be said is that a man's thoughts, whether embodied in symbols or worked out in syllogisms, are more valuable in proportion as they indicate greater philosophical insight; and therefore that, *ceteris paribus,* that man is the greater poet whose imagination is most transfused with reason; who has the deepest truths to proclaim as well as the strongest feelings to utter. . . .

It follows that a kind of collateral test of poetical excellence may be found by extracting the philosophy from the poetry. The test is, of course, inadequate. A good philosopher may be an execrable poet. Even stupidity is happily not inconsistent with sound doctrine, though inconsistent with a firm grasp of ultimate principles. But the vigour with which a man grasps and assimilates a deep moral doctrine is a test of the degree in which he possesses one essential condition of the higher poetical excellence. A continuous illustration of this principle is given in the poetry of Wordsworth, who, indeed, has expounded his ethical and philosophical views so explicitly, one would rather not say so ostentatiously, that great part of the work is done to our hands. Nowhere is it easier to observe the mode in which poetry and philosophy spring from the same root, and owe their excellence to the same intellectual powers. So much has been said by the ablest critics of the purely poetical side of Wordsworth's genius, that I may willingly renounce the difficult task of adding or repeating. I gladly take for granted—what is generally acknowledged—that Wordsworth in his best moods reaches a greater height than any other modern Englishman. The word 'inspiration' is less forced when applied to his loftiest poetry than when used of any of his contemporaries. With defects too obvious to be mentioned, he can yet pierce furthest behind the veil; and embody most efficiently the thoughts and emotions which come to us in our most solemn and reflective moods. Other poetry becomes trifling when we are making our inevitable passages through the Valley of the Shadow of Death. Words-worth's alone retains its power. We love him the more as we grow older and become more deeply impressed with the sadness and seriousness of life; we are apt to grow weary of his rivals when we have finally quitted the regions of youthful enchantment. And I take the reason to be that he is not merely a melodious writer, or a powerful utterer of deep emotion, but a true philosopher. His poetry wears well because it has solid substance. He is a prophet and a moralist, as well as a mere singer. His ethical system, in particular, is as distinctive and capable of systematic exposition as that of Butler. . . .

The great aim of moral philosophy is to unite the disjoined elements, to end the divorce between reason and experience, and to escape from the alternative of dealing with empty but symmetrical formulae or concrete and chaotic facts. No hint can be given here as to the direction in which a final solution must be sought. Whatever the true method, Words-worth's mode of conceiving the problem shows how powerfully he grasped the questions at issue. If his doctrines are not systematically expounded, they all have a direct bearing upon the real difficulties involved. They are stated so forcibly in his noblest poems that we might almost express a complete theory in his own language. . . .

But I must not take to preaching in the place of Words-worth. The whole theory is most nobly summed up in the grand lines already noticed on the character of the Happy Warrior. There Wordsworth has explained in the most forcible and direct language the mode in which a grand character can be formed; how youthful impulses may be changed into manly purpose; how pain and sorrow may be transmuted into new forces; how the mind may be fixed upon lofty purposes; how the domestic affections—which give the truest happiness—may also be the greatest source of strength to the man who is

More brave for this, that he has much to love;

and how, finally, he becomes indifferent to all petty ambition—

Finds comfort in himself and in his cause:
And, while the mortal mist is gathering, draws
His breath in confidence of Heaven's applause.
    This is the Happy Warrior, this is he
    Whom every man in arms should wish to be.

We may now see what ethical theory underlies Wordsworth's teaching of the transformation of instinct into reason.
We must start from the postulate that there is in fact a Divine
order in the universe; and that conformity to this order
produces beauty as embodied in the external world, and is the
condition of virtue as regulating our character. It is by
obedience to the 'stern lawgiver,' Duty, that flowers gain
their fragrance, and that 'the most ancient heavens' preserve
their freshness and strength. But this postulate does not seek
for justification in abstract metaphysical reasoning. The
'Intimations of Immortality' are precisely intimations, not
intellectual intuitions. They are vague and emotional, not
distinct and logical. They are a feeling of harmony, not a
perception of innate ideas. And, on the other hand, our
instincts are not a mere chaotic mass of passions, to be gratified
without considering their place and function in a certain
definite scheme. They have been implanted by the Divine
hand, and the harmony which we feel corresponds to a real
order. . . .

It only remains to be added once more that Wordsworth's
poetry derives its power from the same source as his philosophy. It speaks to our strongest feelings because his speculations rest upon our deepest thoughts. His singular capacity
for investing all objects with a glow derived from early associations; his keen sympathy with natural and simple emotions;
his sense of the sanctifying influences which can be extracted
from sorrow, are of equal value to his power over our
intellects and our imaginations. His psychology, stated systematically, is rational; and, when expressed passionately, turns
into poetry. To be sensitive to the most important phenomena
is the first step equally towards a poetical or a scientific
exposition. To see these truly is a condition of making
the poetry harmonious and the philosophy logical. And it is

often difficult to say which power is most remarkable in Wordsworth.

MATTHEW ARNOLD

The Excursion and *The Prelude*, his poems of greatest bulk, are by no means Wordsworth's best work. His best work is in his shorter pieces, and many indeed are there of these which are of first-rate excellence. . . . Work altogether inferior, work quite uninspired, flat and dull, is produced by him with evident unconsciousness of its defects, and he presents it to us with the same faith and seriousness as his best work. Now a drama or an epic fill the mind, and one does not look beyond them; but in a collection of short pieces the impression made by one piece requires to be continued and sustained by the piece following. In reading Wordsworth the impression made by one of his fine pieces is too often dulled and spoiled by a very inferior piece coming after it. . . .

Long ago, in speaking of Homer, I said that the noble and profound application of ideas to life is the most essential part of poetic greatness. I said that a great poet receives his distinctive character of superiority from his application, under the conditions immutably fixed by the laws of poetic beauty and poetic truth, from his application, I say, to his subject, whatever it may be, of the ideas

On man, on nature, and on human life,

which he has acquired for himself. The line quoted is Wordsworth's own; and his superiority arises from his powerful use, in his best pieces, his powerful application to his subject, of ideas 'on man, on nature, and on human life.'

Voltaire, with his signal acuteness, most truly remarked that 'no nation has treated in poetry moral ideas with more energy and depth than the English nation.' And he adds: 'There, it seems to me, is the great merit of the English poets.' Voltaire does not mean, by 'treating in poetry moral ideas,' the composing moral and didactic poems;—that brings us but a very little way in poetry. He means just the same thing as was meant when I spoke above 'of the noble and profound application of ideas to life'; and he means the application of these ideas under the conditions fixed for us by the laws of poetic beauty and poetic truth. If it is said that to call these ideas *moral* ideas is to introduce a strong and injurious limitation, I answer that it is to do nothing of the kind, because moral ideas are really so main a part of human life. The question, *how to live*, is itself a moral idea; and it is the question which most interests every man, and with which, in some way or other, he is perpetually occupied. . . .

And when we come across a poet like Wordsworth, who sings

> Of truth, of grandeur, beauty, love and hope.
> And melancholy fear subdued by faith,
> Of blessed consolations in distress,
> Of moral strength and intellectual power,
> Of joy in widest commonalty spread,

then we have a poet intent on 'the best and master thing', and who prosecutes his journey home. We say, for brevity's sake, that he deals with *life*, because he deals with that in which life really consists. This is what Voltaire means to praise in the English poets,—this dealing with what is really life. But always it is the mark of the greatest poets that they deal with it; and to say that the English poets are remarkable for dealing with it, is only another way of saying, what is true, that in poetry the English genius has especially shown its power.

Wordsworth deals with it, and his greatness lies in his dealing with it so powerfully. I have named a number of celebrated poets above all of whom he, in my opinion, deserves to be placed. He is to be placed above poets like Voltaire, Dryden, Pope, Lessing, Schiller, because these famous person-ages, with a thousand gifts, and merits, never, or scarcely ever, attain the distinctive accent and utterance of the high and genuine poets—

> *Quique pii vates et Phoebo digna locuti*

at all. Burns, Keats, Heine, not to speak of others in our list, have this accent;—who can doubt it? And at the same time they have treasures of humour, felicity, passion, for which in Wordsworth we shall look in vain. Where, then, is Wordsworth's superiority? It is here; he deals with more of *life* than they do; he deals with *life*, as a whole, more powerfully.

No Wordsworthian will doubt this. Nay, the fervent Wordsworthian will add, as Mr Leslie Stephen does, that Wordsworth's poetry is precious because his philosophy is sound; and his 'ethical system is as distinctive and capable of exposition as Bishop Butler's'; that his poetry is informed by ideas which 'fall spontaneously into a scientific system of thought'. But we must be on our guard against the Wordsworthians, if we want to secure for Wordsworth his due rank as a poet. The Wordsworthians are apt to praise him for the wrong things, and to lay far too much stress upon what they call his philosophy. His poetry is the reality, his philosophy,— so far, at least, as it may put on the form and habit of 'a scientific system of thought,' and the more that it puts them on,—is the illusion. Perhaps we shall one day learn to make this proposition general, and to say: Poetry is the reality, philosophy the illusion. But in Wordsworth's case, at any rate, we cannot do him justice until we dismiss his formal philosophy. . . .

. . . the 'scientific system of thought' in Wordsworth gives us at last such poetry as this, which the devout Wordsworthian accepts—

> O for the coming of that glorious time
> When, prizing knowledge as her noblest wealth
> And best protection, this Imperial Realm,
> While she exacts allegiance, shall admit
> An obligation, on her part, to *teach*
> Them who are born to serve her and obey;
> Binding herself by statute to secure,
> For all the children whom her soil maintains,
> The rudiments of letters, and inform
> The mind with moral and religious truth.

Wordsworth calls Voltaire dull, and surely the production of these un-Voltarian lines must have been imposed on him as a judgment! One can hear them being quoted at a Social Science Congress; one can call up the whole scene. A great room in one of our dismal provincial towns; dusty air and jaded afternoon daylight; benches full of men with bald heads and women in spectacles; an orator lifting up his face from a manuscript written within and without to declaim these lines of Wordsworth; and in the soul of any poor child of nature who may have wandered in thither, an unutterable sense of lamentation, and mourning, and woe!

'But turn we,' as Wordsworth says, 'from these bold, bad men,' the haunters of Social Science Congresses. And let us be on our guard, too, against the exhibitors and extollers of a 'scientific system of thought' in Wordsworth's poetry. The poetry will never be seen aright while they thus exhibit it. The cause of its greatness is simple, and may be told quite simply. Wordsworth's poetry is great because of the extraordinary power with which Wordsworth feels the joy offered to us in nature, the joy offered to us in the simple primary affections and duties; and because of the extraordinary power with which, in case after case, he shows us this joy, and renders it so as to make us share it. . . .

In Wordsworth's case, the accident, for so it may almost be called, of inspiration, is of peculiar importance. No poet, perhaps, is so evidently filled with a new and sacred energy when the inspiration is upon him; no poet, when it fails him, is so left 'weak as is a breaking wave'. I remember hearing him say that 'Goethe's poetry was not inevitable enough'. The remark is striking and true; no line in Goethe, as Goethe said himself, but its maker knew well how it came there. Wordsworth is right. Goethe's poetry is not inevitable; not inevitable enough. But Wordsworth's poetry, when he is at his best, is inevitable, as inevitable as Nature herself. It might seem that Nature not only gave him the matter for his poem, but wrote his poem for him. He has no style. He was too conversant with Milton not to catch at times his master's manner, and he has fine Miltonic lines; but he has no assured poetic style of his own, like Milton. When he seeks to have a style he falls into ponderosity and pomposity. . . .

Wordsworth has in constant possession, and at command,

no style of this kind; but he had too poetic a nature, and had read the great poets too well, not to catch, as I have already remarked, something of it occasionally. We find it not only in his Miltonic lines; we find it in such a phrase as this, where the manner is his own, not Milton's—

> . . . the fierce confederate storm
> Of sorrow barricadoed evermore
> Within the walls of cities;

although even here, perhaps, the power of style, which is undeniable, is more properly that of eloquent prose than the subtle heightening and change wrought by genuine poetic style. It is style, again, and the elevation given by style, which chiefly makes the effectiveness of *Laodameia*. Still the right sort of verse to choose from Wordsworth, if we are to seize his true and most characteristic form of expression, is a line like this from Michael—

> And never lifted up a single stone.

There is nothing subtle in it, no heightening, no study of poetic style, strictly so called, at all; yet it is expression of the highest and most truly expressive kind.

Wordsworth 1879

MARK RUTHERFORD

During the first two years at college my life was entirely external. My heart was altogether untouched by anything I heard, read, or did, although I myself supposed that I took an interest in them. But one day in my third year, a day I remember as well as Paul must have remembered afterwards the day on which he went to Damascus, I happened to find amongst a parcel of books a volume of poems in paper board. It was called *Lyrical Ballads*, and I read first one and then the whole book. It conveyed to me no new doctrine, and yet the change it wrought in me could only be compared with that which is said to have been wrought on Paul himself by the Divine

apparition. Looking over the *Lyrical Ballads* again, as I have
looked over it a dozen times since then, I can hardly see what
it was which stirred me so powerfully, nor do I believe that it
communicated much to me which could be put into words.
But it excited a movement and a growth which went on till,
by degrees, all the systems which enveloped me like a body
gradually decayed from me and fell away into nothing. Of
more importance, too, than the decay of systems was the birth
of a habit of inner reference and a dislike to occupy myself
with anything which did not in some way or other touch
the soul, or was not the illustration or embodiment of some
spiritual law. There is, of course, a definite explanation to be
given of one effect produced by the *Lyrical Ballads*. God is
nowhere formally deposed, and Wordsworth would have been
the last man to say that he had lost his faith in the God of his
fathers. But his real God is not the God of the Church, but
the God of the hills, the abstraction Nature, and to this my
reverence was transferred. Instead of an object of worship
which was altogether artificial, remote, never coming into
genuine contact with me, I had now one which I thought to
be real, one in which literally I could live and move and have
my being, an actual fact present before my eyes. God was
brought down from that heaven of the books, and dwelt on
the downs in the far-away distances, and in every cloud-
shadow which wandered across the valley. Wordsworth unconsciously did for me what every religious reformer has done,
—he re-created my Supreme Divinity; substituting a new and
living spirit for the old deity, once alive, but gradually hardened
into an idol.

The Autobiography of Mark Rutherford 1881

SWINBURNE

It does not seem to me that the highest distinctive qualities
of Wordsworth's genius are to be found in what is usually
considered his most characteristic work. In homely accuracy
and simplicity he is equalled by Cowper and distanced by
Burns: for the great Scotchman is not more certainly his
superior in humour, animation, and variety than in vivid

veracity of accurate and sympathetic representation. Few poets were ever less realistic than Milton: few at least ever depended less on accuracy of transcription from the simple truth and modesty of nature for the accomplishment of their highest and most abiding aims: and yet the place of Wordsworth, whose own professed aim was to study and reproduce in the effects of his verse the effects of nature in their most actual simplicity, is rather with Milton or with Pindar than with Cowper or with Burns. He wants indeed the constancy of impulse, the certitude of achievement, the steadfastness of inspiration, by which Pindar and Milton are exalted and sustained through the whole course of their spiritual flight from summit to summit of majestic imagination and moral ardour; their sovereign sway and masterdom lay hardly within reach of his less imperial spirit; the ethics of Wordsworth are scarcely so solid and profound as theirs, so deeply based on righteousness and reality, on principles of truth and manhood invariable and independent of custom or theology, of tradition and of time. But is there anything in modern poetry so Pindaric—in other words, is there anything at once so exalted and so composed, so ardent and serene, so full of steadfast light and the flameless fire of imaginative thought, as the hymn which assigns to the guardianship of duty or everlasting law the fragrance of the flowers on earth and the splendour of the stars in heaven? Here at least his conception of duty, of righteousness, and of truth is one with the ideal of Aeschylus, of Alighieri and of Hugo: no less positive and pure, no more conventional or accidental than theirs. And in a lesser lyric than this we find the same spontaneous and sublime perfection of inspired workmanship. None but a poet of the first order could have written the eight lines in which the unforeseeing security of a charmed and confident happiness is opposed to the desolate certitude of unforeseen bereavement by a single touch of contrast, a single note of comparison, as profound in its simplicity as the deepest well-spring of human emotion or remembrance itself. No elaboration of elegiac lament could possibly convey that sense of absolute and actual truth, of a sorrow set to music of its own making,—a sorrow hardly yet wakened out of wonder into sense of its own reality,

—which is impressed at once for ever on the spirit of any reader, at any age, by those eight faultless and incomparable verses. . . .

Whether we do or do not agree at all points with the pupil as critic or commentator, it is none the less undeniable that the perfect, the final, the supreme praise of Wordsworth will always be sought, always cherished, and always enjoyed in Mr Arnold's memorial verses on his death. Here if anywhere is the right chord struck, the just and exact meed of honour assigned to a poet whose work was for so long the object of blundering blame and no less blundering praise. 'Wordsworth's healing power', his gift of direct or indirect refreshment, the comfort and support of his perfect and pure sincerity in all his dealings with nature, can best be felt, can only perhaps be felt in full, when we consent to forget and succeed in forgetting his excursion or excursions into the preacher's province, a territory dense and dubious with didactic quags and theosophic briars. In his own far loftier land of natural contemplation, when least meditative with any prepense or prefixed purpose, he could do such work and give such gifts as no other poet has given or has done. . . . In such a poem, for example, as *Resolution and Independence*, there is a breadth of prouder music, a ring of keener sound, than we expect or admit in elegy; it has more in its highest notes of the quality proper to lyric style—when the lyrist is likewise a thinker; to the lyric style of Sophocles or Pindar. And only in such works as the highest and rarest even of theirs may anyone think to find the like of such a verse as this:

The sleepless soul that perished in its pride.

I will back that against any of Mr Arnold's three representative quotations from Homer, from Dante, and from Shakespeare. It is like nothing from any other hand; the unspeakable greatness of its quality is Wordsworth's alone; and I doubt if it would really be as rash as it might seem to maintain that there is not and never will be a greater verse in all the world of song.

Wordsworth and Byron   1884

J. K. STEPHEN

Two voices are there: one is of the deep;
It learns the storm-cloud's thunderous melody,
Now roars, now murmurs with the changing sea,
Now bird-like pipes, now closes soft in sleep;
And one is of an old half-witted sheep
Which bleats articulate monotony,
And indicates that two and one are three,
That grass is green, lakes damp, and mountains steep:
And, Wordsworth, both are thine: at certain times
Forth from the heart of thy melodious rhymes
The form and pressure of high thoughts will burst:
At other times—good Lord, I'd rather be
Quite unacquainted with the ABC
Than write such hopeless rubbish as thy worst.

The Granta   1891

MADARIAGA

'If,' wrote Matthew Arnold, 'Wordsworth's place among
the poets who have appeared in the last two or three centuries
is after Shakespeare, Molière, Milton, Goethe, indeed, but
before all the rest, then in time Wordsworth will have his due.
We shall recognise him in his place, as we recognise Shakespeare and Milton; and not only we ourselves shall recognise
him, but he will be recognised by Europe also.'

Up to the present day, however, this prophecy has not come
true. Nor is it possible to argue, with Matthew Arnold, that
Europe was slow also in recognising Shakespeare and Milton,
for present-day Europe has achieved a unity of culture unknown in Matthew Arnold's time . . . Nowadays the relatively
small community of men of letters who study and speak for
Europe cannot be said to be hindered by any provincialism of
taste in their estimate of an English poet. English is one of the
three or four great languages of the world. It is not the veil of
ignorance which stands between the world and Wordsworth's

glory. If then Europe has not yet 'recognized Wordsworth, it is perhaps not too rash to assume that she never will. We are then confronted with a question of fact. In England, a considerable body of literary opinion, following Matthew Arnold, holds Wordsworth a glorious third after Shakespeare and Milton. In Europe, Wordsworth is hardly known to the reading many and is not considered as a universal poet by the discerning few. A consistent interpretation of his work and character may perhaps provide an explanation of this discrepancy. . . .

. . . . except for a few of his less guarded utterances—in which he shows how great a poet he might have been—Wordsworth never succeeds in casting his thoughts into one beautiful mould. The unity of each of his works, as well as the unity of his work as a whole, is not aesthetic, but philosophical and moral.

If, then, Wordsworth was rarely loved by the muses, the reason is that he was not sufficiently devoted to them. As a worshipper of Beauty he was neither whole-hearted nor trustful enough. He sought to harness Pegasus to the chariot of thought, not only because he was afraid of the winged horse's 'fancy,' but because a cart is a cart and one can always drive it on useful errands. At bottom, he is too utilitarian, too much in a hurry. He wants results, immediate results, from his cult to the muses. And the muses, like all God-like beings, demand disinterested hearts, and only to trustful and disinterested hearts do they grant the gift of creation. . . .

As a work of thought, no less than as a work of art, it is marred by the fact that the *purpose* of Wordsworth 'is too much with us'. His mental 'milieu' is not passive to the light of nature, but on the contrary *refracts* it and therefore gives to things and people seen through his brain a shape all *his* own. An overpowering nature, he forces upon the objects which he absorbs the texture of his own mind. Hence, his powers of observation far exceed his achievements as a truth-seeker just as his powers of intuition exceed his achievements as a poet. . . .

As studies of truth his poems are no more satisfactory than as impressions of beauty. And for the same reason, that

D

their centre of gravity is beyond them, outside of beauty and outside of truth. . . .

Wordsworth's primary deity was neither Truth nor Beauty. It was Virtue . . . Wordsworth was filled with this generous desire to benefit men with the wisdom distilled by his mind. He had a true vocation for teaching. When he says: 'I wish either to be considered as a teacher, or as nothing,' he is neither trying to smuggle his poetic wares under cover of utility, nor indulging in vain metaphor, but tersely expressing a literal truth. . . . Strong and self-controlled as he was, he could not alter the architecture of his spirit, and in his spirit the triangle True-Good-Beautiful was placed with its *Good* point up. The Good was his strongest tendency, and he had to obey it. He was above all an ethical nature, and every other tendency in him was curbed to the service of his ethical impulse. His work cannot be understood unless it is considered as an *act*. Poor in beauty, hesitating in truth, it is a masterpiece of purpose and intention. . . .

To work, think or feel 'in the air' is as contrary to Wordsworth's nature as it is to that of every Englishman. He feels, as do his countrymen, the necessity of incarnating his thought, and thus his social-moral tendency merges into the bodily or material tendency, also typical of his race. Wordsworth is an excellent example of that materialism—not of thought, but of instinct—which leads the Briton towards preferring to all other activities manifestation in the tangible world. Physically, it shows itself in his splendid animal vitality which inspires so many telling lines in his poetry—particularly in *The Prelude*—as to make quotation unnecessary, and in the cleanliness and innocence of his sense of pleasure—for the body is innocent and cannot sin. Mentally, it appears in what Coleridge called his 'matter-of-fact-ness', a certain inability to rise into the realm of the spirit and to part company with 'flesh and blood'; a certain pedestrian turn of mind which is somewhat connected with that other British characteristic, empiricism. It is also from the social-moral stem that his very British power of self-control derives, since self-control presupposes action, *an aim*, a purpose. And this, the British virtue *par excellence*, is the bane of Wordsworth's poetry, for, though neither all nor

perhaps the best poetry is written when overflowing with
Dionysian spirits, it is doubtful whether a mind that never
was possessed by Dionysos can rise to poetry at all. The
British gentleman and the poet are ever in conflict within
Wordsworth's soul. Generally, the British gentleman wins. . . .

Like all living beings, the British Gentleman must die.
He will die to survive in a still more complex type which is
being evoked under our eyes. Who does not see the far-reaching
changes brought about in British manhood by the economic
evolution of the twentieth century, by the closer relationship
between Great Britain and Anglo-Saxon nations overseas, by
the growing intimacy with France. . .? When the new type of
Englishman asserts itself and its tastes, it is safe to predict
that of all the great names of English literature those will
suffer most which will have most intimately and adequately
represented the type that passed, and of them, Wordsworth
is perhaps the first. His glory belongs to Great Britain and to
the nineteenth century.

It is not the smaller for that. Duration and expansion are
after all but gross conceptions, linked with man's two mental
infirmities, space and time. Depth and power are great if
only for one second, if only in one spot of space. Wordsworth's greatness is precisely in that which limits his appeal: in
the fact that he represents his country and his age in a manner
worthy of his country and his age. That he is neither universal
nor permanent detracts nothing from his symbolical value.
Indeed, it adds perhaps to it. Are not Wordsworthians secretly
pleased and flattered in their insularity when they think of
Wordsworth as surrounded by seas of incomprehension?

*Shelley and Calderon and other Essays on English and Spanish
Poetry* 1920

SIDNEY KEYES

No room for mourning: he's gone out
Into the noisy glen, or stands between the stones
Of the gaunt ridge, or you'll hear his shout
Rolling among the screes, he being a boy again.

He'll never fail nor die
And if they lay his bones
In the wet vaults or iron sarcophagi
Of fame, he'd rise at the first summer rain
And stride across the hills to seek
His rest among the broken lands and clouds.
He was a stormy day, a granite peak
Spearing the sky; and look, about its base
Words flower like crocuses in the hanging woods,
Blank though the dalehead and the bony face.

1941

Byron

Byron was the only one of the Romantic poets to leave no extensive discourses on the nature of poetry: nothing to compare with Wordsworth's Prefaces, *Shelley's* Defence, *or the long questionings scattered through Keats' letters. He gave little thought to the matter, because it seemed to him that it needed little thought; it was settled for him in the simple motto, 'Thou shalt believe in Milton, Dryden, Pope.' His conception of poetry was, in fact, one which he accepted as handed down to him ready— made, and his attitude towards his own writing was rather as to a happy natural knack, which was not only enjoyable, but financially profitable.*

The obvious and nevertheless possibly the right view of his work is to dismiss it as one of the clearest examples of all that is involved in what we now call 'a best-seller': writings, that is to say, of reasonable competence, but of no real distinction what- ever, which, by some lucky coincidence of fashion in readers and flair in the author and his publisher, seize on the public with a force somehow beyond mere literature, of legitimate concern to the social historian and the sociologist, but of no concern at all to the literary critic. Much of his poetry was, of course, the more accessible to the essentially illiterate reading public because it was narrative, unencumbered with subtleties of characterization, conception or expression; and his lyrics were at a level not substantially higher than those of a modern pop song. He was, moreover, what every Englishman dearly loves— a lord, with the additionally endearing trait of being rather a naughty nobleman.

Such, or something like it, is the view inevitably suggested by a view of the extracts given in this section, especially when compared with those in the section on Wordsworth. It is strength- ened by the recollection that Byron was uniformly ungenerous in his comments on Wordsworth, or, what is worse, genuinely unappreciative of him. Again and again Byron's admirers shy away from what he actually wrote and fall into talk of the sheer force of his personality, or into comment on his interesting and in many ways admirable life; none of them writes in the tone of Wordsworth's admirers—the tone of a man whose life has been altered by what he has read.

There is, however, one cause for caution. While Wordsworth never attained any recognition outside Britain, Byron became, even before his death, a major influence upon European literature. The passages quoted below from Goethe, Mazzini, and Herzen illustrate, on a very small scale, the scope of this influence. It is at least arguable that an influence so vast and penetrating, upon men of this calibre, could hardly have been exercised by an entirely third-rate imagination. It is here that Byron's personality becomes inseparable from his writing. As a man, he was in temper and temperament an exile, and he wrote the thoughts and feelings of an exile, even before his self-banishment from English society. And it was perhaps his rendering of the exile's temper and temperament that gave him his grip on the imagination of Young Europe in the 1830's—on the hundreds of young men like Mazzini and Herzen who, through a not very different fusion of inward and outward causes, were forced to spend their lives as exiles. To have rendered so resonantly this temper, to have embodied so passionately the superfluous man, the eternal 'outsider' upon whose solitariness the imaginative and spiritual well-being of the multitude of 'insiders' so much depends, is an achievement not lightly to be dismissed. If only it had been rendered in more living, more deeply meditated, language, there could be no question of dismissing it. But as the last two extracts below suggest, the lack of depth in Byron's English was perhaps one of the main reasons for his European vogue. He was eminently translatable, simply because his language lacked all those overtones and profundities of reference which make translation of real poetry impossible.

BYRON

It may be asked, why, having this opinion of the present state of poetry in England, and having had it long, as my

friends and others well knew—possessing, or having possessed
too, as a writer, the ear of the public for the time being—I
have not attempted to correct rather than encourage the
taste of the day. To this I would answer, that it is easier to
perceive the wrong than to pursue the right, and that I have
never contemplated the prospect 'of filling [with *Peter Bell*—
see its Preface] permanently a station in the literature of the
country'. Those who know me best know this, and that I have
been considerably astonished at the temporary success of my
works, having flattered no person and no party, and expressed
opinions which are not those of the general reader. Could I
have anticipated the degree of attention which has been
accorded me, assuredly I would have studied more to deserve
it. But I have lived in far countries abroad, or in the agitating
world at home, which was not favourable to study or reflection;
so that almost all I have written has been mere passion,—
passion, it is true, of different kinds, but always passion: for
me (if it be not an Irishism to say so) my *indifference* was a
kind of passion, the result of experience, and not the philosophy of nature. Writing grows a habit, like a woman's
gallantry; there are women who have had no intrigue, but
few who have had but one only; so there are millions of men
who have never written a book, but few who have written
only one. And thus, having written once, I wrote on; en-
couraged no doubt by the success of the moment, yet by no
means anticipating its duration, and, I will venture to say,
scarcely even wishing it. But then I did other things besides
write, which by no means contributed either to improve my
writings or my prosperity.

Letter to D'Israeli   1820

I perch upon a humbler promontory,
    Amidst life's infinite variety:
With no great care for what is nicknamed glory,
    But speculating as I cast mine eye
On what may suit or may not suit my story,
    And never straining hard to versify,
I rattle on exactly as I'd talk
With anybody in a ride or walk.

I don't know that there may be much ability
   Shown in this sort of desultory rhyme;
But there's a conversational facility,
   Which may round off an hour upon a time.
Of this I'm sure at least, there's no servility
   In mine irregularity of chime,
Which rings what's uppermost of new or hoary
Just as I feel the 'Improvisatore.'

Don Juan, Canto xv 1823

ANON

The poesy of this young lord belongs to the class which neither gods nor men are said to permit. Indeed we do not recollect to have seen a quantity of verse with so few deviations in either direction from that exact standard. His effusions are spread over a dead flat, and can no more get above or below the level, than if they were so much stagnant water. As an extenuation of this offence, the noble author is peculiarly forward in pleading minority. . . .

But, whatever judgment may be passed on the poems of this noble author, it seems we must take them as we find them, and be content; for they are the last we shall ever have from him. He is, at best, he says, but an intruder into the groves of Parnassus: he never lived in a garret, like thorough-bred poets; and 'though he once roved a careless mountaineer in the Highlands of Scotland', he has not of late enjoyed this advantage. Moreover, he expects no profit from his publi-cation; and, whether it succeed or not, 'it is highly improbable, from his situation and pursuits hereafter', that he should again condescend to become an author. There, let us take what we can get, and be thankful. What right have we poor devils to be nice? We are well off to have got so much from a man of this lord's station, who does not live in a garret, but 'has the sway'[1] of Newstead Abbey, Again, we say, let us be thank-

---

[1] A reference, not undeserved, to one of the poems, *Elegy on Newstead Abbey*, and the lines:

   The last and youngest of a noble line
   Now holds thy mouldering turrets in his sway.

ful; and, with honest Sancho, bid God bless the giver, nor look
the gift horse in the mouth.

Edinburgh Review on Hours of Idleness   1808

[In his *Preface*, Byron had very loftily made such observations
as these: 'Poetry, however, is not my primary vocation; to
divert the dull moments of indisposition, or the monotony of
a vacant hour, urged me "to this sin": little can be expected
from so unpromising a muse . . . With slight hopes, and some
fears, I publish this first and last attempt. . . . It is highly
improbable, from my situation and pursuits hereafter, that I
should ever obtrude myself a second time on the public. . . .'
The sincerity of these prefatory emollients, however, is open
to question, and he was very furious when Jeffrey took them
at their face value. 'I well recollect,' he said in 1821, 'the effect
which the critique of the Edinburgh Reviewers on my first
poem, had upon me—it was rage and resistance, and redress;
but not despondency nor despair. A savage review is hemlock
to a sucking author, and the one on me (which produced the
English Bards etc.) knocked me down—but I got up again.
That critique was a masterpiece of low wit, a tissue of scurrilous
abuse. I remember there was a great deal of vulgar trash,
about people being "thankful for what they could get"—"not
looking a gift horse in the mouth", and such stable expressions.
But so far from their bullying me, or deterring me from writing,
I was bent on falsifying their raven predictions, and determined to show them, croak as they would, it was not the last
time they should hear from me'] Jeffrey

If the finest poetry be that which leaves the deepest impression upon the minds of its readers—and this is not the worst
test of its excellence—Lord Byron, we think, must be allowed
to take precedence of all his distinguished contemporaries.
He has not the variety of Scott—nor the delicacy of Campbell
—nor the absolute truth of Crabbe—nor the polished sparkling
of Moore; but in force of diction, and inextinguishable energy
of sentiment, he clearly surpasses them all. 'Words that breathe
and thoughts that burn,' are not merely the ornaments but
the common staple of his poetry; and he is not inspired or

impressive only in some happy passages, but through the whole body and tissue of his composition. . . .

In Lord Byron . . . we have a perpetual stream of thick-coming fancies—an eternal spring of fresh-blown images, which seem called into existence by the sudden flash of those glowing thoughts and overwhelming emotions, that struggle for expression through the whole flow of his poetry—and impart to a diction that is often abrupt and irregular, a force and a charm which frequently realize all that is said of inspiration.

With these undoubted claims to our admiration, however, it is impossible to deny that the noble author before us has still something to learn, and a good deal to correct. He is frequently abrupt and careless, and sometimes obscure. There are marks, occasionally, of effort and straining after an emphasis, which is generally spontaneous; and above all, there is far too great a monotony in the moral colouring of his pictures, and too much repetition of the same sentiments and maxims. He delights too exclusively in the delineation of a certain morbid exaltation of character and of feeling—a sort of demoniacal sublimity, not without some traits of the ruined Archangel. He is haunted almost perpetually with the image of a being feeding and fed upon violent passions, and the recollections of the catastrophes they have occasioned: and, although worn out by their past indulgence, unable to sustain the burden of an existence which they do not continue to animate:—full of pride, and revenge, and obduracy—disdaining life and death, and mankind and himself—and trampling, in his scorn, not only upon the falsehood and formality of polished life, but upon its tame virtues and slavish devotion: yet envying, by fits, the very beings he despises, and melting into mere softness and compassion, when the helplessness of childhood or the frailty of woman makes an appeal to his generosity. . . .

It is impossible to represent such a character better than Lord Byron has done in all these productions—or indeed, to represent anything more terrible in its anger, or more attractive in its relenting. In point of effect, we readily admit, that no one character can be more poetical or impressive: but it is really too much to find the scene perpetually filled by one character. . . .

We do not consider it unfair to say that Lord Byron appears to us to be the zealous apostle of a certain fierce and magnificent misanthropy; which has already saddened his poetry with too deep a shade, and not only led to the misapplication of great talents, but contributed to render popular some very false estimates of the constituents of human happiness and merit.

The Edinburgh Review 1816

Of *Cain, a Mystery*, we are constrained to say, that, though it abounds in beautiful passages, and shows more *power* perhaps than any of the author's dramatical compositions, we regret very much that it should ever have been published. It will give great scandal and offence to pious persons in general —and may be the means of suggesting the most painful doubts and distressing perplexities, to hundreds of minds that might never otherwise have been exposed to such dangerous disturbance. It is nothing less than absurd, in such a case, to observe, that Lucifer cannot well be expected to talk like an orthodox divine—and that the conversation of the first Rebel and the first Murderer was not likely to be very unexceptionable—or to plead the authority of Milton, or the authors of the old mysteries, for such offensive colloquies. The fact is, that here *the whole argument*—and a very elaborate and specious argument it is—is directed against the goodness or the power of the Deity, and against the reasonableness of religion in general; and there is no answer so much as attempted to the offensive doctrines that are so strenuously inculcated. The Devil and his pupil have the field entirely to themselves—and are encountered with nothing but feeble obtestations and unreasoning horrors. . . .

The Edinburgh Review 1822

Lord Byron complains bitterly of the detraction by which he has been assailed—and intimates that his works have been received by the public with far less cordiality than he was entitled to expect. We are constrained to say that this appears to us a very extraordinary mistake. In the whole course of our experience, we cannot recollect a single author who has had so little reason to complain of his reception—to whose genius the public has been so early and so constantly just—to whose faults they have been so long and so signally indulgent. From the very first, he must have been aware that he offended the principles and shocked the prejudices of the majority, by his sentiments, as much as he delighted them by his talents. Yet there never was an author so universally and so warmly applauded, so gently admonished—so kindly entreated to look more heedfully to his opinions. He took the praise, as usual, and rejected the advice. As he grew in fame and authority, he aggravated all his offences—clung more fondly to all he had been reproached with. . . .

This is the charge which *we* bring against Lord Byron. We say that, under some strange misapprehension as to the truth, and the duty of proclaiming it, he has exerted all the powers of his powerful mind to convince his readers, both directly and indirectly, that all ennobling pursuits, and disinterested virtues, are mere deceits or illusions—hollow and despicable mockeries for the most part, and, at best, but laborious follies. Religion, love, patriotism, valour, devotion, constancy, ambition—all are to be laughed at, disbelieved in, and despised!—and nothing is really good, so far as we can gather, but a succession of dangers to stir the blood, and of banquets and intrigues to soothe it again! If this doctrine stood alone, with its examples, it would revolt, we believe, more than it would seduce:—But the author of it has the unlucky gift of personating all those sweet and lofty illusions, and that with such grace and force and truth to nature, that it is impossible not to suppose, for the time, that he is among the most devoted of their votaries—till he casts off the character with a jerk—and, the moment after he has moved and exalted us to the very height of our conception, resumes his mockery at all things serious or sublime—and lets us down at once on some coarse joke, hard-hearted sarcasm, or fierce and relentless personality—as if on purpose to show—

Who'er was edified, himself was not—

or to demonstrate practically as it were, and by example, how possible it is to have all fine and noble feelings, or their appearance, for a moment, and yet retain no particle of respect for them—or of belief in their intrinsic worth or permanent reality.

The Edinburgh Review 1822

ANON

In the composition of this work there is unquestionably a more thorough and intense infusion of genius and vice— power and profligacy—than in any poem which had ever before been written in the English or, indeed, in any other modern language. Had the wickedness been less inextricably mingled with the beauty, and the grace, and the strength of a most inimitable and incomprehensible muse, our task would have been easy. *Don Juan* is by far the most admirable specimen of the mixture of ease, strength, gaiety and seriousness extant in the whole body of English poetry: the author has devoted his powers to the worst of purposes and passions; and it increases his guilt and sorrow, that he has devoted them entire.

The moral strain of the whole poem is pitched in the lowest key. Love—honour—patriotism—religion, are mentioned only to be scoffed at, as if their sole resting-place were, or ought to be, in the bosoms of fools. It appears, in short, as if this miserable man, having exhausted every species of sensual gratification—having drained the cup of sin even to its bitterest dregs—were resolved to show us that he is no longer a human being, even in his frailties; but a cool unconcerned fiend, laughing with a detestable glee over the whole of the better and worst elements of which human life is composed— treating well-nigh with equal derision the most pure of virtues, and the most odious of vices—dead alike to the beauty of the one, and the deformity of the other—a mere heartless despiser of that frail but noble humanity, whose type was never exhibited in a shape of more deplorable degradation than in his own contemptuously distinct delineation of himself. To confess to his Maker, and weep over in secret agonies, the wildest and most fantastic transgressions of heart and mind is the part of a conscious sinner, in whom sin has not become the sole principle of life and action. But to lay bare to the eye of man—and of *woman*—all the hidden convulsions of a wicked spirit—and to do all this without one symptom of contrition, remorse, or hesitation, with a calm ferociousness of contented and satisfied depravity—this was an insult which no man of genius had ever before dared to put upon his Creator or his species. Impiously railing against his God—madly and meanly disloyal to his Sovereign and his country,—and brutally outraging all the best feelings of female honour, affection, and confidence,—how small a part of chivalry is that which remains to the descendant of the Byrons—a gloomy vizor, and a deadly weapon!

Those who are acquainted (as who is not) with the main incidents in the private life of Lord Byron—and who have not seen this production, will scarcely believe that malignity should have carried him so far, as to make him commence a filthy and impious poem, with an elaborate satire on the character and manners of his wife—from whom, even by his own confession, he has been separated only in consequence of his own cruel and heartless misconduct. . . .

. . . Every high thought that was ever kindled in our breast by the muse of Byron—every pure and lofty feeling that ever responded from within us to the sweep of his majestic inspirations—every remembered moment of admiration and enthusiasm, is up in arms against him. We look back with a mixture of wrath and scorn to the delight with which we suffered ourselves to be filled by one who, all the while he was furnishing us with delight, must, we cannot doubt it, have been mocking us with a cruel mockery—less cruel only, because less peculiar than that with which he has now turned him from the lurking-place of his selfish and polluted exile, to pour the pitiful chalice of his contumely on the surrendered devotion of a virgin-bosom, and the holy hopes of the mother of his child. It is indeed a sad and humiliating thing to know, that in the same year there proceeded from the same pen two productions, in all things so different, as the Fourth Canto of *Childe Harold* and this loathsome *Don Juan*.

Blackwood's Magazine 1819

SHELLEY

I entirely agree with what you say about *Childe Harold*. The spirit in which it is written is, if insane, the most wicked and mischievous insanity that ever was given forth. It is a kind of obstinate and self-willed folly, in which he hardens himself. I remonstrated with him in vain on the tone of mind from which such a view of things alone arises. For its real root is very different from its apparent one. Nothing can be less sublime than the true source of these expressions of contempt and desperation. The fact is, that first, the Italian women with whom he associates are perhaps the most contemptible of all who exist under the moon—the most ignorant, the most disgusting, the most bigoted; countesses smell so strongly of garlic, that an ordinary Englishman cannot approach them. Well, L.B. is familiar with the lowest sort of these women, the people his gondolieri pick up in the streets. He associates with wretches who seem almost to have lost the gait and physiognomy of man, and who do not scruple to avow practices, which are not only not named, but I believe seldom even conceived in England. He says he disapproves, but he endures. He is heartily and deeply discontented with himself; and contemplating in the distorted mirror of his own thoughts the nature and destiny of man, what can he behold but objects of contempt and despair? But that he is a great poet, I think the address to Ocean proves.

Letter to Peacock 1818

He has read to me one of the unpublished cantos of *Don Juan*, which is astonishingly fine. It sets him not only above, but far above, all the poets of the day—every word is stamped with immortality. I despair of rivalling Lord Byron, as well I may, and there is no other with whom it is worth contending. This canto is in the style, but totally, and sustained with incredible ease and power, like the end of the second canto. There is not a word which the most rigid assertor of the dignity of human nature would desire to be cancelled. It fulfills, in a certain degree, what I have long preached of producing— something wholly new and relative to the age, and yet sur- passingly beautiful. It may be vanity, but I think I see the trace of my earnest exhortations to him to create something wholly new.

Letter to his wife 1821

What think you of Lord Byron's last volume? In my opinion it contains finer poetry than has appeared in England since the publication of *Paradise Regained. Cain* is apocalyp- tic; it is a revelation not before communicated to man.

Letter to John Gisborne 1822

KEATS

You speak of Lord Byron and me. There is this great difference between us. He describes what he sees, I describe what I imagine. Mine is the hardest task.

Letter to George Keats 1819

A violent storm in the Bay of Biscay lasted for thirty hours, and exposed the voyagers to considerable danger. 'What awful music!' cried Severn, as the waves raged against the vessel. 'Yes,' said Keats, as a sudden lurch inundated the cabin, 'water parted from the sea.' After the tempest had subsided, Keats was reading the description of the storm in *Don Juan*, and cast the book on the floor in a transport of indignation. 'How horrible an example of human nature,' he cried, 'is this man, who has no pleasure left him but to gloat over and jeer at the most awful incidents of life. Oh! this paltry originality, which consists in making solemn things gay, and gay things solemn, and yet it will fascinate thousands, by the very diabolical outrage of their sympathies. Byron's perverted education makes him assume to feel, and try to

impart to others, those depraved sensations which the want of
any education excites in many.'

Lord Houghton's *Life* 1848

COLERIDGE

It seems, to my ear, that there is a sad want of harmony in
Lord Byron's verses. Is it not unnatural to be always con-
necting very great intellectual power with utter depravity?
Does such a combination often really exist *in rerum natura*?

Table Talk 1822

How lamentably the *art* of versification is neglected by the
poets of the present day!—by Lord Byron, as it strikes me, in
particular, among those of eminence for other qualities. Upon
the whole, I think the part of *Don Juan* in which Lambro's
return to his home, and Lambro himself, are described, is the
best, that is, the most individual, thing in all I know of Lord
Byron's works. The festal abandonment puts one in mind of
Nicholas Poussin's pictures.

Table Talk 1824

CRABB ROBINSON

. . . in the evening read Lord Byron's last poems. The
Prisoner of Chillon is but a feeble work, but *The Dream*, a
poetical review of his life, though it exhibits him in a most
unfavourable point of view—thinking of his first love when at
the altar and marrying his wife whom he is still represented as
loving—is a pathetic and interesting composition. *Darkness*,
too, is a powerful picture of all nature suffering under the
horror of darkness—famine and murder being its accompaniments. The idea is, however, contained in Shakespeare's
lines ending: 'And darkness be the burier of the dead.' . . .
Certainly Lord Byron has the elements of poetry in him and
his style is singularly changing. (4)

Diary 1816

Finished Moore's *Life of Byron*—a book of great interest, but giving little satisfaction. The power of Lord Byron cannot be denied; his strength of passion was, however, not accompanied by corresponding *art*; he had neither a sense of moral beauty to attract him to real excellence nor was he under the influence of a sense of duty. His works give me little pleasure. Nor was his poetical imagination strong, but he was a man of wit and an admirable satirist, and occasionally in his noisy expression of his misanthropy, when it seemed to proceed from a consciousness of his own worthlessness, one could feel respect for the truth of the sentiment.

Diary 1832

LAMB

So we have lost another poet. I never much relished his Lordship's mind, and shall be sorry if the Greeks have cause to miss him. He was to me offensive, and I never can make out his great *power*, which his admirers talk of. Why a line of Wordsworth's is a lever to lift the immortal spirit! Byron can only move the Spleen. He was at best a Satyrist,—in any other way he was mean enough. I dare say I do him injustice; but I cannot love him, nor squeeze a tear to his memory.

Letter to Bernard Barton 1824

GOETHE

Don Juan is a work of boundless genius, manifesting the bitterest and most savage hatred of humanity, and then again penetrated with the deepest and tenderest love for mankind. And as we already know and esteem the author and would not have him other than he is, we gratefully enjoy what with excessive licence, nay with audacity, he dares to set before us. The technical handling of the verse is quite in harmony with the strange, wild, ruthless content; the poet spares his language as little as he spares humanity; and as we approach closer we become aware that English poetry is already in possession of something we Germans totally lack: a cultured comic language.

Commentary on the first instalment of Don Juan 1819

As for the rest, although he has died young, the domain of
letters has lost nothing by that as far as the extension of its
territory is concerned. Byron could go no further; he had
attained the maximum of his powers. What he might have
produced subsequently would doubtless still have been beautiful and admirable, but it would have done more for the reader's
entertainment than for himself. It would not have extended the
limits of the field in which his genius could develop. He had
attained the furthest bourne of his imagination in that incon-
ceivable production *The Vision of Judgment.*

Comment on Byron's death, in conversation with Soret   1824

This poet, whose burning spiritual vision penetrates
beyond all comprehension into the past and the present and,
in their train, also into the future, has now conquered new
worlds for his boundless talent; and no human being can
foresee what he will achieve with them. His method on the
other hand can already be defined with some exactitude.

He holds to the letter of the Biblical tradition. By making
the first human pair barter their original purity and innocence
for a guilt mysteriously induced, and by making the penalty
thus incurred the inheritance of all their descendants, he lays
an enormous burden on the shoulders of Cain as the representative of disaffected humanity, plunged into abject misery
owing to no transgression of its own. The primeval son of
man, bowed down beneath his load of sin, is tormented by
the thought of death, of which he has yet no conception; and
although he may wish the end of his present wretchedness, to
exchange it for a state utterly unknown seems to him still
more repugnant. From this it is already clear that the full
burden of a dogmatic theology, expository, interposing, and
perpetually in conflict with itself—a theology which still
preoccupies us—has been laid on the shoulders of the first
distressful son of man.

These calamities, to which humanity is no stranger, surge
in his soul and cannot be allayed by the resigned meekness of
his father and brother, nor by the loving and soothing minis-
trations of his sister-wife. To aggravate them beyond endurance,

Satan now appears, a powerful seductive spirit, who first unsettles him morally and then leads him miraculously through all worlds, showing him the past as colossally great, the present as small and trivial, the future without consolation.

He returns to his own people, more distraught but not worse than he was before; and finding everything in the family going on in the same way, he feels the importunity of Abel in forcing him to take part in the sacrifice to be utterly intolerable. We say no more than that the scene in which Abel is killed is wonderfully prepared, and what follows is equally great and beyond praise. There lies Abel! This is death, of which we have heard so much, and the race of man knows just as much about it as before.

But we must not forget that through the whole piece there runs a kind of presentiment of the coming Saviour, and that in this as in all other points, the poet has succeeded in approximating to our interpretations and doctrines.

Of the scene with the parents, when Eve finally curses the silent Cain, a scene which our Western neighbour has so admirably singled out for praise, there is nothing more to be said; we can only approach the conclusion with awe and admiration.

Review of Cain   1824

. . . you must not take it evil, but Byron owes these fine views of the Old Testament to the *ennui* he suffered at school. He must have been terribly annoyed at the absurdities and in his own mind he ruminated over them and turned them to account.

Conversation with Crabb Robinson   1829

Lord Byron is to be regarded as a man, as an Englishman and as a great talent. His good qualities derive in the main from the man; his bad from the fact that he was an Englishman and a peer of England; and his talent was incommensurable.

All Englishmen as such are without the power to reflect;

dissipation and party-spirit prevent quiet mental development. But they are great as practical men.

That is why Lord Byron could never attain self-knowledge, and why his reflections are altogether wide of the mark. . . .

Byron's high rank as an English peer was very disadvantageous to him; for if every talent is hindered by the outside world, how much more is that the case for one of such high birth and great wealth!

Conversation with Eckerman 1825

SCOTT

It has been, however, reserved for our own time to produce one distinguished example of the Muse having descended upon a bard of a wounded spirit, and lent her lyre to tell, and we trust, to soothe, afflictions of no ordinary description; afflictions originating probably in that singular combination of feeling which has been called the poetical temperament, and which has so often saddened the days of those on whom it has been conferred. If ever a man could lay claim to that character in all its strength and all its weakness, with its unbounded range of enjoyment, and its exquisite sensibility of pleasure and of pain, it must certainly be granted to Lord Byron. Nor does it require much time, or a deep acquaintance with human nature, to discover why these extraordinary powers should in many cases have contributed more to the wretchedness than to the happiness of their possessor.

Edinburgh Weekly Journal 1824

HAZLITT

Intensity is the great and prominent distinction of Lord Byron's writings. He seldom gets beyond force of style, nor has he produced any regular work or masterly whole. He does not prepare any plan beforehand, nor revise and retouch what he has written with polished accuracy. His only object seems to be to stimulate himself and his readers for the moment —to keep both alive, to drive away *ennui*, to substitute a feverish and irritable state of excitement for listless indolence or even calm enjoyment. For this purpose he pitches on any subject at random without much thought or delicacy—he is only impatient to begin—and takes care to adorn and enrich it as he proceeds with 'thoughts that breathe and words that burn'. He composes (as he himself has said) whether he is in the bath, in his study, or on horseback—he writes as habitually as others talk or think—and whether we have the inspiration of the Muse or not, we always find the spirit of the man of genius breathing from his verse. He grapples with his subject, and moves, penetrates, and animates it by the electric force of his own feelings. He is often monotonous, extravagant, offensive; but he is never dull, or tedious, but when he writes prose. Lord Byron does not exhibit a new view of nature, or raise insignificant objects into importance by the romantic associations with which he surrounds them; but generally (at least) takes commonplace thoughts and events, and endeavours to express them in stronger and statelier language than others. His poetry stands like a Martello tower by the side of his subject. He does not, like Mr Wordsworth, lift poetry from the ground, or create a sentiment out of nothing. He does not describe a daisy or a periwinkle, but the cedar or the cypress: not 'poor men's cottages, but princes' palaces'. His *Childe Harold* contains a lofty and impassioned review of the great events of history, of the mighty objects left as wrecks of time, but he dwells chiefly on what is familiar to the mind of every schoolboy; has brought out few new traits of feeling or thought; and has done no more than justice to the reader's preconceptions by the sustained force and brilliancy of his style and imagery. . . .

The *Don Juan* indeed has great power; but its power is owing to the force of the serious writing, and to the oddity of the contrast between that and the flashy passages with which it is interlarded. From the sublime to the ridiculous there is but one step. You laugh and are surprised that any one should turn round and *travestie* himself: the drollery is in the utter discontinuity of ideas and feelings. He makes virtue serve as a foil to vice; *dandyism* is (for want of any other) a variety of genius. A classical intoxication is followed by the splashing of soda-water, by frothy effusions of ordinary bile. After the lightning and the hurricane, we are introduced to the interior of the cabin and the contents of the wash-hand basins. The solemn hero of tragedy plays *Scrub* in the farce. This is 'very tolerable and not to be endured'. The Noble Lord is almost the only writer who has prostituted his talents in this way. He hallows in order to desecrate; takes pleasure in defacing the images of beauty his hand wrought; and raises our hopes and our beliefs in goodness to heaven only to dash them to earth again, and break them in pieces the more effectually from the height they have fallen. Our enthusiasm for genius or virtue is thus turned into a jest by the very person who has kindled it, and who thus fatally quenches the spark of both. It is not that Lord Byron is sometimes serious and sometimes trifling, sometimes profligate, and sometimes moral—but when he is most serious and most moral, he is only preparing to mortify the unsuspecting reader by putting a pitiful *hoax* upon him. This is a most unaccountable anomaly. It is as if the eagle were to build its eyry in a common sewer, or the owl were seen soaring to the mid-day sun. Such a sight might make one laugh, but one would not wish or expect it to occur more than once.

In fact, Lord Byron is the spoiled child of fame as well as fortune. He has taken a surfeit of popularity, and is not contented to delight, unless he can shock the public. He would force them to admire in spite of decency and common sense— he would have them read what they would read in no one but himself, or he would not give a rush for their applause. . . .

We had written thus far when news came of the death of Lord Byron, and put an end at once to a strain of somewhat peevish invective, which was intended to meet his eye, not to insult his memory. Had we known that we were writing his epitaph, we must have done it with a different feeling. As it is, we think it better and more like himself, to let what we had written stand, than to take up our leaden shafts, and try to melt them into 'tears of sensibility', or mould them into dull praise, and an unaffected show of candour. We were not silent during the author's life-time, either for his reproof or his encouragement (such as we could give, and *he* did not disdain to accept) nor can we now turn undertaker's men to fix the glittering plate upon his coffin, or fall into the procession of popular woe. Death cancels everything but truth; and strips a man of everything but genius and virtue. It is a sort of natural canonization. It makes the meanest of us sacred—it installs the poet in his immortality, and lifts him to the skies. Death is the great assayer of the sterling ore of talent. At his touch the drossy particles fall off, the irritable, the personal, the gross, and mingle with the dust—the finer and more ethereal part mounts with the winged spirit to watch over our latest memory, and protect our bones from insult. We consign the least worthy qualities to oblivion, and cherish the nobler and imperishable nature with double pride and fondness. Nothing could show the real superiority of genius in a more striking point of view than the idle contests and the public indifference about the place of Lord Byron's interment, whether in West-minster Abbey or his own family vault. A king must have a coronation—a nobleman a funeral procession.—The man is nothing without the pageant. The poet's cemetery is the human mind, in which he sows the seeds of never-ending thought—his monument is to be found in his works:

> Nothing can cover his high fame but heaven;
> No pyramids set off his memory,
> But the eternal substance of his greatness.

Lord Byron is dead: he also died a martyr to his zeal in the cause of freedom, for the last, best hopes of man. Let that be his excuse and his epitaph!

The Spirit of the Age 1825

WORDSWORTH

Lord Byron has spoken severely of my compositions. However faulty they may be, I do not think that I ever could have prevailed upon myself to print such lines as he has done.
. . .
Byron seems to me deficient in *feeling*.

Opinions Expressed 1827

MOORE

It will be found . . . on reflection, that this very versatility, which renders it so difficult to fix, 'ere it change', the fairy fabric of his character is, in itself, the true clue through all that fabric's mazes,—is in itself the solution of whatever was most dazzling in his might or startling in his levity, of all that most attracted and repelled, whether in his life or his genius. A variety of powers almost boundless, and a pride no less vast in displaying them,—a susceptibility of new impressions and impulses, even beyond the usual allotment of genius, and an uncontrolled impetuosity, as well from habit as temperament, in yielding to them,—such were the two great and leading sources of all that varied spectacle which his life exhibited; of that succession of victories achieved by his genius, in almost every field of mind that genius ever trod, and of all those sallies of character in every shape and direction that un- checked feeling and dominant self-will could dictate.

It must be perceived by all endowed with quick powers of association how constantly, when any particular thought or sentiment presents itself to their minds, its very opposite, at the same moment, springs up there also:—if any thing sublime occurs, its neighbour, the ridiculous, is by its side;— with a bright view of the present or future, a dark one mixes also its shadow;—and, even in questions respecting morals and conduct, all the reasonings and consequences that may suggest themselves on the side of one of two opposite courses will, in such minds, be instantly confronted by an array just as cogent on the other. A mind of this structure,—and such, more or less, are all those in which the reasoning is made subservient to the imaginative faculty,—though enabled, by such rapid powers of association to multiply its resources without end, has need of the constant exercise of a controlling judgment to keep its perceptions pure and undisturbed between the contrasts it thus simultaneously calls up; the obvious danger being that, where matters of taste are con- cerned, the habit of forming such incongruous juxtapositions— as that, for example, between the burlesque and sublime—

should at last vitiate the mind's relish for the nobler and
higher quality; and that, on the yet more important subject of
morals, a facility in finding reasons for every side of a question
may end, if not in the choice of the worst, at least in a sceptical
indifference to all.

In picturing to oneself so awful an event as a shipwreck,
its many horrors and perils are what alone offer themselves
to ordinary fancies. But the keen, versatile imagination of
Byron could detect in it far other details, and, at the same
moment with all that is fearful and appalling in such a scene,
could bring together all that is most ludicrous and low. That
in this painful mixture he was but too true to human nature,
the testimony of De Retz (himself an eye-witness of such an
event) attests:—'*Vous ne pouvez vous imaginer* (says the
Cardinal) *l'horreur d'une grande tempête;—vous en pouvez
imaginer aussi peu le ridicule.*' But, assuredly, a poet less
wantoning in the variety of his power, and less proud of
displaying it, would have paused ere he mixed up, thus
mockingly, the degradation of humanity with its sufferings,
and, content to probe us to the core with the miseries of our
fellow-men, would have forborne to wring from us, the next
moment, a bitter smile at their baseness. . . .

Among the less serious ills flowing from this abuse of his
great versatile powers,—more especially as exhibited in his
most characteristic work, *Don Juan,*—it will be found that even
the strength and impressiveness of his poetry is sometimes not
a little injured by the capricious and desultory flights into
which this pliancy of wing allures him. It must be felt, indeed,
by all readers of that work, and particularly by those who,
being gifted with but a small portion of such ductility themselves, are unable to keep pace with his changes, that the
suddenness with which he passes from one strain of sentiment
to another,—from the frolic to the sad, from the cynical to
the tender,—begets a distrust in the sincerity of one or both
moods of mind which interferes with, if not chills, the sympathy that a more natural transition would inspire. In general
such a suspicion would do him injustice; as, among the
singular combinations which his mind presented, that of
uniting at once versatility and depth of feeling was not the

least remarkable. But, on the whole, favourable as was all this quickness and variety of association to the extension of the range and resources of his poetry, it may be questioned whether a more select concentration of his powers would not have afforded a still more grand and precious result. Had the minds of Milton and Tasso been thus thrown open to the incursions of light, ludicrous fancies, who can doubt that those solemn sanctuaries of genius would have been as much injured as profaned by the intrusion?—and it is at least a question whether, if Lord Byron had not been so actively versatile, so totally under the domination of

> A fancy, like the air, most free,
> And full of mutability,

he would not have been less wonderful, perhaps, but more great.

Letters and Journals of Lord Byron   1830

MACAULAY

There can be no doubt that this remarkable man owed the vast influence which he exercised over his contemporaries at least as much to his gloomy egotism as to the real power of his poetry. We never could very clearly understand how it is that egotism, so unpopular in conversation, should be so popular in writing; or how it is that men who affect in their compositions qualities and feelings which they have not impose so much more easily on their contemporaries than on posterity. . . .

. . . a few more years will destroy whatever yet remains of that magical potency which once belonged to the name of Byron. To us he is still a man, young, noble, and unhappy. To our children he will be merely a writer; and their impartial judgment will appoint his place among writers, without regard to his rank or his private history. That his poetry will undergo a severe sifting, that much of what has been admired by his contemporaries will be rejected as worthless, we have little doubt. But we have as little doubt that, after the closest scrutiny, there will still remain much that can only perish with the English language. . . .

He [Voltaire], like Lord Byron, put himself at the head of an intellectual revolution, dreading it all the time, murmuring at it, sneering at it, yet choosing rather to move before his age in any direction than to be left behind and forgotten. . . .

Though always sneering at Mr Wordsworth, he was yet, though perhaps unconsciously, the interpreter between Mr Wordsworth and the multitude. In the *Lyrical Ballads* and *The Excursion* Mr Wordsworth appeared as the high priest of a worship, of which nature was the idol. No poems have ever indicated a more exquisite perception of the beauty of the outer world, or a more passionate love and reverence of that beauty. Yet they were not popular; and it is not likely that they ever will be popular as the poetry of Sir Walter Scott is popular. The feeling which pervaded them was too deep for general sympathy. Their style was often too mysterious for general comprehension. They made a few esoteric disciples, and many scoffers. Lord Byron founded what may be called an esoteric Lake school; and all the readers of verse in England, we might say in Europe, hastened to sit at his feet. What Mr Wordsworth had said like a recluse, Lord Byron said like a man of the world, with less profound feeling, but with more perspicuity, energy and conciseness. We would refer our readers to the last two cantos of *Childe Harold* and to *Manfred*, in proof of these observations.

The Edinburgh Review   1831

HENRY TAYLOR

The poetical taste to which some of the popular poets of this century gave birth, appears at present to maintain a more unshaken dominion over the writers of poetry, than over its readers.

These poets were characterised by great sensibility and fervour, by a profusion of imagery, by force and beauty of language, and by a versification peculiarly easy and adroit, and abounding in that sort of melody, which, by its very obvious cadences, makes itself most pleasing to an unpractised ear. They exhibited, therefore, many of the most attractive graces and charms of poetry—its vital warmth not less than its external embellishments; and had not the admiration which they excited, tended to produce an indifference to higher, graver, and more various endowments, no one would have said that it was, in any evil sense, excessive. But from this unbounded indulgence in the mere luxuries of poetry, has there not ensued a want of adequate appreciation for its intellectual and immortal part? . . .

So keen was the sense of what the new poets possessed, that it never seemed to be felt that any thing was deficient in them. Yet their deficiencies were not unimportant. They wanted, in the first place, subject matter. A feeling came more easily to them than a reflection, and an image was always at hand when a thought was not forthcoming. Either they did not look upon mankind with observant eyes, or they did not feel it to be any part of their vocation to turn what they saw to account. It did not belong to poetry, in their apprehension, to thread the mazes of life in all its classes and under all its circumstances, common as well as romantic, and, seeing all things, to infer and to instruct: on the contrary, it was to stand aloof from everything that is plain and true; to have little concern with what is rational and wise; it was to be, like music, a moving and enchanting art, acting upon the fancy, the affections, the passions, but scarcely connected with the exercise of the intellectual faculties. These writers had, indeed, adopted a tone of language which is hardly consistent with the state of mind in which a man makes use of his understanding. . . .

Poetry of which sense is not the basis, though it may be excellent of its kind, will not long be reputed to be poetry of the highest order. It may move the feelings and charm the fancy; but failing to satisfy the understanding, it will not take permanent possession of the strong-holds of fame. Lord Byron, in giving the most admirable example of this species of poetry, undoubtedly gave the strongest impulse to the appetite for it. Yet the impulse is losing its force, and even Lord Byron himself repudiated, in the latter years of his life, the poetical taste which he had espoused and propagated. . . .

Had he united a philosophical intellect to his peculiarly poetical temperament, he would probably have been the greatest poet of his age. But no man can be a very great poet which is not also a great philosopher. Whatever Lord Byron's natural powers may have been, idleness and light reading, an early acquisition of popularity by the exercise of a single talent, and an absorbing and contracting self-love, confined the field of his operations within narrow limits. He was in knowledge merely a man of Belles-lettres; nor does he appear at any time to have betaken himself to such studies as would have tended to the cultivation and discipline of his reasoning powers, or the enlargement of his mind. He had, however, not only an ardent and brilliant imagination, but a clear under-standing; and the signs both of what he had and of what he wanted, are apparent in his poetry. There is apparent in it a working and moulding spirit, with a want of material to work up,—a great command of language, with a want of any views or reflections which, if unembellished by imagery, or un-associated with passionate feelings, it would be very much worth while to express. . . .

Lord Byron's conception of a hero is an evidence, not only of scanty materials of knowledge from which to construct the ideal of a human being, but also of a want of perception of what is great or noble in our nature. His heroes are creatures abandoned to their passions, and essentially, there-fore, weak of mind. Strip them of the veil of mystery and the trappings of poetry, resolve them into their plain realities, and they are such beings as, in the eyes of a man of masculine judgment, would certainly excite no sentiment of admiration, even if they did not provoke contempt.

Preface to Philip van Artevelde   1834

MAZZINI

Byron appears at the close of one epoch, and before the dawn of the other; in the mist of a community based upon an aristocracy which has outlived the vigour of its prime; sur-rounded by a Europe containing nothing grand, unless it be Napoleon on one side and Pitt on the other, genius degraded to minister to egotism; intellect bound to the service of the past. No seer exists to foretell the future: belief is extinct;

there is only its pretence: prayer is no more; there is only a
movement of the lips at a fixed day or hour, for the sake of the
family, or what is called *the people*: love is no more; desire
has taken its place; the holy warfare of ideas is abandoned;
the conflict is that of interests. The worship of great thoughts
has passed away. That which *is*, raises the tattered banner of
some corpse-like traditions; that which *would be*, hoists only
the standard of physical wants, of material appetites: around
him are ruins, beyond him the desert; the horizon is a blank.
A long cry of suffering and indignation bursts from the heart
of Byron; he is answered by anathemas. He departs; he
hurries through Europe in search of an ideal to adore; he
traverses it distracted, palpitating, like Mazeppa on the wild
horse; borne onwards by a fierce desire; the wolves of envy
and calumny follow in pursuit. He visits Greece, he visits
Italy; if anywhere a lingering spark of the sacred fire, a ray of
divine poetry, is preserved, it must be *there*. Nothing. A glorious
past, a degraded present; none of life's poetry; no movement,
save that of the sufferer turning on his couch to relieve his
pain. Byron, from the solitude of his exile, turns his eyes again
towards England; he sings. What does he sing? What springs
from the mysterious and unique conception which rules, one
would say in spite of himself, over all that escapes him in his
sleepless vigil? The funeral hymn, the death-song, the epitaph
of the aristocratic idea; we discovered it, we Continentalists;
not his own countrymen. He takes his types from amongst
those privileged by strength, beauty, and individual power.
They are grand, poetical, heroic, but solitary . . . Each of them
is the personification, slightly modified, of a single type, a
single idea—the *individual*; free, but nothing more than free;
such as the epoch now closing has made him;—Faust, but
without the compact which submits him to the enemy; for
the heroes of Byron make no such compact. . . . What can they
do with the liberty so painfully won? On whom, on what
expend the exuberant vitality within them? *They are alone*;
this is the secret of their wretchedness and impotence. They
'thirst for good'—Cain has said it for all of them—but cannot
achieve it; for they have no mission, no belief, no comprehension even of the world around them. They have never

realized the conception of *Humanity* in the multitudes that
have preceded, surround, and will follow after them; never
thought on their own place between the past and future; on
the continuity of labour that unites all the generations into one
Whole; on the common end and aim, only to be realized by
the common effort; on the spiritual post-sepulchral life even
on earth of the individual, through the thoughts he transmits
to his fellows; and, it may be—when he lives devoted and dies
in faith—through the guardian agency he is allowed to exercise
over the loved ones left on earth.

Gifted with a liberty they know not how to use; with a
power and energy they know not how to apply; with a life
whose purpose and aim they comprehend not;—they drag
through their useless and convulsed existence. Byron destroys
them one after the other, as if he were the executioner of a
sentence decreed by heaven. . . . This, for those who can read
with the soul's eyes, is what Byron sings; or rather what
Humanity sings through him. The emptiness of the life and
death of solitary individuality has never been so powerfully
and efficaciously summed up as in the pages of Byron. . . .

The day will come when Democracy will remember all
that it owes to Byron. England too, will, I hope, one day
remember the mission—so entirely English, yet hitherto overlooked by her—which Byron fulfilled on the Continent; the
European rôle given by him to English literature, and the
appreciation and sympathy for England which he awakened
amongst us.

Before he came, all that was known of English literature
was the French translation of Shakespeare, and the anathema
hurled by Voltaire against the 'intoxicated barbarian'. It is
since Byron that we Continentalists have learned to study
Shakespeare and other English writers. From him dates the
sympathy of all the true-hearted amongst us for this land of
liberty, whose true vocation he so worthily represented among
the oppressed. He led the genius of Britian on a pilgrimage
throughout all Europe.

Byron and Goethe 1839

LANDOR

Landor: He had drawn largely from his imagination, penuriously from his heart. He distrusted it: what wonder, then, if he had little faith in another's! Had he lived among the best of the ancient Greeks, he would have satirised and reviled them; but their characters caught his eye softened by time and distance; nothing in them of opposition, nothing of rivalry; where they are, they must stand; they cannot come down nearer. Of all great poets, for such I consider him, Byron has borrowed most from others, not excepting Ariosto, of whose description he reminds me—

> Salta a cavallo e per *diversa strada*
> Va discorrendo, e *molti pone a sacco*.

Not only in the dresses which he puts on expressly for the ladies, not only in the oriental train and puffy turban, but also in the tragic pall, his perfumery has somewhat too large a proportion of musk in it; which so hangs about those who are accustomed to spend many hours with him, that they seldom come forth again with satisfaction into what is fresher and purer. Yet Byron is, I think, the keenest and most imaginative of satirists.

English Visitor: Those who spoke the most malignantly of him in his lifetime have panegyrized him since his decease, with so little truth, discretion and precision, that we may expect it to have been done designedly; and the rather, as the same insincerity hath been displayed towards others, both where there might be and where there could not be a jealousy of rivalship. After his hot and stimulating spicery, we are now running to those sager poets who give us lemonade and ices; just by the same direction as dogs recur to grass. We rush out of the sudatory of Byron to roll in the snow of Wordsworth.

Landor: He suited the times. The rapid excitement and easy reading of novels, the only literature (if such it may be called) which interests the public, outrun the graver and measured steps of poetry. We have no longer decennial epics

E

and labyrinthine tragedies. Our steeplechases are out of vogue: we canter up and down the narrow green lane with the ladies, and return with an appetite and small fatigue. Byron dealt chiefly in felt and furbelow, wavy Damascus daggers, and pocket pistols studded with paste. He threw out frequent and brilliant sparks; but his fire burnt to no purpose; it blazed furiously when it caught muslin, and it hurried many a pretty wearer into an untimely blanket.

English Visitor: They who were lately his most zealous admirers now disown him.

Landor: Dress, medicine, poetry, are subject to fashion and variation. The same people have extolled and reviled both Wordsworth and Byron. Public taste must first be vitiated and then consulted. To praise immoderately the poet who before was immoderately depreciated, is the easiest way to knock out a gilt nail-head from the coffin.

Imaginary Conversations: Landor, English Visitor, and
Florentine 1846

HERZEN

Imagine a hothouse-reared youth—the one, for instance, who has described himself in *The Dream*; imagine him face to face with the most boring, with the most tedious society, face to face with the monstrous Minotaur of English life, uncouthly welded together of two beasts—the one sinking into decrepitude, the other knee-deep in filthy mire, weighed down like the Caryatides whose everlastingly strained muscles leave not a drop of blood for the brain. If he could have adapted himself to this life, he would, instead of dying at thirty in Greece, by now have been Lord Palmerston or Lord John Russell. But since he could not, there is nothing surprising in his saying, like his Harold to his ship:

> Nor care what land thou bearest me to,
> But not again to mine.

But what awaited him in the distance? Spain devastated by Napoleon, Greece sunk back into barbarism, the general resurrection after 1814 of all the stinking Lazaruses; there was no getting away from them in Ravenna or in Diodati. Byron could not be satisfied like a German with theories *sub specie aeternitatis*, nor like a Frenchman with political chatter; he was crushed, but crushed like a menacing Titan, flinging his scorn in men's faces and not troubling to soften the blow.

This discordance and disharmony, of which Byron as a poet and a genius was conscious forty years ago, has, after a succession of painful experiences, after the filthy transition from 1830 to 1848, and the infamous one from 1848 to the present, overwhelmed many of us to-day. And we, like Byron, do not know what to do with ourselves, where to lay our heads.

The realist Goethe, like the romantic Schiller, knew nothing of this rending of the spirit. The one was too religious, the other too philosophical. Both could find peace in abstract spheres. When the 'spirit of negation' appears as such a jester as Mephistopheles, then the disharmony is not yet tragic; his mocking and ever contradictory nature is still blended in the higher harmony, and in its own due time will chime in with everything—*sieist gerettet*. Lucifer in *Cain* is very different; he is the gloomy angel of darkness, on whose brow shines with dim lustre the star of bitter thought, full of inner discords which can never be harmonised.

He does not jest with negation, he does not amuse with the impudence of his infidelity, he does not allure by sensuality, he does not procure simple maidens, wine, and diamonds, but calmly impels to murder, by some inexplicable force, like the lure of still moonlit water, that promises nothing but death in its comfortless, cold, glimmering embraces.

Neither Cain nor Manfred, neither Don Juan nor Byron, has any deduction, any solution, any 'moral'. Perhaps from the point of view of dramatic art this is a defect, but it gives a stamp of sincerity and shows the depths of the gulf. Byron's epilogue, his last word, if you like, is *The Darkness*; that is the logical conclusion of a life that begins with *The Dream*. Complete the picture for yourselves.

Two enemies, hideously disfigured by hunger, are dead, they are devoured by some crab-like monsters . . . a ship is rotting—the tarred rope sways in the muddy waters in the darkness, there is fearful cold, the animals are dying out, history has already perished and the place is cleared for new life; our period will be reckoned as the fourth formation—that is, if the new world arrives at being able to count up to four. . . .

That is why I prize now so highly the courageous thought of Byron. He saw that there is *no escape*, and proudly said so.

My Past and Thoughts 1850

KINGSLEY

Now it is worth remarking, that it is Shelley's form of fever, rather than Byron's, which has been of late years the prevailing epidemic. Since Shelley's poems have become known in England, and a timid public, after approaching in fear and trembling the fountain which was understood to be poisoned, has begun first to sip, and then, finding the magic water at all events sweet enough, to quench its thirst with unlimited draughts, Byron's fiercer wine has lost favour. Well—at least the taste of the age is more refined, if that be a matter of congratulation. And there is an excuse for preferring champagne to waterside porter, heady with grains of paradise and quassia, salt and cocculus indicus. Nevertheless, worse ingredients than œnanthic acid may lurk in the delicate draught, and the Devil's Elixir may be made fragrant, and sweet, and transparent enough, as French moralists well know, for the most fastidious palate. The private sipping of eau-de-cologne, say the London physicians, has increased mightily of late; and so has the reading of Shelley. It is not surprising. Byron's Corsairs and Laras have been, on the whole, impossible during the thirty years' peace! and piracy and profligacy are at all times, and especially nowadays, expensive amusements, and often require a good private fortune—rare among poets. They have, therefore, been wisely abandoned as ideals, except among a few young persons, who used to wear turn-down collars, and are now attempting moustaches and Mazzini hats. But even among them, and among their betters—rather their more-respectables—nine-tenths of the bad influence which is laid at Byron's door is really owing to Shelley. Among the many good-going gentlemen and ladies, Byron is generally spoken of with horror—he is 'so wicked', forsooth; while poor Shelley, 'poor dear Shelley', is 'very wrong, of course,' but 'so refined', 'so beautiful', 'so tender',—a fallen angel, while Byron is a satyr and a devil. We boldly deny the verdict. . . .

At all events, Byron never set to work to consecrate his own sin into a religion and proclaim the worship of uncleanliness as the last and highest ethical development of 'pure' humanity. No—Byron may be brutal; but he never cants. If at moments he finds himself in hell, he never turns round to the world and melodiously informs them that it is heaven, if they could but see it in its true light.

The truth is, that what has put Byron out of favour with the public of late has not been his faults but his excellences. His artistic good taste, his classical polish, his sound shrewd sense, his hatred of cant, his insight into humbug above all, his shallow pitiable habit of being intelligible—these are the sins which condemn him in the eyes of a mesmerising, table-turning, spirit-rapping, spiritualising, Romanising generation, who read Shelley in secret, and delight in his bad taste, mysticism, extravagance, and vague and pompous sentimentalism. The age is an effeminate one, and it can well afford to pardon the lewdness of the gentle and sensitive vegetarian, while it has no mercy for that of the sturdy peer proud of his bull neck and his boxing, who kept bears and bull-dogs, drilled Greek ruffians at Missolonghi, and 'had no objection to a pot of beer'; and who might, if he had reformed, have made a gallant English gentleman; while Shelley, if once his intense self-opinion had deserted him, would probably have ended in Rome as an Oratorian or a Passionist.

We would that it were only for this count that Byron has had to make way for Shelley. There is, as we have said before, a deeper moral difference between the men, which makes the weaker, rather than the stronger, find favour in young men's eyes. For Byron has the most intense and awful sense of moral law—of law external to himself. Shelley has little or none; less, perhaps, than any known writer who has ever meddled with moral questions. Byron's cry is, I am miserable because law exists; and I have broken it, broken it so habitually, that now I cannot help breaking it. . . . This idea, confused, inter-mitted, obscured by all forms of evil—for it was not discovered, but only in the process of discovery—is the one which comes out with greater and greater strength, through all Corsairs, Laras, and Parasinas, till it reaches its completion in *Cain* and in *Manfred*, of both of which we do boldly say, that if any sceptical poetry at all be right, which we often question, they are right and not wrong; that in *Cain* as in *Manfred*, the awful problem which, perhaps, had better not have been put at all, is nevertheless fairly put, and the solution, as far as it is seen, fairly confessed; namely, that there is an absolute and eternal law in the heart of man which sophistries of his own or of other beings may make him forget, deny, blaspheme; but which exists eternally, and will assert itself. . . .

Yes; that law exists, let it never be forgotten, is the real meaning of Byron, down to that last terrible *Don Juan*, in which he sits himself down, in artificial calm, to trace the gradual rotting and degradation of a man without law, the slave of his own pleasures; a picture happily never finished, because he who painted it was taken away before he had learnt, perhaps when he was beginning to turn back from—the lower depth within the lowest depth.

Now, to this whole form of consciousness, poor Shelley's mind is altogether antipodal. His whole life through was a denial of external law, and a substitution in its place of internal sentiment. Byron's cry is: There is a law, and there-fore I am miserable. Why cannot I keep the law? Shelley's is: There is a law, and therefore I am miserable. Why should not the law be abolished? Away with it, for it interferes with my sentiments—Away with marriage, 'custom and faith, the foulest birth of time'.

Thoughts on Shelley and Byron 1853

RUSKIN

And thus the richest and sweetest passages of Byron, which usually address themselves most to the imagination of youth, became an inspiration to Turner in his later years: and an inspiration so compelling, that, while he only illustrated here and there a detached passage from other poets, he endeavoured, as far as in him lay, to delineate the whole mind of Byron. He fastened on incidents related in other poems; this is the only picture he ever painted to illustrate the poet's own mind and pilgrimage.

And the illustration is imperfect, just because it misses the *manliest* characters of Byron's mind: Turner was fitter to paint Childe Harold when he himself could both mock and weep, than now, when he can only dream: and, beautiful as the dream may be, he but joins in the injustice too many have done to Byron, in dwelling rather on the passionate than the reflective and analytic elements of his intellect. I believe no great power is sent on earth to be wasted, but that it must, in some sort, do an appointed work: and Byron would not have done this work, if he had only given melody to the passions, and majesty to the pangs, of men. His clear insight into their foibles; his deep sympathy with justice, kindness, and courage; his intense reach of pity, never failing, however far he had to stoop to lay his hand on a human heart, have all been lost sight of, either in too fond admiration of his slighter gifts, or in narrow judgement of the errors which burst into all the more flagrant manifestation, just because they were inconsistent with half his soul, and could never become incarnate, accepted, silent sin, but had still to fight for their hold on him.

Childe Harold's Pilgrimage   1856

ARNOLD

To the poetry of Byron the world has ardently paid homage; full justice from his contemporaries, perhaps even more than justice, his torrent of poetry received. His poetry was admired, adored, 'with all its imperfections on its head',—in spite of negligence, in spite of diffuseness, in spite of repetitions, in spite of whatever faults it possessed. His name is still great and brilliant. Nevertheless the hour of irresistible vogue has passed away for him; even for Byron it could not but pass away. The time has come for him, as it comes for all poets, when he must take his real and permanent place, no longer depending upon the vogue of his own day and upon the enthusiasm of his

contemporaries. Whatever we may think of him, we shall not
be subjugated by him as they were; for, as he cannot be for us
what he was for them, we cannot admire him so hotly and
indiscriminately as they. His faults of negligence, of diffuseness, of repetition, his faults of whatever kind, we shall
abundantly feel and unsparingly criticise; the mere interval
of time between us and him makes disillusion of this kind
inevitable. But how then will Byron stand, if we relieve him
too, as far as we can, of the encumbrance of his inferior and
weakest work, and if we bring before us his best and strongest
work in one body together? That is the question which I who
can even remember the latter years of Byron's vogue, and have
myself felt the expiring wave of that mighty influence, but
who certainly also regard him, and have long regarded him,
without illusion, cannot but ask myself, cannot but seek to
answer. . . .

Now if we take the two parts of Goethe's criticism of Byron,
the favourable and the unfavourable, and put them together,
we shall have, I think, the truth. On the one hand, a splendid
and puissant personality—a personality 'in eminence such as
has never been yet, and is not likely to come again'; of which
the like, therefore, is not to be found among the poets of our
nation, by which Byron 'is different from all the rest, and in the
main greater'. Byron is, moreover, 'the greatest talent of the
century'. On the other hand, this splendid personality and
unmatched talent, this unique Byron, 'is quite too much in
the dark about himself''; nay, 'the moment he begins to reflect
he is a child'. There we have, I think, Byron complete; and in
estimating him and ranking him we have to strike a balance
between the gain which accrues to his poetry, as compared
with the productions of other poets, from his superiority, and
the loss which accrues to it from his defects. . . .

The power of Byron's personality lies in 'the splendid and
imperishable excellence which covers all his offences and
outweighs all his defects: *the excellence of sincerity and
strength*'. . . .

There is the Byron who posed, there is the Byron with his
affectations and silliness, the Byron whose weakness Lady
Blessington, with a woman's acuteness, so admirably seized:

'His great defect is flippancy and a total want of self-possession.'
But when this theatrical and easily criticised personage betook
himself to poetry, and when he had fairly warmed to his work,
then he became another man; then the theatrical personage
passed away; then a higher power took possession of him and
filled him; then at last came forth into light that true and
puissant personality, with its direct strokes, its ever-welling
force, its satire, its energy, and its agony. This is the real
Byron; whoever stops at the theatrical preludings does not
know him. . . .

True, as a man, Byron could not manage himself, could not
guide his ways aright, but was all astray. True, he has no light,
cannot lead us from the past to the future; 'the moment he
reflects, he is a child'. The way out of the false state of
things which enraged him he did not see,—the slow and
laborious way upward; he had not the patience, knowledge,
self-discipline, virtue, requisite for seeing it. True, also, as a
poet, he has no fine and exact sense for word and structure
and rhythm; he has not the artist's nature and gifts. Yet a
personality of Byron's force counts for so much in life, and a
rhetorician of Byron's force counts for so much in literature!
But it would be unjust to label Byron . . . as a rhetorician only.
Along with his astounding power and passion he had a strong
and deep sense for what is beautiful in nature, and for what is
beautiful in human action and suffering. . . .

I place Wordsworth's poetry . . . above Byron's on the
whole, although in some points he was greatly Byron's inferior,
and although Byron's poetry will always, probably, find more
readers than Wordsworth's, and will give pleasure more
easily. But these two, Wordsworth and Byron, stand, it
seems to me, first and pre-eminent in actual performance, a
glorious pair, among the English poets of this century. Keats
had probably, indeed, a more consummate poetic gift than
either of them; but he died having produced too little and being
as yet too immature to rival them. I for my part can never even
think of equalling with them any other of their contemporaries;
—either Coleridge, poet and philosopher wrecked in a mist of
opium; or Shelley, beautiful and ineffectual angel, beating in
the void his luminous wings in vain. Wordsworth and Byron

stand out by themselves. When the year 1900 is turned, and our nation comes to recount her poetic glories in the century which has then just ended, the first names with her will be these.

The Poetry of Byron 1881

SWINBURNE

But in Byron—of all remembered poets the most wanting in distinction of any kind, the most dependent for his effects on the most violent and vulgar resources of rant and cant and glare and splash and splutter—in Byron the apostle of culture, and the author of such nobly beautiful and blameless work as *Thyrsis* and the songs of Callicles finds a seed of immortality more promising than in Coleridge or Shelley, the two coequal kings of English lyric poetry. All Mr Arnold's readers will remember the effect produced on him by the case of 'that poor girl Wragg' (5); a remembrance which emboldens me to quote from a later newspaper report a singular example of critical coincidence or sympathy with his tastes on the part of 'the Sunderland murderer Fury'. Of that inarticulate poet, who 'beat his music out', if I remember, in a very 'grim and earnest', not to say Titanic and lurid-spectral, though not undivine fashion—if the Calvinistic or Carlylesque idea of the divine nature be in any degree consonant with Fact—the journals of his day have placed on record the following memoranda, here cited from the *Pall Mall Gazette*: 'He has great taste for poetry, can recite long passages from popular poets, Byron's denunciations of the pleasures of the world having for him great attraction, as a description of his own experiences. Wordsworth is his favourite poet. He confesses himself a villain.' . . .

Setting aside mere instances of passionately cynical burlesque, and perhaps one or two exceptional examples of apparently sincere though vehemently demonstrative personal feeling, we find little really living or really praiseworthy work of Byron's which has not in it some direct or indirect touch of political emotion.

But, without wishing to detract from the just honour

which has been paid to him on this score, and paid at least in full if not with over-measure, we must not overlook, in common justice, the seamy side of his unique success among readers who did not read him in English. It is something, undoubtedly, to be set down to a man's credit, that his work —if his work be other than poetic—should lose nothing by translation: always assuming that it has anything to lose. But what shall be said of a poet whose work not only does not lose, but gains, by translation into foreign prose? and gains so greatly and indefinitely by that process as to assume a virtue which it has not? On taking up a fairly good version of *Childe Harold's Pilgrimage* in French or Italian prose, a reader whose eyes and ears are not hopelessly sealed against all distinction of good from bad in rhythm or in style will infallibly be struck by the vast improvement which the text has undergone in the course of translation. The blundering, floundering, lumbering and stumbling stanzas, transmuted into prose and trans-figured into grammar, reveal the real and latent force of rhetorical energy that is in them: the gasping, ranting, wheezing, broken-winded verse has been transformed into really effective and fluent oratory. . . . Not that even under these improved conditions Byron's is comparable to the work of a first-rate orator or preacher; but one may perceive how men to whom English poetry was a strange tongue might mistake it for an impressive and effective example of English poetry.

Wordsworth and Byron   1884

ELIOT

Of a Scottish quality in Byron's poetry, I shall speak when I come to *Don Juan*. But there is a very important part of the Byronic make-up which may appropriately be mentioned before considering his poetry, for which I think his Scottish antecedence provided the material. That is his peculiar diabolism, his delight in posing as a damned creature—and in providing evidence for his damnation in a rather horrifying way. Now, the diabolism of Byron is very different from any-thing that the Romantic Agony (as Mr Praz calls it) produced in Catholic countries. And I do not think it is easily derived from the comfortable compromise between Christianity and paganism arrived at in England and characteristically English. It could come only from the religious background of a people steeped in Calvinistic theology.

Byron's diabolism, if indeed it deserves the name, was of a mixed type. He shared, to some extent, Shelley's Promethean attitude, and the Romantic passion for Liberty; and this passion, which inspired his more political outbursts, combined with the image of himself as a man of action to bring about the Greek adventure. And his Promethean attitude merges into a Satanic (Miltonic) attitude. The romantic conception of Milton's Satan is semi-Promethean, and also contemplates Pride as a *virtue*. It would be difficult to say whether Byron was a proud man, or a man who liked to pose as a proud man —the possibility of the two attitudes being combined in the same person does not make them any less dissimilar in the abstract. Byron was certainly a vain man, in quite simple ways:

> I can't complain, whose ancestors are there,
>   Erneis, Radulphus—eight-and-forty manors
> (If that my memory doth not greatly err)
>   Were their reward for following Billy's banners. . . .

His sense of damnation was also mitigated by a touch of un-reality: to a man so occupied with himself and with the figure he was cutting nothing outside could be altogether real. It is therefore impossible to make out of his diabolism anything coherent or rational. He was able to have it both ways, it seems; and to think of himself both as an individual isolated and superior to other men because of his own crimes, and as a naturally good and generous nature distorted by the crimes committed against it by others. It is this inconsistent creature that turns up as the Giaour, the Corsair, Lara, Manfred and Cain; only as Don Juan does he get nearer to the truth about himself. But in this strange composition of attitudes and beliefs the element that seems to me most real and deep is that of a perversion of the Calvinist faith of his mother's ancestors. . . .

One reason for the neglect of Byron is, I think, that he has been admired for what are his most ambitious attempts

to be poetic; and these attempts turn out, on examination, to
be fake: nothing but sonorous affirmations of the common-
place with no depth of significance. A good specimen of such
imposture is the well-known stanza at the end of Canto XV of
Don Juan:

> Between two worlds life hovers like a star,
>   'Twixt night and morn, upon the horizon's verge.
> How little do we know that which we are!
>   How less what we may be! The eternal surge
> Of time and tide rolls on, and bears afar
>   Our bubbles; as the old burst, new emerge,
> Lashed from the foam of ages; while the graves
> Of empire heave but like some passing waves

—verses which are not too good for the school magazine.
Byron's real excellence is on a different level from this.

The qualities of narrative verse which are found in *Don
Juan* are no less remarkable in the earlier tales. Before under-
taking this essay I had not read these tales since the days of
my schoolboy infatuation, and I approached them with
apprehension. They are readable. However absurd we find
their view of life, they are, as tales, very well told. As a *tale-
teller* we must rate Byron very high indeed: I can think of none
other than Chaucer who has a greater readability, with the
exception of Coleridge whom Byron abused and from whom
Byron learned a great deal. And Coleridge never achieved a
narrative of such length. Byron's plots, if they deserve that
name, are extremely simple. What makes the tales interesting
is first a torrential fluency of verse and a skill in varying it
from time to time to avoid monotony; and second a genius
for divagation. Digression, indeed, is one of the valuable arts
of the story-teller. The effect of Byron's digressions is to keep
us interested in the story-teller himself, and through this
interest to interest us more in the story. On contemporary
readers this interest must have been strong to the point of
enchantment; for even still, once we submit ourselves to the
point of reading a poem through, the attraction of the
personality is powerful. . . .

It is all the more difficult, in a period which has rather lost the appreciation of the kind of virtues to be found in Byron's poetry, to analyse accurately his faults and vices. Hence we fail to give credit to Byron for the instinctive art by which, in a poem like *Childe Harold* and still more efficiently in *Beppo* or *Don Juan*, he avoids monotony by a dexterous turn from one subject to another. He has the cardinal virtue of being never dull. But, when we have admitted the existence of forgotten virtues, we still recognize a falsity in most of those passages which were formerly most admired. To what is this falsity due?

Whatever it is, in Byron's poetry, that is 'wrong', we should be mistaken in calling it rhetoric. Too many things have been collected under that name; and if we are going to think that we have accounted for Byron's verse by calling it 'rhetorical', then we are bound to avoid using that adjective about Milton and Dryden, about both of whom (in their very different kinds) we seem to be saying something that has meaning, when we speak of their 'rhetoric'. Their failures, when they fail, are of a higher kind than Byron's success, when he succeeds. Each had a strongly individual idiom, and a sense of language; at their worst, they have an interest in the *word*. You can recognize them in the single line, and can say: here is a particular way of using the language. There is no such individuality in the line of Byron. If one looks at the few single lines, from the Waterloo passage in *Childe Harold*, which may pass for 'familiar quotations', you cannot say that any of them is great poetry:

> And all went merry as a marriage bell . . .
> On with the dance! let joy be unconfined . . .

Of Byron one can say, as of no other English poet of his eminence, that he added nothing to the language, that he discovered nothing in the sounds, and developed nothing in the meaning, of individual words. I cannot think of any other poet of his distinction who might so easily have been an accomplished foreigner writing English. The ordinary person talks English, but only a few people in every generation can write it; and upon this undeliberate collaboration between a great many people talking a living language and a very few people writing it, the continuance and maintenance of a language depends. Just as an artisan who can talk English beautifully while about his work or in a public bar, may compose a letter painfully written in a dead language bearing some resemblance to a newspaper leader, and decorated with words like 'maelstrom' and 'pandemonium': so does Byron write a dead or dying language. (6)

This imperceptiveness of Byron to the English word—so that he has to use a great many words before we become aware of him—indicates for practical purposes a defective sensibility. I say 'for practical purposes' because I am concerned with the sensibility of his poetry, not with his private life; for if a writer has not the language in which to express feelings they might as well not exist. We do not even need to compare his account of Waterloo with that of Stendhal to feel the lack of minute particulars; but it is worth remarking that the prose sensibility of Stendhal, being sensibility, has some values of poetry that Byron completely misses. Byron did for the language very much what the leader writers of our journals are doing day by day. I think that this failure is much more important than the platitude of his intermittent philosophizing. Every poet has uttered platitudes, every poet has said things that have been said before. It is not the weakness of the ideas, but the schoolboy command of the language, that makes his lines seem trite and his thought shallow:

Mais que Hugo aussi était dans tout ce peuple. The words of Péguy have kept drifting through my mind while I have been thinking of Byron:

Non pas vers qui chantent dans la mémoire, mais vers qui dans la mémoire sonnent et rétentissent comme une fanfare, vibrants, trépidants, sonnant comme une fanfare, sonnant comme une charge, tambour éternel, et qui battra dans les mémoires françaises longtemps après que les réglementaires tambours auront cessé de battre au front des régiments.

But Byron was not 'in *this* people', either of London or of England, but in his mother's people, and the most stirring stanza of his Waterloo is this:

And wild and high the 'Cameron's gathering' rose!
The war-note of Lochiel, which Albyn's hills

Have heard, and heard, too, have her Saxon foes;—
How in the noon of night that pibroch thrills,
Savage and shrill! But with the breath which fills
Their mountain-pipe, so fill the mountaineers
With the fierce native daring which instils
The stirring memory of a thousand years,
And Evan's, Donald's fame rings in each clansman's ears! . . .

What puts the last cantos of *Don Juan* at the head of Byron's works is, I think, that the subject matter gave him at last an adequate object for a genuine emotion. The emotion is hatred of hypocrisy; and if it was reinforced by more personal and petty feelings, the feelings of the man who as a boy had known the humiliation of shabby lodgings with an eccentric mother, who at fifteen had been clumsy and unattractive and unable to dance with Mary Chaworth, who remained oddly alien among the society that he knew so well—this mixture of the origin of his attitude towards English society only gives it greater intensity. And the hypocrisy of the world that he satirized was at the opposite extreme from his own. Hypocrite, indeed, except in the original sense of the word, is hardly the term for Byron. He was an actor who devoted immense trouble to *becoming* a rôle that he adopted; his superficiality was something that he created for himself. It is difficult, in considering Byron's poetry, not to be drawn into an analysis of the man: but much more attention has already been devoted to the man than to the poetry, and I prefer, within the limits of such an essay as this, to keep the latter in the foreground. My point is that Byron's satire upon English society, in the latter part of *Don Juan*, is something for which I can find no parallel in English literature. He was right in making the hero of his house-party a Spaniard, for what Byron understands and dislikes about English society is very much what an intelligent foreigner in the same position would understand and dislike.

Byron   1937

Shelley

This array of comments differs from the others in one interesting respect: in the magnitude of the change registered in the general view of the object. Nowadays it is almost universally assumed that the most obvious quality in Shelley's verse is a lack of hard and tangible substance; to some tastes this is a defect of vagueness, to others, a splendid evanescence, but both admirers and detractors agree as to the fact itself. Yet the merest glance at the comments of the Establishment of his own day—and they deserve no more than this merest glance—is enough to prove beyond all doubt that once upon a time there must have been some very tangible substance in Shelley. And it need not be forgotten that he was sent down from Oxford in 1811 for atheism, and deprived of the custody of his children for the same pious reason by the Court of Chancery in 1817; nor that in 1841 it took a jury (suitably egged on by a judge) only a quarter of an hour to decide that Queen Mab *was a 'libel on God' and its publisher indictable for blasphemy. Substance there must have been. The question is, what has become of it in the meantime?*

The atheism, of course, was at its crudest in the least readable of the early poems, and its expression in the later ones is more shadowy, easier for the reader to evade. But apart from this purely literary consideration, atheism in general has lost much of its offensiveness, and also of its potential sting and attraction. Dogmatic religion has grown to be so rare that there is not much fun to be got out of being an atheist now, and religious belief so vague and liberal that a militantly atheist posture is very hard to assume. A century ago Browning found it possible to argue that Shelley was well on the way to becoming a Christian when he was drowned, and fifty years ago Francis Thompson, a devout Catholic poet, found behind 'the mask of revolutionary metaphysics' nothing worse—or better—than 'the winsome face of the child'.

The political rebellion, the Godwinism, has melted away even more surely and painlessly. Its generous violence had expressed itself characteristically in large declarations of principle, rather than in sharply defined practical proposals, and on its purely practical side it fell a good long way short of the Welfare State. The difficulty now is to recapture any glimpse of its pristine offensiveness: a difficulty the greater because even in its original expression there was, as Blackwood's *gratefully observed, the note of 'a scholar and a gentleman'. The extent of the modern sanctification can be richly sensed in the discourse pronounced by the Master of the College which had sent him down from Oxford at the erection of the Shelley Memorial in 1893.*

Once these inflammable substances had burned themselves out, what was left? Something, certainly, for there have always been some enthusiasts for what remains in Shelley's verse. Unfortunately, their precise sense of what remains can only be —or has only been—expressed in terms which are barely comprehensible to those who have never experienced it. The language both of his admirers and of his detractors is curiously similar; it is one of seas, winds, clouds, fireworks, skies, planets, angels, luminous wings in a void, ethereality, and incandescence. That they mean something by such words must of course be allowed, and it is to be hoped that they have the pleasant privilege of understanding one another. But they offer little help to the unprivileged, who have never, even for a brief moment in youth, felt the sensation of being somewhere inside Shelley's world, and making something of it. Without any such personal experience one is left helplessly outside the whole discussion, as at a conversation about ghosts and telepathy when one has never been lucky enough to see a ghost or receive a telepathic communication. And from such a personal distance, the whole hubbub resolves itself into a sound uncomfortably like 'All Aboard for the Skylark'.

Two tendencies emerge more or less clearly from this survey of Shelley criticism. First, an enthusiasm for his poetry has not seldom been an affair of youth, something almost naturally destined to be grown out of; it was so, largely, with Tennyson and his circle, who grew out of Shelley into Keats, and turned

*their attempt to compare the two poets into a routine exercise
of critical gymnastics. Secondly, his reputation has on the
whole been on the decline, with a steadiness of tendency which
makes any large upward movement in the future unlikely;
unless, indeed, it is pure folly to envisage poetic reputations
rather as lines on a graph which may be extrapolated a little
once some general trend has become apparent.*

*If this is so, and is to be so, it is a thousand pities, for he was
certainly a very charming man, and even in literature there is
room for youthful aberrations whose correction is one of the
means to eventual ripeness of judgment.*

SHELLEY

. . . in this have I long believed, that my power consists in
sympathy and that part of imagination which relates to sentiment and contemplation. I am formed, if for anything not in
common with the herd of mankind, to apprehend the minute
and remote distinctions of feeling, whether relative to external
nature or the living beings which surround us, and to communicate the conceptions which result from considering either
the moral or the material universe as a whole.

Letter to William Godwin   1817

The *Epipsychidion* is a mystery; as to real flesh and blood,
you may know that I do not deal in those articles; you might
as well go to a gin shop for a leg of mutton, as expect anything human or earthly from me.

Letter to John Gisborne   1821

We have more moral, political, and historical wisdom than
we know how to reduce into practice; we have more scientific
and economical knowledge than can be accommodated to the
just distribution of the produce which it multiplies. The poetry
in these systems of thought is concealed by the accumulation
of facts and calculating processes. There is no want of knowledge respecting what is wisest and best in morals, government,

and political economy, or at least, what is wiser and better than what men now practise and endure. But we let '*I dare not* wait upon *I would*, like the poor cat in the adage'. We want the creative faculty to imagine that which we know; we want the generous impulse to act that which we imagine; we want the poetry of life: our calculations have outrun conception; we have eaten more than we can digest. The cultivation of those sciences which have enlarged the limits of the empire of man over the external world has, for want of the poetical faculty, proportionally circumscribed those of the internal world; and man, having enslaved the elements, remains himself a slave. To what but a cultivation of the mechanical arts in a degree disproportioned to the presence of the creative faculty, which is the basis of all knowledge, is to be attributed the abuse of all invention for abridging and combining labour, to the exasperation of the inequality of mankind? From what other cause has it arisen that the discoveries which should have lightened have added a weight to the curse imposed on Adam? Poetry, and the principle of Self, of which money is the visible incarnation, are the God and Mammon of the world.

Poetry is indeed something divine. It is at once the centre and circumference of knowledge; it is that which comprehends all science, and that to which all science must be referred. It is at the same time the root and blossom of all other systems of thought; it is that from which all spring, and that which adorns all; and that which, if blighted, denies the fruit and the seed, and withholds from the barren world the nourishment and the succession of the scions of the tree of life. It is the perfect and consummate surface and bloom of all things; it is as the odour and the colour of the rose to the texture of the elements which compose it, as the form and splendour of unfaded beauty to the secrets of anatomy and corruption. What were virtue, love, patriotism, friendship—what were the scenery of this beautiful universe which we inhabit; what were our consolations on this side of the grave—and what were our aspirations beyond it, if poetry did not ascend to bring light and fire from those eternal regions where the owl-winged faculty of calculation dare not soar. . . .

Poetry is the record of the best and happiest moments of the happiest and best minds. We are aware of evanescent visitations of thought and feeling sometimes associated with place and person, sometimes regarding our own mind alone, and always arising unforeseen and departing unbidden, but elevating and delightful beyond all expression: so that even in the desire and regret they leave there cannot but be pleasure, participating as it does in the nature of its object. It is as it were the interpenetration of a diviner nature through our own; but his footsteps are like those of a wind over the sea, which the coming calm erases, and whose traces remain only as on the wrinkled sand which paves it. These and corresponding conditions of being are experienced principally by those of the most delicate sensibility and the most enlarged imagination; and the state of mind produced by them is at war with every base desire. The enthusiasm of virtue, love, patriotism, and friendship, is essentially linked with such emotions; and whilst they last, self appears as what it is, an atom to a universe. Poets are not only subject to these experiences as spirits of the most refined organization, but they can colour all that they combine with the evanescent hues of this ethereal world; a word, a trait in the representation of a scene or a passion, will touch the enchanted chord, and reanimate, in those who have ever experienced these emotions, the sleeping, the cold, the buried image of the past. Poetry thus makes immortal all that is best and most beautiful in the world; it arrests the vanishing apparitions which haunt the interlunations of life, and veiling them, or in language or in form, sends them forth among mankind, bearing sweet news of kindred joy to those with whom their sisters abide—abide, because there is no portal of expression from the caverns of the spirit which they inhabit into the universe of things. Poetry redeems from decay the visitations of the divinity in man.

A Defence of Poetry 1821

LEIGH HUNT

We are sure that he will be much better pleased to see obstructions cleared away from the progress of such opinions

as his, than the most minute account given of them in particular. It may be briefly repeated, that they are at war with
injustice, violence, and selfishness of every species, however
disguised; that they represent, in a very striking light, the
folly and misery of systems, either practical or theoretical,
which go upon penal and resentful grounds, and add 'pain
to pain': and that they would have men, instead of worshipping
tyrannies and terrors of any sort, worship goodness and
gladness, diminish the vices and sorrows made by custom
only, encourage the virtues and enjoyments which mutual
benevolence may realize; and in short, make the best and
utmost of this world, as well as hope for another.

The beauties of *The Revolt of Islam* consist in depth of
sentiment, in grandeur of imagery, and a versification remark-
ably sweet, various, and noble, like the placid playing of a
great organ. If the author's genius reminds us of any other
poets, it is of two very opposite ones, Lucretius and Dante.
The former he resembles in the Daedalian part of it, in the
boldness of his speculations, and in his love of virtue, of
external nature, and of love itself. It is his gloomier or more
imaginative passages that sometimes remind us of Dante.
This sort of supernatural architecture in which he delights has
in particular the grandeur as well as obscurity of that great
genius, to whom however he presents this remarkable and
instructive contrast, that superstition and pain and injustice
go hand in hand even in the pleasantest parts of Dante, like
the three Furies, while philosophy, pleasure, and justice,
smile through the most painful passages of our author, like
the three Graces.

Mr Shelley's defects as a poet are obscurity, inartificial
and yet not natural economy, violation of costume, and too
great a sameness and gratuitousness of image and metaphor,
too drawn from the elements, particularly the sea. The book
is full of humanity; and yet it certainly does not go the best
way to work for appealing to it, because it does not appeal
to it through the medium of its common knowledges. It is for
this reason that we must say something, which we would
willingly leave unsaid, both from admiration of Mr Shelley's
genius and love of his benevolence; and this is, that the work

cannot possibly become popular. It may set others thinking and writing, and we have no doubt it will do so; and those who can understand and relish it, will relish it exceedingly; but the author must forget his metaphysics and sea-sides a little more in his future works, and give full effect to that nice knowledge of man and things which he otherwise really possesses to an extraordinary degree. We have no doubt he is destined to be one of the leading spirits of his age, and indeed has already fallen into his place as such; but however resolute, as to his object, he will only be doing it justice to take the most effectual means in his power to forward it.

Examiner   1818

Among the many reasons which his friends had to deplore the premature death of this splendid poet and noble hearted man, the greatest was his not being able to repeat, to a more attentive public, his own protest, not only against some of his earlier effusions (which he did in the newspapers), but against all which he had written in a wailing and angry, instead of an invariable calm, loving and therefore thoroughly helping spirit. His works, in justice to himself, require either to be winnowed from what he disliked, or to be read with remembrance of that dislike. He had sensibility almost unique, seemingly fitter for a planet of a different sort, or in a more final condition, than ours: he has said of himself—so delicate was his organization—that he could

> hardly bear
> The weight of the superincumbent hour;

and the impatience which he vented for some years against that rough working towards good, called evil, which he carried out into conduct too hasty, subjected one of the most naturally pious of men to charges which hurt his name, and thwarted his philanthropy. Had he lived, he would have done away all mistakes on these points, and made everybody know him for what he was—a man idolized by his friends—studious, temperate, of the gentlest life and conversation, and willing to have died to do the world a service. . . .

. . . in general if Coleridge is the sweetest of our poets,

Shelley is at once the most ethereal and most gorgeous; the one who has clothed his thoughts in draperies of the most evanescent and most magnificent words and imagery. Not Milton himself is more learned in Grecisms, or nicer in etymological propriety; and nobody has a style so Orphic and primeval. His poetry is as full of mountains, seas, and skies, of light, and darkness, and the seasons, and all the elements of our being, as if Nature herself had written it, with the creation and its hopes newly cast around her; not, it must be confessed, without too indiscriminate a mixture of great and small, and a want of sufficient shade—a certain chaotic brilliancy, 'dark with excess of light'. Shelley (in the verses to a *Lady with a Guitar*) might well call himself Ariel. All the most enjoying part of this poetry is Ariel—the 'delicate' yet powerful 'spirit', jealous of restraint, yet able to serve; living in the elements and the flowers; treading the 'ooze' of the salt deep, and running 'on the sharp wind of the north'; feeling for creatures unlike himself; 'flaming amazement' on them too, and singing exquisitest songs. Alas! and he suffered for years, as Ariel did in the cloven pine: but now he is out of it, and serving the purposes of Beneficence with a calmness befitting his knowledge and his love.

Imagination and Fancy 1844

THE ESTABLISHMENT

Shall I turn to Shelley?—Yes!—No!—Yes!—I wish that such a mind had not ranked itself among those depraved Spirits, who make it doubtful whether we should more admire their powers, or lament and condemn the abuse of them!—that he had rested contented with the admiration, without extorting the censure, of mankind. He is one of the many whom we cannot read without wonder, or without pain: when I consider his powers of mind, I am proud that he was an Etonian: when I remember their perversion, I wish he had never been one. However, he has made his election; and where Justice cannot approve, Charity can at least be silent!

The Etonian 1821

The writer was probably W. M. Praed]

To the last part of the painful duty which we have imposed upon ourselves we turn with pleasure, because it is the last, for nothing else could induce us to revert to that most execrable publication, *Queen Mab*, with any other feelings than those of unmingled horror and disgust. Compared with this *Don Juan* is a moral poem and *Cain* a homily. It does not merely question or sneer at revelation, nor is it satisfied with denying it—deism is too mean a flight for its author's wondrous powers—the providence of the Deity too insignificant an object of his attack—his being therefore is denied, and the atheist-bard confidently assures us, that there is no God. Our blood curdled in our veins as we waded through nine cantos of blasphemy and impiety, such as we never thought that any one, on the outside of bedlam, could have uttered; nor dare we transcribe any portion of it in our pages, save one of the very mildest of its author's attacks upon religion, the slightest of his insults to his God, whom again and again—our hand trembles as we write it—the impious wretch has dared to brand as a tyrant, a murderer, a cheat, a demon and a fiend.

The Investigator   1822

Concerning the talents of Mr Shelley, we know no more than that he published certain convulsive caperings of Pegasus labouring under cholic pains; namely, some purely fantastic verse, in the hubble bubble, toil and trouble style; and as to Mr Shelley's virtues, if he belonged (as we understand he did), to a junta, whose writings tend to make our sons profligates, and our daughters strumpets, we ought as justly to regret the decease of the Devil (if that were possible), as one of his coadjutors. Seriously speaking, however, we feel no pleasure in the untimely death of this Tyro of the Juan school, that pre-eminent academy of Infidels, Blasphemers, Seducers, and Wantons. We had much rather have heard, that he and the rest of the fraternity had been consigned to a Monastery of La Trappe, for correction of their dangerous principles, and expurgation of their corrupt minds. Percy Bysshe Shelley is a fitter subject for a penitentiary dying speech, than a lauding elegy; for the muse of the rope, rather than that of the cypress; the muse that advises us 'warning to take by other's harm, and we shall do full well'.

The Gentleman's Magazine   1822

BEDDOES

Write it in gold—a Spirit of the sun,
An Intellect ablaze with heavenly thoughts,
A Soul with all the dews of pathos shining,
Odorous with love, and sweet to silent woe
With the dark glories of concentrate song,
Was sphered in mortal earth. Angelic sounds
Alive with panting thoughts sunned the dim world.
The bright creations of an human heart
Wrought magic in the bosoms of mankind.
A flooding summer burst on Poetry;
Of which the crowning sun, the night of beauty,
The dancing showers, the birds whose anthems wild
Note after note unbind the enchanted leaves
Of breaking buds, eve, and the flow of dawn,
Were centered and condensed in his one name
As in a providence—and that was SHELLEY.

Written by Beddoes at Oxford, on a blank leaf of his
Prometheus Unbound   1822

LOCKHART

Why, up to this blessed hour, has the *Edinburgh Review* never hinted that there has been such a man in the world as Percy Bysshe Shelley? Surely, his fancy and invention were in the proportion of 1000 to 1 compared to those of Johnny Keats. Surely, surely he was abused by the *Quarterly*, fully as bitterly as Keats ever was. But no—there is a reason for everything. Shelley, with all his faults, was a gentleman, a scholar, and a poet; and his merits as such were uniformly acknowledged in *Blackwood's Magazine*. That work, if there was a cry against Shelley, did not join it. On the contrary, it was in that work that he was *first* praised in a style worthy of his genius; and while many severe criticisms appeared there, of and concerning his bad principles, political and religious, there never appeared one word which Shelley, or the friends of Shelley, could complain of, as either illiberal or indecorous towards the man or towards the poet. In a word, the *Edinburgh Review* neglected his fine qualities, however obvious, and *Blackwood* praised them warmly and zealously, in spite of his bad qualities, however obvious.

Blackwood's Magazine   1823

W. S. WALKER

If we might venture to express a general opinion of what far surpasses our comprehension, we should compare the poems contained in this volume to the visions of gay colours mingled with darkness, which often in childhood, when we shut our eyes, seem to revolve at an immense distance around us. In Mr Shelley's poetry all is brilliance, vacuity, and confusion. We are dazzled by the multitude of words which sound as if they denoted something very grand or splendid: fragments of images pass in crowds before us; but when the procession has gone by, and the tumult of it is over, not a trace of it remains upon the memory. The mind, fatigued and perplexed, is mortified by the consciousness that its labour has not been rewarded by the acquisition of a single distinct conception; the ear, too, is dissatisfied: for the rythm of the verse is often harsh and unmusical; and both the ear and the understanding are disgusted by new and uncouth words, and by the awkward and intricate construction of the sentences. The predominating characteristic of Mr Shelley's poetry, however, is its frequent and total want of meaning. . . .

The want of meaning in Mr Shelley's poetry takes different shapes. Sometimes it is impossible to attach any significance to his words; sometimes they hover on the verge between

meaning and no meaning, so that a meaning may be obscurely
conjectured by the reader though none is expressed by the
writer; and sometimes they convey ideas, which, taken separately, are sufficiently clear, but, when connected, are altogether
incongruous. We shall begin with a passage which exhibits in
some parts the first species of nonsense, and in others the
third.

> Lovely apparitions, dim at first,
> Then radiant, as the mind arising bright
> From the embrace of beauty, whence the forms
> Of which these are the phantoms, casts on them
> The gathered rays which are reality,
> Shall visit us, the immortal progeny
> Of painting, sculpture, and wrapt poesy,
> And arts, tho' unimagin'd, yet to be.

The verses are very sonorous; and so many fine words are
played off upon us, such as, *painting, sculpture, poesy, phantoms,
radiance, the embrace of beauty, immortal progeny,* &c. that a
careless reader, influenced by his habit of associating such
phrases with lofty or agreeable ideas, may possibly have his
fancy tickled into a transient feeling of satisfaction. But let
any man try to ascertain what is really said, and he will
immediately discover the imposition that has been practised.

Quarterly Review 1821

Amidst the crowd of feeble and tawdry writers with which
we are surrounded, tantalizing us with a mere show of power,
and rendering their native baldness more disgusting by the
exaggerations and distortions with which they attempt to hide
it, it is refreshing to meet with a work upon which the genuine
mark of intellectual greatness is stamped.

We had intended to add something like a delineation of
Shelley's poetical character; but we feel the task would
demand many qualifications which we do not possess. It
may suffice to say, as a general description, that his element
lay in the mixture of passion and imagination—the imagery
being, as it were, impregnated with the passion which brooded

over it. His extraordinary sensitive power overbalanced his power of reflection; he would otherwise have been even greater than he was. He wants pliancy of genius; no first-rate poet ever possessed less variety of powers; there is not merely a want of thought, but a want of human interest in his productions. But no words can do justice to the mixed sublimity and sweetness of his images. It is as if the solid grandeur of Milton were combined with the thrilling vividness and overpowering sweetness of Jeremy Taylor. It is like glory of the noontide sun, and the glory of the lightning, united in one. We have left ourselves no room to speak of his marvellous command of language, and the delicious melody of his versification; the sweetness of which would be cloying, were it not supported by a strength equally remarkable.

Knight's Quarterly 1824

HAZLITT

Mr Shelley's style is to poetry what astrology is to natural science—a passionate dream, a straining after impossibilities, a record of fond conjectures, a confused embodying of vague abstractions—a fever of the soul, thirsting and craving after what it cannot have, indulging its love of power and novelty at the expense of truth and nature, associating ideas by contraries, and wasting great powers by their application to unattainable objects.

Poetry, we grant, creates a world of its own; but it creates it out of existing materials. Mr Shelley is the maker of his own poetry—out of nothing. Not that he is deficient in the true sources of strength and beauty, if he had given himself fair play (the volume before us, as well as his other productions, contains many proofs to the contrary): but, in him, fancy, will, caprice, predominated over and absorbed the natural influences of things; he had no respect for any poetry that did not strain the intellect as well as fire the imagination— and was not sublimed into a high spirit of metaphysical philosophy. Instead of giving a language to thought, or lending the heart a tongue, he utters dark sayings, and deals in allegories and riddles. His Muse offers her services to clothe shadowy doubts and inscrutable difficulties in a robe of glittering words, and to turn nature into a brilliant paradox. We thank him—but we must be excused. Where we see the dazzling beacon-lights streaming over the darkness of the abyss, we dread the quicksands and the rocks below. Mr Shelley's mind was of 'too fiery a quality' to repose [for any continuance] on the probable or the true—it soared 'beyond the visible diurnal sphere', to the strange, the improbable, and the impossible. He mistook the nature of the poet's calling, which should be guided by involuntary not by voluntary impulses. He shook off, as an heroic and praiseworthy act, the trammels of sense, custom and sympathy, and became the creature of his own will. He was 'all air', disdaining the bars and ties of mortal mould. He ransacked his brain for incongruities, and believed in whatever was incredible. Almost all is effort, almost all is extravagant, almost all is quaint, incomprehensible, and abortive, from aiming to be more than it is. Epithets are applied, because they do not fit: subjects are chosen because they are repulsive: the colours of his style, for their gaudy, changeful, startling effect, resemble the display of fire-works in the dark, and, like them, have neither durability, nor keeping, nor discriminate form. Yet Mr Shelley, with all his faults, was a man of genius; and we lament that uncontrollable violence of temperament which gave it a forced and false direction. He has simple thoughts of great force and depth, single images of rare beauty, detached passages of extreme tenderness; and, in his smaller pieces, where he has attempted little he has done much. If some casual and interesting idea touched his feelings or struck his fancy, he expressed it in a pleasing and unaffected verse: but give him a larger subject and time to reflect, and he was sure to get entangled in a system. The fumes of vanity rolled volumes of smoke, mixed with sparkles of fire, from the cloudy tabernacle of his thought. The success of his writings is therefore in general in the inverse ratio of the extent of his undertakings; inasmuch as his desire to teach, his ambition to excel, as soon as it was brought into play, encroached upon, and outstripped his powers of execution.

The Edinburgh Review 1824

MRS SHELLEY

His life was spent in the contemplation of nature, in arduous study, or in acts of kindness and affection. He was an elegant scholar and a profound metaphysician; without possessing much scientific knowledge, he was unrivalled in the justness and extent of his observations on natural objects; he knew every plant by its name, and was familiar with the history and habits of every production of the earth; he could interpret without a fault each appearance in the sky; and the varied phenomena of heaven and earth filled him with deep emotion. He made his study and reading-room of the shadowed copse, the stream, the lake, and the waterfall. . . .

Such was his love for nature that every page of his poetry is associated, in the minds of his friends, with the loveliest scenes of the countries which he inhabited. . . .

Preface to the Posthumous Poems   1824

These characteristics breathe throughout his poetry. The struggle for human weal; the resolution firm to martyrdom; the impetuous pursuit, the glad triumph in good; the determination not to despair; such were the features that marked those of his works which he regarded with most complacency, as sustained by a lofty subject and useful aim. . . .

No poet was ever warmed by a more genuine and unforced inspiration. His extreme sensibility gave the intensity of passion to his intellectual pursuits; and rendered his mind keenly alive to every perception of outward objects, as well as to his internal sensations. Such a gift is, among the sad vicissitudes of human life, the disappointments we meet, and the galling sense of our own mistakes and errors, fraught with pain; to escape from such, he delivered up his soul to poetry, and felt happy when he sheltered himself from the influence of human sympathies, in the wildest regions of fancy. His imagination has been termed too brilliant, his thoughts too subtle. He loved to idealize reality; and this is a taste shared by few. We are willing to have our passing whims exalted into passions, for this gratifies our vanity; but few of us understand or sympathize with the endeavour to ally the love of abstract beauty, and adoration of abstract good, the τὸ ἀγαθὸν καὶ τὸ καλὸν of the Socratic philosophers, with our sympathies with our kind. In this Shelley resembled Plato; both taking more delight in the abstract and the ideal than in the special and tangible. This did not result from imitation; for it was not till Shelley resided in Italy that he made Plato his study. . . . The luxury of imagination, which sought nothing beyond itself (as a child burthens itself with Spring flowers, thinking of no use beyond the enjoyment of gathering them), often showed itself in his verses: they will be only appreciated by minds which have resemblance to his own; and the mystic subtlety of many of his thoughts will share the same fate. The metaphysical strain that characterizes much of what he has written was, indeed, the portion of his works to which, apart from those whose scope was to awaken mankind to aspirations for what he considered the true and good, he was himself particularly attached. There is much, however, that speaks to the many. When he would consent to dismiss these huntings after the obscure (which, entwined with his nature as they were, he did with difficulty), no poet ever expressed in sweeter, more heart-reaching, or more passionate verse, the gentler or more forcible emotions of the soul.

Preface to Shelley's Poems   1839

WORDSWORTH

Shelley is one of the best *artists* of us all: I mean in work-manship of style.

Opinions Expressed   1827

THE APOSTLES

On another occasion Manning took a part, and a part highly creditable to himself, in a memorable debate [in 1829] on the comparative poetical merits of Byron and Shelley. This discussion, which I, under Cambridge influences, brought forward, was attended by three distinguished members of the

Cambridge Union, Arthur Hallam, Richard Milnes, and
Sunderland. They came over from the sister university by
what was then called the Pluck coach . . . Lord Houghton . . .
has picturesquely introduced Mr Gladstone—who really had
very little to do with the business, except that he came afterwards to supper—a feat that might have been accomplished
with equal success by a man of much inferior genius. The
Cardinal fancies that Hallam and Milnes spoke before Sunderland . . . This was not so. Sunderland . . . spoke first and spoke
with great effect, though scarcely, I believe, with the same fire
that he often put forth on more congenial subjects. Then
followed Hallam, with equal if not superior force . . . Lord
Houghton then stood up, and showed consummate skill
as an advocate. In order to prove Shelley's gradual approxima-
tion out of his boyish atheism to the principles of Christian
truth, he read, with great taste and feeling, that fine chorus
from the *Hellas*, one of Shelley's latest works, the chorus I
mean containing this stanza:

> A power from the unknown God,
> A Promethean conqueror came;
> Like a triumphal path, he trod
> The thorns of death and shame.

Anxious, however, perhaps over-anxious, to inculcate, or as
somebody once phrased it, to tread the truth into the unthinking and ignorant multitude before him, he passed somewhat
lightly over the fact that the chorus in question is a dramatic
chorus, and put by the poet into the mouths of captive Christian
women. After him there was silence in the Union for several
minutes, and then Mr Manning of Balliol, perhaps at that
particular moment the actual leader of our debates, with
great propriety rose. He felt that it would be a somewhat
clownish and inhospitable proceeding if these bold guests
went away unchallenged—if their shields were not touched
with the arms of courtesy, by some daring Oxford cavalier.
He spoke well, exceedingly well, but the framework of his
argument—the backbone of his oration—amounted just to
this: Byron is a great poet, we have all of us read Byron; but
(and this is my justification for introducing the topic at all)

F

if Shelley had been a great poet, we should have read him also; but we have none of us done so. Therefore Shelley is not a great poet—a fortiori he is not so great a poet as Byron. *In hanc sententiam*, an immense majority of the Union went *pedibus*: the debate was over, and we all of us, including Mr Gladstone, adjourned . . . to supper.

Sir Francis Doyle, Reminiscences   1885

J. S. MILL

[This passage is a continuation of that given on pp. 71–3]

Shelley is the very reverse of all this. Where Wordsworth is strong, he is weak; where Wordsworth is weak, he is strong. Culture, that culture by which Wordsworth has reared from his own inward nature the richest harvest ever brought forth by a soil of so little depth, is precisely what was wanting to Shelley; or let us rather say, he had not, at the period of his deplorably early death, reached sufficiently far in that intellectual progression of which he was capable, and which, if it has done so much for far inferior natures, might have made of him the greatest of our poets. For him, intentional mental discipline had done little; the vividness of his emotions and of his sensations had done all. He seldom follows up an idea; it starts into life, summons from the fairy-land of his inexhaustible fancy some three or four bold images, then vanishes, and straight he is off on the wings of some casual association into quite another sphere. He had not yet acquired the consecutiveness of thought necessary for a long poem; his more ambitious compositions too often resemble the scattered fragments of a mirror; colours brilliant as life, single images without end, but no picture. It is only when under the overruling influence of some one state of feeling, either actually experienced, or summoned up in almost the vividness of reality by a fervid imagination, that he writes as a great poet; unity of feeling being to him the harmonizing principle which a central idea is to minds of another class, and supplying the coherency and consistency which would else have been wanting. Thus it is in many of his smaller, and especially his lyrical poems. They are obviously written to exhale, perhaps to relieve, a state of feeling, or of conception of feeling, almost oppressive from its vividness. The thoughts and imagery are suggested by the feeling, and are such as it finds unsought. The state of feeling may be either of soul or of sense, or oftener (might we not say invariably?) of both; for the poetic temperament is usually, perhaps always, accompanied by exquisite senses. The exciting cause may be either an object or an idea. But whatever of sensation enters into the feeling, must not be local, or consciously bodily; it is a state of the whole frame, not of a part only; like the state of sensation produced by a fine climate, or indeed like all strongly pleasurable or painful sensations in an impassioned nature, it pervades the entire nervous system. States of feeling, whether sensuous or spiritual, which thus possess the whole being, are the fountains of that poetry, which we have called the poetry of poets; and which is little else than the utterance of the thoughts and images that pass across the mind while some permanent state of feeling is occupying it.

To the same original fineness of organization, Shelley was doubtless indebted for another of his rarest gifts, that exuberance of imagery, which when unrepressed, as in many of his poems it is, amounts even to a vice. The susceptibility of his nervous system, which made his emotions intense, made also the impressions of his external senses deep and clear: and agreeably to the law of association by which, as already remarked, the strongest impressions are those which associate themselves the most easily and strongly, these vivid sensations were readily recalled to mind by all objects or thoughts which had co-existed with them, by all feelings which in any degree resembled them. Never did a fancy so teem with sensuous imagery as Shelley's. Wordsworth economizes an image, and detains it until he has distilled all the poetry out of it, and it will not yield a drop more: Shelley lavishes his with a profusion which is unconscious because it is inexhaustible. The one like a thrifty housewife, uses all his materials and wastes none; the other scatters them with a reckless prodigality of wealth of which there is perhaps no similar instance.

The Two Kinds of Poetry   1833

. . . Where the poetic temperament exists in its greatest degree, while the systematic culture of the intellect has been neglected, we may expect to find, what we do find in the best poems of Shelley—vivid representations of states of passive and dreamy emotion, fitted to give extreme pleasure to persons of similar organization to the poet, but not likely to be sympathized in, because not understood, by any other persons; and scarcely conducing at all to the noblest end of poetry as an intellectual pursuit, that of acting upon the desires and characters of mankind through their emotions, to raise them towards the perfection of their nature.

Tennyson's Poems 1835

HENRY TAYLOR

It may be proper to take a distinction between the ordinary Byronian poetry, and that which may be considered as the offspring, either in the first or second generation, of the genius of Mr Shelley. Mr Shelley was a person of a more powerful and expansive imagination than Lord Byron, but he was inferior to him in those practical abilities, which (unacceptable as such an opinion may be to those who believe themselves to be writing under the guidance of inspiration) are essential to the production of consummate poetry. . . . In Mr Shelley's case, there seems to have been an attempt to unrealise every object in nature, presenting them under forms and combinations in which they are never to be seen through the mere medium of our eye-sight. Mr Shelley seems to have written under the notion that no phenomena can be perfectly poetical, until they shall have been so decomposed from their natural order and coherency, as to be brought before the eader in the likeness of a phantasma or vision. A poet is, in his estimation . . . purely and pre-eminently a visionary. Much beauty, exceeding splendour of diction and imagery, cannot but be perceived in his poetry, as well as exquisite charms of versification; and a reader of an apprehensive fancy will doubtless be entranced whilst he reads: but when he shall have closed the volume, and considered within himself what it has added to his stock of permanent impressions, of recurring thoughts,

he will probably find his stores in this kind no more enriched
by having read Mr Shelley's poems, than by having gazed on
so many gorgeously coloured clouds in an evening sky. Sur-
passingly beautiful they were whilst before his eyes; but for-
asmuch as they had no relevancy to his life, past or future, the
impression upon the memory barely survived that upon the
senses. . . .

Mr Shelley and his disciples—the followers (if I may so
call them) of the PHANTASTIC SCHOOL, labour to effect a
revolution. . . . They would transfer the domicile of poetry
to regions where reason, far from having any supremacy or
rule, is all but unknown, an alien and an outcast; to seats of
anarchy and abstraction, where imagination exercises the
shadow of an authority, over a people of phantoms, in a land
of dreams.

Preface to Philip van Artevelde 1834

THE LAW

The passages selected as specimens of the indicted libel are
found in a complete edition of Percy Bysshe Shelley, a work
comprising more than twenty thousand lines of verse, and
occupy something less than the three-hundredth part of the
volume which contains them. The book presents the entire
intellectual history,—true and faithful because traced in the
series of those works which were its events,—of one of the
most extraordinary persons ever gifted and doomed to illustrate the nobleness, the grandeur, the imperfections, and the
progress of human genius, whom it pleased God to take from
this world while the process harmonising his stupendous
powers was yet incomplete, but not before it had indicated
its beneficent workings.

The first of these works is a poem, written at the age of
eighteen, entitled *Queen Mab*; a composition marked with
nothing to attract the casual reader—irregular in versification,
wild, disjointed, visionary; often difficult to be understood
even by a painful student of poetry, and sometimes wholly

unintelligible even to him; but containing as much to wonder at, to ponder on, to weep over, as any half-formed work of genius which ever emanated from the vigour and the rashness of youth. This poem, which I shall bring before you presently, is followed by the marvellous series of works of which *Alastor*, *The Revolt of Islam*, the *Prometheus Unbound*, and *The Cenci* form the principal, exhibiting a continuous triumph of mellowing and consecrating influences, down to the moment when sudden death shrouded the poet's career from the observation of mortals. Now the question is, whether it is blasphemy to present to the world—say rather to the calm, the laborious, the patient searchers after wisdom and beauty, who alone will peruse this volume—the awful mistakes, the mighty struggles, the strange depressions, and the imperfect victories of such a spirit, because the picture has some passages of frightful gloom. . . .

Lord Denman said 'it was difficult to quit the captivating subject on which the learned Sergeant had addressed them with so much animation and eloquence, but he and the jury were bound to take the law as it had been handed down to them. The only question for their consideration was, whether in their opinion the work which had been made the subject of prosecution deserved the imputations that were cast upon it by the indictment, and whether the publisher had sent it forth deliberately into the world, knowing its character to be such. The purpose of the passage cited from *Queen Mab* was, he thought, to cast reproach and insult upon what in Christian minds were the peculiar objects of veneration. It was not however, sufficient that mere passages of such an offensive character should exist in a work in order to render the publication of it an act of criminality. It must appear that no condemnation of such passages appeared in the context. It has been said that the extraordinary poem in question was the production of a mere youth. Were the lines indicted calculated to shock the feelings of any Christian reader? Were their points of offence explained, or was their virus neutralised by any remarks in the margin, by any note of explanation or apology? If not, they were libels on God, and indictable.'

The jury, after deliberating for a quarter of an hour, declared the defendant Guilty.

> *From the Trial of Mr Moxon for Blasphemy in*
> *publishing Shelley's Works* 1841

[The eloquent pleader for Shelley is Sergeant Talfourd]

G. H. LEWES

Of poetry, as Thomas Jouffroy, the French metaphysician, remarks, 'It gives utterance in song to the sentiments of the epoch, on the good, the beautiful, and the true. It expresses the indistinct thought of the masses, in a manner that is more vivid, but not more clear, because he feels his thought more vividly, but comprehends it as little. This is comprehended only by philosophy. If poetry comprehended it, it would become philosophy and disappear.' Hence the reason of cycles in poetry—the true poet can only arise to give birth to a new *credo*. Note, however, that as no one individual can epitomise but one section of the spirit of his age, so we can only see one section of it in his works—hence the band of simultaneous poets. We cannot, therefore, regard Leigh Hunt's notion, 'that for ordinary or immediate purposes a great deal of Mr Shelley's poetry ought to have been written in prose', otherwise than as a mistake of the poet's mission. He was a poet, not a politician, and he himself said as much:

> But it is a mistake to suppose that I dedicate my poetical compositions solely to the direct enforcement of reform, or that I consider them in any degree as containing a reasoned system on the theory of human life. Didactic poetry is my abhorrence; nothing can be equally well expressed in prose that is not tedious and superogatory in verse. My purpose has hitherto been simply to familiarise the highly refined imagination of the more select classes of poetical readers with beautiful idealisms of moral excellence; aware that until the mind can love, and admire, and trust, and hope, and endure, reasoned principles of moral conduct are seeds cast upon the highway of life,

which the unconscious passenger tramples into dust,
although they would bear the harvest of his happiness.

Shelley does not so much preach as inspire. He knew that
it is not what we absolutely learn and can carry away with us,
but what we *become*, which the poet's works effect. The French
Revolution was the proclamation, written in blood, that the
world had outgrown its clothes, and would have others.
England followed, and in that turbulent period there arose a
band of poets to utter the new doctrines, such as will never
pass out of literature. But let us look at their positions. They
all saw that the existing state of things was corrupt—how far
did they tend towards its alleviation? Scott resorted to the
past, called up the dead spirit of chivalry before our eyes, and
passed in panoramic manner the whole bygone days, with
their border forays, pageants, tourneys, merry men of the
forest, brawny fighters clad in buff and steel, quick-blooded,
vigorous-fibred men, bearing about them the tangible reality
and excitement of existence, full of

Dance and provençal song and sunburnt mirth,

performing prodigies of valour, living in the wild eddies of
danger, beacon-lighted by war and intrigue. But it was the
dead past, and bore in its womb no living future. Wordsworth,
Southey, and Coleridge—these men began life with their wild
youthful theories of Pantisocracy, but they all three started
back at the apparition of Liberty they had called up; in none
of them lay the heroic endurance to carry out at all costs the
gospel they had received, and so we find them all three resort-
ing to other worlds than the present. Wordsworth, to an
impossible state of country life or nature—hymning nature as
the only healthy nurse, but stopping short whenever he came
to any important point. Southey (of whom this present
reviewer, having never read his poetry, will prefer silence),
we see altogether choosing foreign and past scenes, Madoes,
Rodericks, Thalabas, &c. Coleridge, also dreaming in the
slumbers of the past, but unsettled, remote, altogether vague
and intangible. Byron mirroring the disease of the age—the
disease of unbelief and self-anatomy—giving the world

terrible glimpses of all the 'Bluebeard chambers of his heart', to use Carlyle's fine expression, talking about liberty, but the next moment laughing and mocking it and all things—he was no 'spiritual leader of his people' to any goal of happiness or wisdom. Moore, bursting lyrically out into occasional nationalism, but in all his larger works seeking the remote past—orientalism, voluptuousness, nature's beauty, &c., *but no Gospel.* Keats, remote and unsettled, seeing much that was wrong, but not clearly seeing where and how it could be righted. Leigh Hunt, seeing the disease, and devoting himself with heroic endurance to the cure—but this as a philosopher— as a poet merely girding at conventional morals, and trying to bring round broader and truer ones.

Shelley alone was the poet standing completely on his truth; giving up his life to it, and eternally preaching it. Look where you will throughout his various works, there you see this gospel ever lying underneath, even under the smallest poems. It stands written there, unchangeable as the word in a firework illumination remains burning visible through all the varieties of fire which play around it and from out of it. One may see also from this why these other men, mirroring, as they did, the immediate restlessness and disease of the period, were more *notable* than this other man who was speaking of futurity in which he could be joined but by the minority; but his fame has been rapidly widening as the morn since his death, and has not yet nearly attained its culminating point.

The vital truth Shelley everywhere enforced, although treated as a chimera by most of his contemporaries, and indulged as a dream by some others, has become the dominant Idea—the philosophy and faith of this age, throughout Europe —it is progression, humanity, perfectibility, civilization, democracy—call it what you will—this is the truth uttered unceasingly by Shelley, and universally received by us. . . .

Thus much concerning the deeper significance of his condition as a poet. Of his claims as an artist we do not think so highly, for although not one of his contemporaries has produced a single work equal to *The Cenci,* yet in the artistic parts Shelley was not so great. He had a most marvellous command of language, music, and imagery, but in most of his larger poems there is too much glare and brilliancy (7)— there is a want of proper 'keeping'—of light and shade; he does not sufficiently subdue his 'tones' (to finish this painter's language) so as to produce the essential harmony of colouring. He is too remote—too fond of talking about 'eyes drinking being' from the form of a beloved. To illustrate this he some- times uses the epithet *'wingless* boat'. A prosaic critic would say that boats not usually having wings, to call one wingless is superfluous; and although the prosaic critic would thereby prove himself, as he always does, to be a discoverer of mares' nests, and one might ask him if Shelley did not know that as well as he, yet his objection to the epithet would be well founded, though ill expressed. By 'wingless' the student of Shelley knows that he means to intimate extreme swiftness by some supernatural means, but this meaning is too remote for poetry (8). Further, one may note a certain want of *objectivity* —a want of plastic powers in his descriptions; you can never identify them—they seem rather to have been broken memories of many a scene woven into one than the description of any particular scene. It has the effect of dreaminess—as one who has basked in the sun with his eyes closed in some lovely spot, and on opening them looks around and all seems unreal; a dim, dreamy haze is spread between the scene and him. We should characterise his mind as sensitive and reflective, rather than plastic and creative. These are artistic faults which must be taken into the scale while instituting a comparison with his contemporaries.

Percy Bysshe Shelley 1841

BROWNING

Whatever Shelley was, he was with an admirable sincerity. It was not always truth that he thought and spoke; but in the purity of truth he spoke and thought always. Everywhere is apparent his belief in the existence of Good, to which Evil is an accident; his faithful holding by what he assumed to be the former, going everywhere in company with the tenderest pity for those acting or suffering on the opposite hypothesis. For

he was tender, though tenderness is not always the characteristic of very sincere natures; he was eminently both tender
and sincere. . . .

Gradually he was raised above the contemplation of spots
and the attempt at effacing them to the great Abstract Light,
and through the discrepancy of the creation to the sufficiency
of the First Cause. Gradually he was learning that the best way
of removing abuses is to stand fast by truth. Truth is one, as
they are manifold; and innumerable negative effects are
produced by the upholding of one positive principle. I shall
say what I think—had Shelley lived he would have finally
ranged himself with the Christians; his very instinct for helping
the weaker side (if numbers make strength), his very 'hate
of hate', which at first translated itself into delirious *Queen
Mab* notes and the like, would have got clearer-sighted by
exercise. . . .

Meantime, as I call Shelley a moral man, because he was
true, simple-hearted, and brave, and because what he acted
corresponded to what he knew, so I call him a man of religious
mind, because every audacious negative cast up by him against
the Divine was interpenetrated with a mood of reverence and
adoration—and because I find him everywhere taking for
granted some of the capital dogmas of Christianity, while most
vehemently denying their historical basement. . . .

Let me conclude with a thought of Shelley as a poet. In the
hierarchy of creative minds, it is the presence of the highest
faculty that gives first rank, in virtue of its kind, not degree;
no pretension of a lower nature, whatever the completeness of
development of variety of effect, impeding the precedency of
the rarer endowment though only in the germ. The contrary is
sometimes maintained; it is attempted to make the lower gifts
(which are potentially included in the higher faculty) of
independent value, and equal to some exercise of the special
function. For instance, should not a poet possess common
sense? Then the possession of abundant common sense implies
a step towards becoming a poet. Yes; such a step as the lapi-
dary's, when, strong in the fact of carbon entering largely into
the composition of the diamond, he heaps up a sack of charcoal
in order to compete with the Koh-i-noor. I pass at once,

therefore, from Shelley's minor excellences to his noblest and predominating characteristic.

This I call his simultaneous perception of Power and Love in the absolute, and of Beauty and Good in the concrete, while he throws, from his poet's station between both, swifter, subtler, and more numerous films for the connexion of each with each, than have been thrown by any modern artificer of whom I have knowledge; proving how, as he says,

> The spirit of the worm within the sod,
> In love and worship blends itself with God.

I would rather consider Shelley's poetry as a sublime fragmentary essay towards a presentment of the correspondency of the universe to Deity, of the natural to the spiritual, and of the actual to the ideal, than I would isolate and separately appraise the worth of many detachable portions which might be acknowledged as utterly perfect in a lower moral point of view, under the mere conditions of art. It would be easy to take my stand on successful instances of objectivity in Shelley: there is the unrivalled *Cenci*; there is the *Julian and Maddalo* too; there is the magnificent *Ode to Naples*: why not regard, it may be said, the less organised matter as the radiant elemental foam and solution, out of which would have been evolved, eventually, creations as perfect even as those? But I prefer to look for the highest attainment, not simply the high,—and, seeing it, I hold by it. There is surely enough of the work 'Shelley' to be known enduringly among men, and, I believe, to be accepted of God, as human work may; and around the imperfect proportions of such, the most elaborated productions of ordinary art must arrange themselves as inferior illustrations.

Essay on Shelley 1852

KINGSLEY

'Lawless love' is Shelley's expressed ideal of the relation of the sexes; and his justice, his benevolence, his pity, are all equally lawless. 'Follow your instincts' is his one moral rule, confounding the very lowest animal instincts with those lofty ideas of right, which it was the will of Heaven that he should

retain, ay, and love, to the very last, and so reducing them all
to the level of sentiments. 'Follow your instincts'—But what
if our instincts lead us to eat animal food? 'Then you must
follow the instincts of me, Percy Bysshe Shelley. I think it
horrible, cruel, it offends my taste.' What if our instincts lead
us to tyrannise over our fellow-men? 'Then you must repress
those instincts. I, Shelley, think that, too, horrible and cruel.'
Whether it be vegetarianism or liberty, the rule is practically
the same—sentiment: which, in his case, as in the case of all
sentimentalists, turns out to mean at last, not the sentiments of
mankind in general, but the private sentiments of the writer.
This is Shelley; a sentimentalist pure and simple; incapable of
anything like inductive reasoning; unable to take cognisance
of any facts but those which please his taste, or to draw any
conclusion from them but such as also pleases his taste; as, for
example, in that eighth stanza of his *Ode to Liberty*, which, had
it been written by any other man but Shelley, possessing the
same knowledge as he, one would have called a wicked and
deliberate lie—but in his case, is to be simply passed over with
a sigh, like a young lady's proofs of table-turning and rapping
spirits. She wished to see it so—and therefore she saw it so.

For Shelley's nature is utterly womanish. Not merely his
weak points, but his strong ones, are those of a woman. Tender
and pitiful as a woman; and yet, when angry, shrieking, railing,
hysterical as a woman. The physical distaste for meat and
fermented liquors, coupled with the hankering after physical
horrors, are especially feminine. The nature of a woman looks
out of that wild, beautiful, girlish face—the nature: but not
the spirit; not

> The reason firm, the temperate will,
> Endurance, foresight, strength and skill.

The lawlessness of the man, with the sensibility of the
woman. . . . His cries are like the wails of a child, inarticulate,
peevish, irrational; and yet his pain fills his whole being,
blackens the very face of nature to him: but he will not confess
himself in the wrong. . . .

A recipe for the production of milleniums which has this
one advantage, that it is small enough to be comprehended by

the very smallest minds, and reproduced thereby, with a difference, in such spasmodic melodies as seem to those small minds to be imitations of Shelley's nightingale notes.

For nightingale notes they truly are. In spite of all his faults—and there are few poetic faults in which he does not indulge, to their very highest power—in spite of his 'interfluous' and 'innumerous', and the rest of his bad English—in spite of bombast, horrors, maundering, sheer stuff and nonsense of all kinds, there is a plaintive natural melody about this man, such as no other English poet has ever uttered, except Shakespeare in some few immortal songs. Who that has read Shelley does not recollect scraps worthy to stand by Ariel's song— chaste, simple, unutterably musical? Yes, when he will be himself—Shelley the scholar and the gentleman and the singer —and leave philosophy and politics, which he does not understand, and shriekings and cursings, which are unfit for any civilised and self-respecting man, he is perfect.

Thoughts on Shelley and Byron   1853

PEACOCK

Now, I could have wished that, like Wordsworth's Cuckoo, he had been allowed to remain a voice and a mystery: that, like his own Skylark, he had been left unseen in his congenial region,

> Above the smoke and stir of this dim spot
> Which men call earth,

and that he had been only heard in the splendour of his song.

Frazer's Magazine   1858

So perished Percy Bysshe Shelley, in the flower of his age, and not perhaps even yet in the full flower of his genius; a genius unsurpassed in the description and imagination of scenes of beauty and grandeur; in the expression of impassioned love of ideal beauty; in the illustration of deep feeling by congenial imagery; and in the infinite variety of harmonious versification. What was, in my opinion, deficient in his poetry was, as I have already said, the want of reality in the characters with which he peopled his splendid scenes, and to which he addressed or imparted the utterance of his impassioned feeling. He was advancing, I think, to the attainment of this reality. It would have given his poetry the only element of truth which it wanted; though at the same time, the more clear development of what men were would have lowered his estimate of what they might be, and dimmed his enthusiastic prospect of the future destiny of the world.

Memoirs of Shelley   Frazer's Magazine   1860

AN ALTERCATION BETWEEN ARNOLD AND SWINBURNE:

ARNOLD

In the literary movement of the beginning of the nineteenth century the signal attempt to apply freely the modern spirit was made in England by two members of the aristocratic class, Byron and Shelley. Aristocracies are, as such, naturally impenetrable by ideas; but their individual members have a high courage and a turn for breaking bounds; and a man of genius, who is the born child of the idea, happening to be born in the aristocratic ranks, chafes against the obstacles which prevent him from freely developing it. But Byron and Shelley did not succeed in their attempt freely to apply the modern spirit in English literature; they could not succeed in it; the resistance to baffle them, the want of intelligent sympathy to guide and uphold them, were too great. Their literary creation, compared with the literary creation of Shakespeare and Spenser, compared with the literary creation of Goethe and Heine, is a failure. The best literary creation of that time in England proceeded from men who did not make the same bold attempt as Byron and Shelley.

Heinrich Heine   1863

SWINBURNE

Mr Arnold, with whose clear and critical spirit it is always good to come in contact, as disciple or as dissenter, has twice spoken of Shelley, each time, as I think, putting forth a brilliant error, shot through and spotted with glimpses of truth. Byron and Shelley, he says, 'two members of the aristocratic class', alone in their day, strove 'to apply the modern spirit' to English literature. . . . So far we must go with Mr Arnold; but I cannot follow him when he adds that Byron and Shelley failed in their attempt; that 'the best literary creation' of their time, work 'far more solid and complete than theirs', was due to men in whom the new spirit was dead or was unborn; that, therefore, 'their names will be greater than their writings'. First, I protest against the bracketing of the two names. With all reserve of reverence for the noble genius and memory of Byron, I can no more accept him as a poet equal or even akin to Shelley on any side but one, than I could imagine Shelley endowed with the various, fearless, keen-eyed and triumphant energy which makes the greatest of Byron's works so great. With all his glory of ardour and vigour and humour, Byron was a singer who could not sing; Shelley outsang all poets on record but some two or three throughout all time; his depths and heights of inner and outer music are as divine as nature's, and not sooner exhaustible. He was alone the perfect singing-god; his thoughts, words, deeds, all sang together.

Notes on the Text of Shelley 1869

ARNOLD

. . . poetry is interpretation both by having *natural magic* in it, and by having *moral profundity*. . . . in Shelley there is not a balance of the two gifts, nor even a co-existence of them, but there is a passionate straining after them both, and this is what makes Shelley, as a man, so interesting: I will not now inquire how much Shelley achieves as a poet, but whatever he achieves, he in general fails to achieve natural magic in his expression; in Mr Palgrave's charming *Treasury* may be seen a gallery of his failures. Compare, for example, his *Lines Written in the Euganean Hills*, with Keats's *Ode to Autumn*. The latter piece *renders* Nature; the former *tries to render her*. I will not deny, however, that Shelley has natural magic in his rhythm; what I deny is, that he has it in his language. It always seemed to me that the right sphere for Shelley's genius was the sphere of music, not of poetry; the medium of sounds he can master, but to master the more difficult medium of words he has neither intellectual force enough nor sanity enough.

Maurice de Guérin 1863

SWINBURNE

Mr Arnold, in my view, misconceives and misjudges him not less when set against Keats than when bracketed with Byron. Keats has indeed a divine magic of language applied to nature; here he is unapproachable; this is his throne, and he may bid all kings of song come bow to it. But his ground is not Shelley's ground; they do not run in the same race at all. The *Ode to Autumn*, among other such poems of Keats, renders nature as no man but Keats ever could. Such poems as the *Lines written among the Euganean Hills* cannot compete with it. But do they compete with it? The poem of Keats, Mr Arnold says, '*renders* Nature'; the poem of Shelley '*tries to render her*'. It is this that I deny. What Shelley tries to do he does; and he does not try to do the same thing as Keats. The comparison is as empty and profitless as one between the sonnets of Shakespeare and the sonnets of Milton. Shelley never in his life wrote a poem of that exquisite contraction and completeness, within that round and perfect limit. This poem of the Euganean Hills is no piece of spiritual sculpture or painting after the life of natural things. I do not pretend to assign it a higher or a lower place; I say simply that its place is not the same. It is a rhapsody of thought and feeling coloured by contact with nature, but not born of the contact; and such as it is all Shelley's work is, even when most vague and vast in its elemental scope of labour and of aim. A soul as great as the world lays hold on the things of the world; on all life of plants, and beasts, and men; on all likeness of time, and death, and good things and evil. His aim is rather to render the effect of a thing than a thing itself; the soul and spirit of life rather than the living form, the growth rather than the thing grown. And herein he too is unapproachable.

Notes on the Text of Shelley 1869

ARNOLD

As a man, Shelley is at a number of points immeasurably Byron's superior; he is a beautiful and enchanting spirit, whose vision, when we call it up, has far more loveliness, more charm for our soul, than the vision of Byron. But all the personal charm of Shelley cannot hinder us from at last discovering in his poetry the incurable want, in general, of a sound subject-matter, and the incurable fault, in consequence, of unsubstantiality. Those who extol him as the poet of clouds, the poet of sunsets, are only saying that he did not, in fact, lay hold upon the poet's right subject-matter; and in honest truth, with all his charm of soul and spirit, and with all his gift of musical diction and movement, he never, or hardly ever, did. . . . Shelley, beautiful and ineffectual angel, beating in the void his luminous wings in vain.

Byron 1881

SWINBURNE

Averting our faces from the clouds and sunsets whose admirers give so much offence to Mr Arnold, what we see in his own judgment on Shelley and Byron might be symbolically described as a sunset of critical judgment in a cloud of hazy paradox. It is a singular certainty that on the subject of Shelley this noble poet and brilliant critic has never got beyond what may be called the 'Johnny Keats' stage of criticism. The Shelley of his imagination has exactly as much in common with the author of the *Ode to Liberty* as the Keats of Gifford's or Wilson's had in common with the author of the *Ode to a Nightingale*. The main features of the phantom's character are apparently these: enthusiastic puerility of mind, incurable unsoundness of judgment, resistless excitability of emotion and helpless inability of intelligence, consumptive wakefulness of fancy and feverish impotence of reason, a dreamily amiable uselessness and a sweetly fantastic imbecility: in a word, the qualities of a silly angel. I venture, in the face of a very general opinion, to doubt whether such a poet as this ever existed: but

I do not doubt at all that none was ever further from any resemblance to such a type than Percy Bysshe Shelley. . . .

As a spiritual poet, and as the poet of nature, Wordsworth won at last, and wore for a generation, the palm of pre-eminence to which his patient and severe ambition had from the first made tacit or explicit claim. And yet, setting aside the poets of pure theology or formal religion, we may find else-where higher flights of strenuous contemplation, purer notes of spiritual passion, than in any but one or two quite excep-tional poems of Wordsworth's. Even at his highest, he can hardly be said to have shown for so long together such an even strength of wing, such a sweeping and soaring harmony of upward and forward flight, as Donne, despite one or two slips and flaws, has displayed in the ardent and majestic rapture of his magnificent *Anniversaries*. Nor did his systematic and studious love of nature, even in those days of more passionate delight in it on which at the age of twenty-eight he could already look back as belonging to a stage of life and feeling irrevocably past and ended, give ever such wings to his words or such fire to their music as any note or any touch of Shelley's is sufficient to show that he could command—that he could not but assume—if he had to deal but for a moment with the glories of nature or the emotions evoked by transitory or enduring sense of them. There is much study, there is much knowledge, there is much sober and sedate enjoyment of nature, much deep and thoughtful thankfulness for such enjoyment, made manifest in the poetry of Wordsworth: there is a singular intensity, a matchless refinement, of relish for the pure delight of communion with natural beauty, perceptible in the poetry of Keats: but to neither was it given, as it was given to Shelley, to rise beyond these regions of contemplation and sensation into that other where the emotion of Keats and the emotion of Wordsworth become one, and are superseded by a greater; to transcend at once the sensuous and the medita-tive elements of poetry, and to fuse their highest, their keenest, their most inward and intimate effects, in such verse as utters what none before could utter, and renders into likeness of form and sound such truths of inspired perception, such raptures of divine surprise, as no poet of nature may think to render again. At the sound of the *Ode to the West Wind*, the stars of Wordsworth's heaven grow fainter in our eyes, and the nightingale of Keats' garden falls silent in our ears. The poet who wrote that, and the poet who wrote *Christabel*,—but these alone of their generation—are indeed to be counted among the very chiefest glories of English poetry: and it is surely no inadequate reward for the noble labour of a long and strenuous life, to stand where Wordsworth stands—but a little lower than these.

Wordsworth and Byron   1884

MASSON

After all, however, less than almost any other poet, is Shelley to be adequately represented in detached passages. His poetry is like an intellectual ether, that must be breathed and lived in for some time ere its influence can be appreciated. To minds of sufficient culture, who have in this way become acquainted with Shelley's poetry (and only minds of considerable culture are ever likely to read much of it), it has always presented itself as something very peculiar in quality—totally different, for example, from the poetry of Milton, or of Wordsworth, or of Byron, or of any other preceding poet. To this, at least, Shelley's poetry can lay claim—that, whether great or not, whether useful or hurtful in its influence, it is very peculiar. . . .

Argument and metaphysics apart, there is, at least, no way in which the *fancy* may more easily apprehend the peculiarity of Shelley's genius than by thinking of him as one who surveyed the world not from a point within it or on it, but from a point in distant space. Better still, perhaps, one might think of him as not a native of the earth at all, but some fluttering spirit of a lighter sphere, that had dropped on the earth by chance, unable to be in happy relation to it as a whole, though keenly sensitive to some of its beauties. Were our science of pedigree worth anything, it might save us the necessity of any such figure. Remembering that the year of Shelley's birth was that of the utmost agony of the French Revolution, when convulsion was shaking all things established, and new social principles

were everywhere abroad, we might then have a glimmering
how it happened that the genius of the time took a whim to
appear even in Sussex, and bespeak as one of its incarnations
the child of a commonplace English Baronet, who had never
bargained for such an honour. But, unable to make anything
to the purpose of such a scientific fancy, we may resort to the
other. Shelley's personal friends used to resort to it. 'I used to
tell him,' says Leigh Hunt, 'that he had come from the planet
Mercury.' One may vary the form of the fancy; and, though
the pale planet Mercury, the sickly darling of the sun, seems
such an orb as Shelley might have come from, had he come
from any, it might be fitter to fancy that he had come from
none, but, till he touched our earth, had been winging about
in unsubstantial ether. When Milton's rebel host left the
celestial realms, angels flocking on angels and the great
Archangel leading, might we not suppose that some small
seraph, who had joined the rebellion, lagged behind the rest
in his flight, became detached from them by regret or weakness,
and, unable to overtake them, was left to flutter disconsolate
and alone amid the starry spaces? Excluded from Heaven, but
not borne down with the rest into Pandemonium, if this
creature did at last come near our orb in his wanderings,
might it not become his refuge; and then might we not suppose
that, when the Highest was named, he would shriek against
the name—yet his recollections of his original would be purer,
and his nature less impaired, than if, instead of transparent
space, populous Pandemonium had been his intermediate home?

Whatever form we give to the fancy, the characteristics of
Shelley's poetry are such as to accord with it. Intense as is his
ethical spirit, his desire to act upon man and society, his
imagination cannot work with things as he finds them, with the
actual stuff of historical life. His mode of thinking is not
according to the terrestrial conditions of time, place, cause and
effect, variety of race, climate, and costume. His persons are
shapes, winged forms, modernized versions of Grecian
mythology, or mortals highly allegorized; and their movements are vague, swift, and independent of ordinary physical
laws.

The Life and Poetry of Shelley 1860

WILLIAM ROSSETTI

As regards the poems, the only observation I wish to add here is that their astonishing beauty of musical sound—admitted on all hands as one of their quite exceptional excellences—is combined with, perhaps partly dependent on, an indifference, uncommon in degree among finished poetical writers, to mere *correctness* of rhyming structure. The precise attention I have had to bestow on this point has brought the fact very forcibly before me—has revealed a looseness of rhyming very much greater than I had before observed in my less technical readings of Shelley. Now, as Shelley himself opined, 'the canons of taste are to be sought in the most admirable works of art'; and the combination, in his poems, of inexactitude of rhyming with almost unrivalled music of sound, impresses itself strongly upon my mind that this may after all be the *right way* to attain the highest forms of verbal harmony in poetry—of course, given the true and great master. I will not enlarge upon the point; but simply append a list of loose rhymes to be found upon five pages taken absolutely at random; a list selected with a purpose would exhibit a still stronger case: 'Lot, thought—alone, shone—afar, war—stood, flood—evil, revel—strong, among—none, groan—drove, love—sinecure, fewer—count, front, account—require, Oliver—off, enough—down, one—promotion, motion—amid, pyramid—floors, alligators—river, ever, wheresoever—harmony, sky—thee, thee (twice over)—low, how—fail (rhymeless)—despair, dear—accept not, reject not.'

A Memoir of Percy Bysshe Shelley 1870

J. A. SYMONDS

As a poet, Shelley contributed a new quality to English literature—a quality of ideality, freedom, and spiritual audacity, which severe critics of other nations think we lack. Byron's daring is in a different region: his elemental worldliness and pungent satire do not liberate our energies, or cheer us with new hopes and splendid vistas. Wordsworth, the very

SHELLEY

antithesis to Shelley in his reverent accord with institutions, suits our meditative moods, sustains us with a sound philosophy, and braces us by healthy contact with the Nature he so dearly loved. But in Wordsworth there is none of Shelley's magnetism. What remains of permanent value in Coleridge's poetry—such work as *Christabel*, the *Ancient Mariner*, or *Kubla Khan*—is a product of pure artistic fancy, tempered by the author's mysticism. Keats, true and sacred poet as he was, loved Nature with a somewhat sensuous devotion. She was for him a mistress rather than a Diotima; nor did he share the prophetic fire which burns in Shelley's verse, quite apart from the direct enunciation of his favourite tenets. In none of Shelley's greatest contemporaries was the lyrical faculty so paramount; and whether we consider his minor songs, his odes, or his more complicated choral dramas, we acknowledge that he was the loftiest and the most spontaneous singer of our language. In the range of power he was also conspicuous above the rest. Not only did he write the best lyrics, but the best tragedy, the best translations, the best familiar poems of his century. As a satirist and humourist, I cannot place him so high as some of his admirers do; and the purely polemical portions of his poems, those in which he puts forth his antagonism to tyrants and religions and custom in all its myriad forms, seem to me to degenerate at intervals into poor rhetoric.

While his genius was so varied and its flight so unapproached in swiftness, it would be vain to deny that Shelley, as an artist, had faults from which the men with whom I have compared him were more free. The most prominent of these are haste, incoherence, verbal carelessness, incompleteness, a want of narrative force, and a weak hold on objective realities. Even his warmest admirers, if they are sincere critics, will concede that his verse, taken altogether, is marked by inequality. In his eager self-abandonment to inspiration, he produced much that is unsatisfying simply because it is not ripe. There was no defect of power in him, but a defect of patience; and the final word to be pronounced in estimating the larger bulk of his poetry is immature. Not only was the poet young; but the fruit of his young mind had been plucked before it had been duly mellowed by reflection. Again, he did not care enough for common things to present them with artistic fulness. He was intolerant of detail, and thus failed to model with the roundness that we find in Goethe's work. He flew at the grand, the spacious, the sublime; and did not always succeed in realising for his readers what he had imagined. A certain want of faith in his own powers, fostered by the extraordinary discouragement under which he had to write, prevented him from finishing what he began, or from giving that ultimate form of perfection to his longer works which we admire in shorter pieces like the *Ode to the West Wind.* When a poem was ready, he had it hastily printed, and passed on to fresh creative efforts. If anything occurred to interrupt his energy, he flung the sketch aside. Some of these defects, if we may use this word at all to indicate our sense that Shelley might by care have been made equal to his highest self, were in a great measure the correlative of his chief quality—the ideality, of which I have already spoken. He composed with all his faculties, mental, emotional, and physical, at the utmost strain at a white heat of intense fervour, striving to attain one object, the truest and most passionate investiture for the thoughts which had inflamed his ever-quick imagination. The result is that his finest work has more the stamp of some-thing natural and elemental—the wind, the sea, the depth of air—than of a mere artistic product.

Shelley   1878

J. M. ROBERTSON

. . . the true Shelleyite adores *Prometheus Unbound* in its nebulous entirety; and when people of culture are found thus fascinated by a coruscating haze we are forced to raise the question whether their own intellectual furniture is of a very substantial kind. Who are the people who find mental nourish-ment and abiding charm in the soft or strained falsettos of Shelley's nymphs and spirits, and the vapourings of his phantoms? Do they combine with a critical literary taste a clear vision of the great issues of life? Are they close students of men and things; and do they affect any harder thinking than that of belles-lettres? It would be unwarrantable to say that there are not out-and-out Shelleyites whose intellectual outfit is of the completest kind; but it may be suspected that a large proportion are to be classified as lovers of the sentimental in philosophy and the mythical in history; and that the competent minds which delight in Shelley generally set aside as valueless two-thirds of his work. . . .

We shall not, however, rightly understand the case until we fully recognise the remarkable faculty which underlies Shelley's worst as well as his best work—the freedom in the use of words, in which, judgment apart, he excels all previous English poets save Shakespeare. It is no doubt this extraordinary capacity for mere verbal movement which overpowers most Shelleyites; it seems so wonderful, so superhuman, so independent of the ordinary trammels of thought and speech, that men in their surprise cease to be critical, and simply bow down and worship. And it must be acknowledged that this faculty of ecstatic speech is at times exhibited by Shelley in sustained flights which do not get lost in cloudland. If I were asked to say in which of the poems over a few hundred lines he is most successful, I should name *Epipsychidion* and the *Lines written among the Euganean Hills*. In these pieces, though they have not, as it were, gone through the process of gestation which made possible the ripest of his short pieces, he is working in the stuff of human feeling; not versifying delirious aspirations, but pouring out his own heart; and though we have agreed that to the poet no subject is tabu, it stands to reason that he has a much better chance of attaining excellence of song when he uses the material of his deepest experience than when spinning the cloud-webs of his wandering fantasy. And so the poem *written among the Euganean Hills*, though done in haste and not free from weaknesses, has a touching quality for all lovers of poetry, the throb of the poet's heart running through all its swift transitions. It really attains the indispensable quality of intension, the poet in the stress of his emotion becoming one, as it were, with all he sees, and attaining in his commentary a white heat of thought. So too in *Epipsychidion* he achieves a transfiguration of passion, moving in the process, it is true, towards his favourite cloudland, but never letting the note of his eager passion die away, never getting quite lost sight of. It is a unique poetic faculty which has produced these two poems, with their eager rush of ideas, that 'pard-like, beautiful and swift' motion which charms so many readers into measure-less applause; and we shall do well to take pains to appreciate their fine qualities, for they stand alone among Shelley's poems of more than two hundred lines in respect of combined intensity and finish. With the *Ode to the West Wind*, they represent his highest lyrical poetry, and give us the measure of his mentality. Wild, passionate yearning, undefined aspiration, expressed with an eagerness always tending towards inco-herence and unintelligibility—this is what Shelley has to give us in the most strenuous of his prosperous flights; and it may be left to readers to say for themselves finally whether at his highest such a poet is one of the greatest poets. . . .

And, to come to perhaps the most delicate point in our summing up, even *Adonais*, one of the poems of 1821, partakes of the nature of a brilliant failure. It has certainly a compara-tively small percentage of quite bad or absurd lines; but none the more does it exhibit ripe art or pregnant utterance. The show of passion, the 'wild and whirling words' in which the poet pours his plaint for his dead fellow singer, have the effect of impressing many readers; and indeed it is impossible to be quite cold to such a storm of eloquent wailing; but I doubt whether anyone of a fairly judicial habit of mind can go through the poem thoughtfully and, mindful of the actual facts of Shelley's relation to the dead man, yet laying no stress on his blunder as to the cause of Keats' death, pro-nounce it the moving expression of a sincere human grief. It has neither the symptoms nor the contagious pathos of heartfelt mourning. Milton's *Lycidas*, with all its noble beauty, had partly set a precedent for rhetorical requiems; but where Milton's rhetoric is august and golden, Shelley's is shrill, hysterical, almost bombastic. It is not by declamatory lamenta-tion of this sort that we are moved to mourn for poets or any one else. Take against the whole profuse outcry of *Adonais* a few sad stanzas of *In Memoriam*, with their controlled but potent feeling. . . .

But let it be reiterated in conclusion that mere failure to criticize life soundly is not the condemnation of a poet. What has been contended in this inadequate inquiry is that not the rightness of a poet's thinking but the charm of his expression of it is his title to praise; and what is rightly to be decided against Shelley is that in his longer works his thought, such as it was, is quite inadequately meditated for the purposes of beautiful expression. With counter arguments to the effect that Shelley's personality glorifies his poetry for us we have nothing to do.

Shelley and Poetry   1884

FRANCIS THOMPSON

Coming to Shelley's poetry we peep over the wild mask of revolutionary metaphysics, and we see the winsome face of the child. Perhaps none of his poems is more purely and typically Shelleian than *The Cloud*, and it is interesting to note how essentially it springs from the faculty of make-believe. The same thing is conspicuous, though less purely conspicuous, throughout his singing; it is the child's faculty of make-believe raised to the *n*th power. He is still at play, save only that his play is such as manhood stops to watch, and his playthings are those which the gods give their children. The universe is his box of toys. He dabbles his fingers in the day-fall. He is gold-dusty with tumbling amidst the stars. He makes bright mischief with the moon. The meteors nuzzle their noses in his hand. He teases into growling the kennelled thunder, and laughs at the shaking of its fiery chain. He dances in and out of the gates of heaven: its floor is littered with his broken fancies. He runs wild over the fields of ether. He chases the rolling world. He gets between the feet of the horses of the sun. He stands in the lap of patient Nature, and twines her loosened tresses after a hundred wilful fashions, to see how she will look nicest in his song.

This it was which, in spite of his essentially modern character as a singer, qualified Shelley to be the poet of *Prometheus Unbound*, for it made him, in the truest sense of the word, a mythological poet. This childlike quality assimilated him to the childlike peoples among whom mythologies have their rise. . . .

But if Shelley, instead of culling Nature, crossed with its pollen the blossoms of his own soul, that Babylonian garden is his marvellous and best apology. For astounding figurative opulence he yields only to Shakespeare, and even to Shakespeare not in absolute fecundity but in range of images. The sources of his figurative wealth are specialized, while the sources of Shakespeare's are universal. It would have been a conscious effort for him to speak without figure as it is for most men to speak with figure. Suspended in the dripping well of his imagination the commonest object becomes encrusted with imagery. Herein again he deviates from the true Nature poet, the normal Wordsworth type of nature poet: imagery was to him not a mere means of expression, not even a mere means of adornment; it was a delight for its own sake. And herein we find the trail by which we would classify him. He belongs to a school of which not impossibly he may hardly have read a line—the Metaphysical School. To a large extent, he *is* what the Metaphysical School should have been. That school was a certain kind of poetry trying for a range. Shelley is the range found. Crashaw and Shelley sprang from the same seed; but in the one case the seed was choked with thorns, in the other it fell on good ground. The Metaphysical School was in its direct results an abortive movement, though indirectly much came of it—for Dryden came of it. Dryden, to a greater extent than is (we imagine) generally perceived, was Cowley systematized; and Cowley, who sank into the arms of Dryden, rose from the lap of Donne. But the movement was so abortive that few will thank us for connecting with it the name of Shelley. This is because to most people the Metaphysical School means Donne, whereas it ought to mean Crashaw. We judge the direction of a development by its highest form, though that form may have been produced but once, and produced imperfectly. Now the highest product of the Metaphysical School was Crashaw, and Crashaw was a Shelley *manqué*; he never reached the Promised Land, but he had fervid visions of it. The Metaphysical School, like Shelley, loved imagery for its own sake: and how beautiful a thing the frank toying with imagery may be, let *The Skylark* and *The Cloud* witness. It is only evil when the poet, on the straight way to a fixed object, lags continually from the path to play. This is commendable neither in poet nor errand-boy. The Metaphysical School failed, not because it toyed with imagery, but because it toyed with it frostily. To sport with the tangles of Neaera's hair may be trivial idleness or caressing tenderness, exactly as your relation to Neaera is that of heartless gallantry or of love. So you may toy with imagery in mere intellectual ingenuity, and then you might as well go write acrostics: or you may toy with it in raptures, and then you may write a *Sensitive Plant*. In fact, the Metaphysical poets when they went astray cannot be said to have done anything so dainty as is implied in *toying* with imagery. They cut into shapes with a pair of scissors. From all such danger Shelley was saved by his passionate spontaneity; no trappings are too splendid for the swift steeds of sunrise. His sword-hilt may be rough with jewels, but it is the hilt of an Excalibur. His thoughts scorch through all the folds of expression. His cloth of gold bursts at the flexures, and shows the naked poetry.

It is this gift of not merely embodying but apprehending everything in figure which co-operates towards creating one of his rarest characteristics, so almost preternaturally developed in no other poet, namely his well-known power to condense the most hydrogenic abstraction. Science can now educe threads of such exquisite tenuity that only the feet of the tiniest infant-spiders can ascend them; but up the filmiest unsubstantiality Shelley runs with agile ease. To him, in truth, nothing is abstract. The dustiest abstractions

> Start, and tremble under his feet,
> And blossom in purple and red.

The coldest moon of an idea rises haloed through his vaporous imagination. The dimmest-sparked chip of a conception blazes and scintillates in the subtile oxygen of his mind. The most wrinkled Æson of an abstruseness leaps rosy out of his bubbling genius. In a more intensified signification than it is probable that Shakespeare dreamed of, Shelley gives to nothing a local habitation and a name. Here afresh he touches the Metaphysical School, whose very title was drawn from this habitual pursuit of abstractions, and who failed in that pursuit from the one cause omnipresent with them, because in all their poetic smithy they had left never a place for a forge. They laid their fancies chill on the anvil.

Shelley   Published in 1908, but written in 1889

THE MASTER OF HIS COLLEGE

The memorial to the poet Shelley which has been presented to University College, Oxford, by Lady Shelley, was opened yesterday in the presence of a distinguished company . . . Lady Shelley, the Bishop of Southwark, the Master of University (Dr Bright), the Master of Balliol (Professor Jowett) . . .

The *Master of University* returned thanks on behalf of the corporation of which he was the head for the generous gift which Lady Shelley had bestowed upon them, adding that the gift received fresh charms from the tender way in which she had delivered it over to them. It was not often that a college in Oxford had a modern work of art given to it. The reason for that was, he thought, that there was a sort of erroneous fancy that Oxford belonged completely to the old. There could not be a greater error. If Oxford was to be what it claimed to be— the very centre and heart of the growth of young England— it seemed to him clear that Oxford must advance with the world, must expand and be open to new influences, and he could not conceive any more true emblem of the present century than the great poet whose effigy they had now received. For if they came to think of what really happened to him, he thought it was this—that he was prophetic in all directions of what was to come to the world. Their thanks were very largely due to this fact—that the gift of the memorial was a sort of emblem and symbol to them of a rubbing out of old ill-wills and old ill-feelings, and of a perfectly peaceful feeling towards that great man. He did not think they ought to judge of their predecessors very harshly, or to say that the action of the College was very extraordinarily wrong, for he believed there was hardly any place in Oxford which would not have acted in the same way as University College acted. But what they had to observe was this—that the very greatness of the man had rendered him open to that sort of treatment. It was because there was in him such a well-spring of hatred of all that was false and oppressive, and because he had such a strong feeling of all that was gloomy and sad in the history of the world and mankind, that he could not but become a rebel; and, being a rebel, he was treated as a rebel. But the rebel of 80 years ago was the hero of the present century. In other words, the great aspirations which he had, the intense love of the human race which he had, the intense admiration of all objects that met his eyes in the natural world, the intense hatred of all that was evil and all that was sad, what was it but the very thing they had been learning for these last 80 years? And when at this time they had constant repetitions of very sad and pessimist sorts of views as to what the world was going to become, it was very cheerful to come across a prophet who prophesied good things and not bad.

The Times   1893

YEATS

I still believe that one cannot help believing him, as this scholar I know believes him, a vague thinker, who mixed occasional great poetry with a phantastic rhetoric, unless one compares such passages, and above all such passages as describe the liberty he praised, till one has discovered the system of belief that lay behind them. It should seem natural to find his thought full of subtlety, for Mrs Shelley has told how he hesitated whether he should be a metaphysician or a poet, and has spoken of his 'huntings after the obscure' with regret, and said of that *Prometheus Unbound*, which so many for three generations have thought *Political Justice* put into rhyme, 'It requires a mind as subtle and penetrating as his own to understand the mystic meanings scattered throughout the poem. They elude the ordinary reader by their abstraction and delicacy of distinction, but they are far from vague. It was his design to write prose metaphysical essays on the *Nature of Man*, which would have served to explain much of what is obscure in his poetry; a few scattered fragments of observation and remarks alone remain. He considered these philosophical views of mind and nature to be instinct with the intensest spirit of poetry.' From these scattered fragments and observations, and from many passages read in their light, one soon comes to understand that his liberty was so much more than the liberty of *Political Justice* that it was one with intellectual beauty, and that the regeneration he foresaw was so much more than the regeneration many political dreamers have foreseen, that it could not come in its perfection till the hours bore 'Time to his grave in eternity'.

Ideas of Good and Evil 1903

A. C. BRADLEY

Swinburne used to insist that the first business of a singer is to sing. Suppose, to avoid controversy, you confine this statement to lyrical poetry, can you hesitate where to place Shelley among English singers? I cannot. His range here is immensely wider than that of Keats, a good deal wider than that of Wordsworth; and the music of his song is the very echo of his mood, whether that be longing, aspiration, triumph, gaiety, deep dejection, uncomplaining sadness, the peace or the rapture of momentary harmony. Naturally, the compass of his voice is not unlimited, and he is not equally master of all rhythms and metres. Where a full-toned slow-moving rhythm is wanted Keats surpasses him; and Keats at his best does so also, as Milton and Wordsworth certainly do, in feeling for the movement of a sonnet. But to attempt *in general* to put Keats beside him as a lyrical poet appears to me an error almost grotesque; and to put Milton or Wordsworth beside him still an error. And I would go yet further. In Shakespeare's day the subject-matter or province of lyrical poetry was much more restricted than in Shelley's day. If this had been otherwise, I suppose Shakespeare would have been our greatest lyrist: but, as things are, I cannot doubt that that title belongs to Shelley.

'Shelley and Arnold's Critique of his Poetry', *an enlargement of a part of a Leslie Stephen Lecture given at Newnham College* 1919

ELIOT

Shelley both had views about poetry and made use of poetry for expressing views. With Shelley we are struck from the beginning by the number of things poetry is expected to do; from a poet who tells us in a note on vegetarianism, that 'the orang-outang perfectly resembles man both in the order and the number of his teeth', we shall not know what to expect. The notes to *Queen Mab* express, it is true, only the views of an intelligent and enthusiastic schoolboy, but a schoolboy who knows how to write; and throughout his work, which is of no small bulk for a short life, he does not, I think, let us forget that he took his ideas seriously. The ideas of Shelley seem to me always to be ideas of adolescence—as there is every reason why they should be. And an enthusiasm for Shelley seems to me also to be an affair of adolescence: for most of us, Shelley has marked an intense period before maturity, but for how many does Shelley remain the companion of age? I confess that I never open the volume of his poems simply because I want to read poetry, but only with some special reason for reference. I find his ideas repellent; and the difficulty of separating Shelley from his ideas and beliefs is still greater than with Wordsworth. And the biographical interest which Shelley has always excited makes it difficult to read the poetry without remembering the man: and the man was humourless, pedantic, self-centred, and sometimes almost a blackguard. Except for an occasional flash of shrewd sense, when he is speaking of someone else and not concerned with his own affairs or with fine writing, his letters are insufferably dull. He makes an astonishing contrast with the attractive Keats. On the other hand, I admit that Wordsworth does not present a very pleasing personality either; yet I not only enjoy his poetry as I cannot enjoy Shelley's, but I enjoy it more than when I first read it. I can only fumble (abating my prejudices as best I can) for reasons why Shelley's abuse of poetry does me more violence than Wordsworth's.

Shelley seems to have had to a high degree the unusual faculty of passionate apprehension of abstract ideas. Whether

G

he was not sometimes confused about his own feelings, as we may be tempted to believe when confounded by the philosophy of *Epipsychidion*, is another matter. I do not mean that Shelley had a metaphysical or philosophical mind; his mind was in some ways a very confused one: he was able to be at once and with the same enthusiasm an eighteenth-century rationalist and a cloudy Platonist. But abstractions could excite in him strong emotion. His views remained pretty fixed, though his poetic gift matured. It is open to us to guess whether his mind would have matured too; certainly, in his last, and to my mind his greatest though unfinished poem, *The Triumph of Life*, there is evidence not only of better writing than in any previous poem, but of greater wisdom.

The Use of Poetry and the Use of Criticism   1933

HERBERT READ

Byron, who was a very honest critic, even of his friends, was the first to be aware of Shelley's *particular* quality. 'You know my high opinion of your own poetry,' he wrote to Shelley, and added the reason: '—because it is of *no* school.' To Byron all the rest of his contemporaries seemed 'second-hand' imitators of antique models or doctrinaire exponents of a mannerism. Shelley alone could not be so simply classified; his verse was too honestly original, too independently thought and wrought, to be accepted as 'fashionable literature'. For there are always these two types of originality: originality that responds like the Aolian harp to every gust of contemporary feeling, pleasing by its anticipation of what is but half-formed in the public consciousness; and originality that is not influenced by anything outside the poet's own consciousness, but is the direct product of his individual mind and independent feeling. The latter type is always long in winning recognition and since Shelley's originality was essentially of this type, we need not be surprised that only a few of his contemporaries appreciated his poetry for its proper qualities. . . .

The whole tendency of Shelley is towards a clarification and abstraction of thought—away from the personal and particular towards the general and universal. . . .

But the highest beauties of Shelley's poetry are evanescent and imponderable—thought so tenuous and intuitive, that it has no visual equivalent; no positive impact. . . .

. . . such poetry has no precision, and the process of its unfolding is not logical. It does not answer to the general definition of any kind. It is vain to apply to it that method of criticism which assumes that the ardour of a verse can be analysed into separate vocables, and that poetry is a function of sound. Poetry is mainly a function of language—the exploitation of a medium, a vocal and mental material, in the interests of a personal mood or emotion, or of the thoughts evoked by such moods or emotions. I do not think we can say much more about it; according to our sensitivity we recognize its success. The rest of our reasoning about it is either mere prejudice, ethical anxiety, or academic pride.

In Defence of Shelley 1935

Keats

After so many previous performances by abler gymnasts it is difficult to summon up much enthusiasm for going through the motions of comparing Shelley and Keats yet again: especially as the comparison was never a very promising critical exercise, the two being so different in kind. But to compare the criticism written on the one with that written on the other promises at least a little freshness in the variation, and may not be without its bearing on the qualities of the two subjects.

The vagueness, or incommunicativeness, of Shelley's critics has already been remarked. It offers an immediate and striking contrast with the tone and content of Keats' critics. They have, and from the beginning, been pretty clear about what they found in him; they are in broad agreement one with another; and what is perhaps most striking, they have been in general very close to Keats' own view of what he had done, and what he ought to do. That his poetry had sensuousness and passion—this is what he felt and said of it himself, and what all his critics have allowed. That it needed to be strengthened by a 'philosophy', a deeper perception of the moral existence of humanity: this too is what he thought himself, and what his critics have thought. The only matter for dispute, and that not very acrid, has been about the precise extent to which he had succeeded in bringing this added strength into his last poems. On the whole, verdicts have been more favourable since the publication of the letters, a century ago, made it easier to identify the more philosophic problems which occupied his mind and feelings in that last astonishing year of his life as a writer. The first notable instance of this type of exegesis is Masson's study, published in 1860, and it would not be very misleading to say that all later critics of Keats have followed the general lines there sketched, though with growing precision of definition and detail. This coherence, this cumulative homogeneity in Keats' criticism, when contrasted with the comparative incoherence of Shelley's critics, may perhaps be allowed to count—though of course indirectly—in his favour, as being evidence of a real superiority of integrity and purpose in his poetry.

Again, while the general estimate of Shelley has more or less steadily fallen, that of Keats has fairly regularly risen, and one of its most obvious effects has been on the shifts of emphasis within the corpus of his writing. For his earlier admirers, for Hunt, Tennyson, and Hallam, he was above all the poet of La Belle Dame *and the* Nightingale Ode: *the 'magic casements' lines were those on which their resonant memories dwelt most fondly. His later critics, however, have turned to the second* Hyperion, *and to those three Odes,* On a Grecian Urn, To Melancholy, *and* To Autumn, *which most fully depend upon the deeper reflections of his last year.*

Perhaps the only problem about which there has been wide difference of opinion is the cause of his early death. Was it Koch's tubercle bacillus, or the Quarterly Magazine *? It is, of course,* prima facie, *merely a biographical or medical problem ; but upon it literary and critical implications have come to depend, for it has been taken for evidence bearing on the essential strength, or lack of strength, in his personality as a writer. To be killed by tubercle would be a merely medical disaster. But to be killed by a savage review would be a moral defeat, and might well indicate some moral vulnerability. The truth is probably neither on the one side nor on the other, but something of both. Unless Keats had first been sapped by his disease he would not have been so wounded by the damage—the quite real damage— inflicted on him by the reviewers. But it is only fair to remember —and no reader of the following pages will readily forget—that he was subjected to an attack by the Tory reviewers of altogether exceptional virulence and meanness.*

The causes of this savagery are not at first sight obvious, but they become clearer if a slight leap of the imagination is made to the Britain of the days before the Reform Bill—to a society organized by a parliament, democratic in principle, but in practice resting upon rotten boroughs, and a fractional franchise. To the defenders of this venerable system, it was of the last *importance to maintain that the great majority of the population, who had no vote, was undeserving of a voice in the affairs of the nation, because it lacked education and intelligence, and positively required to be kept in subjection for its own good. Any sign of exceptional ability in these voiceless and nameless ranks was a potential threat to this constitutional doctrine, and was dealt with on that basis. In literature, it was allowed and accepted that a few writers should rise from the ranks; in verse, they had their own amiable little niche under the general heading of 'peasant poets' such as Burns, Bloomfield, and Keats' acquaintance John Clare. Socially, they were not felt as a menace, for they could be treated as peasants, in the still surviving framework of feudal manners; thus Clare, invited by the Marquis of Exeter to visit Burghley House, was quite naturally dismissed to take his refreshment in the kitchen after a pleasant interview with his noble patron. And from a more strictly literary point of view, it was of course understood that their business, their speciality, was to write about fields and trees and flowers and cattle. It was precisely against these assumptions that Keats offended. Socially, he was not a peasant, but one of the inflammable urban lower classes—those classes which had so lately made the deplorable revolution in France. Moreover, he was associated with Leigh Hunt, a libeller of his monarch—and guilt by association is a doctrine which has always had a natural appeal to the right wing of politics. Worst of all, both he and Hunt were mere 'cockneys', men of low birth and no station in life. As* Blackwood's *expressed it, in its first attack upon the* 'Cockney School of Poetry', 'All the great poets of our country have been men of some rank in society, and there is no vulgarity in their writings; but Mr Hunt cannot utter a dedication, or even a note, without betraying the Shibboleth of low birth and low habits.' *Keats, of course, did not bring very much pestilential democracy into his poetry—nothing like as much as Shelley or Hunt. But he did something which, in its own way, was even worse. Though he had never been to a proper school, and had never learned a word of Greek, he wrote about Greek gods and goddesses, all from some wretched dictionary.* Blackwood's *never tired of making this telling point:* 'What in the name of wonder tempts all these fellows to write on* Greek *fables?—*

'*There they are, a pack of poor illiterate creatures* (*not one of whom could tell, within fifty miles, what is the meaning of a Middle Voice*), *all piping about Pan, and Apollo, and Endymion, and the Muses. . . .*' *Byron himself felt the same sense of aristocratic, Harrovian outrage, and in his last gibe about Keats' death and the* Quarterly *did not omit to mention that this peasant had*

> without Greek
> Contrived to talk about the gods of late,
> Much as they might have been supposed to speak.

It is, then, on these general lines—though they need much more ample illustration than can be given here—that the savagery of the attacks on Keats are to be understood, and also their capacity to wound their victim. The mere existence of such a writer was a threat to the Tory cause, altogether more serious, because more real, than the elegantly expressed apostasies of 'a scholar and a gentleman' such as Shelley.

It may be added that the mere existence of such a writer was, in its own way, no less a portent than the Tories took it for. It was not the least of Keats' achievements to demonstrate that an English writer can do very well without public schooling and station in life ; that all he needs is his own endowment of ability, and the education which consists in nothing more, nor less, than a real reading of English literature.

KEATS

It is a sorry thing for me that any one should have to overcome Prejudices in reading my Verses—that affects me more than any hyper-criticism on any particular passage. In *Endymion* I have most likely but moved into the Go-cart from the leading strings. In Poetry I have a few Axioms, and you will see how far I am from their Centre. 1st. I think Poetry should surprise by a fine excess and not by Singularity—it should strike the Reader as a wording of his own highest thoughts, and appear almost a Remembrance—2nd. Its touches of Beauty should never be half way thereby making the reader breathless instead of content: the rise, the progress, the setting of imagery should like the Sun come natural to him—shine

over him and set soberly although in magnificence leaving him
in the Luxury of twilight—but it is easier to think what Poetry
should be than to write it—and this leads me to another
axiom. That if Poetry comes not as naturally as the Leaves to a
tree it had better not come at all. However it may be with me I
cannot help looking into new countries with 'O for a Muse of
fire to ascend!' If *Endymion* serves me as a Pioneer perhaps I
ought to be content. I have great reason to be content, for
thank God I can read and perhaps understand Shakespeare
to his depths, and I have I am sure many friends, who, if I fail,
will attribute any change in my Life and Temper to Humbleness rather than to Pride—to a cowering under the Wings of
great Poets rather than to a Bitterness that I am not appreciated. I am anxious to get *Endymion* printed that I may forget
it and proceed.

Letter to John Taylor   February 1818

You say 'I fear there is little chance of anything else in this
life.' You seem by that to have been going through with a more
painful and acute zest the same labyrinth that I have—I have
come to the same conclusion thus far. My Branchings out
therefrom have been numerous: one of them is the consideration of Wordsworth's genius and as a help, in the manner of
gold being the meridian Line of worldly wealth—how he
differs from Milton. And here I have nothing but surmises,
from an uncertainty whether Milton's apparently less anxiety
for Humanity proceeds from his seeing further or no than
Wordsworth: And whether Wordsworth has in truth epic
passion, and martyrs himself to the human heart, the main
region of his song—In regard to his genius alone—we find what
he says true as far as we have experienced and we can judge
no further but by larger experience—for axioms in philosophy
are not axioms until they are proved upon our pulses. We
read fine things but never feel them to the full until we have
gone the same steps as the Author. . . .

I compare human life to a large Mansion of Many Apart-
ments, two of which I can only describe, the doors of the rest
being as yet shut upon me. The first we step into we call the

infant or thoughtless Chamber, in which we remain as long as
we do not think—We remain there a long while, and notwithstanding the doors of the second Chamber remain wide
open, showing a bright appearance, we care not to hasten to it;
but are at length imperceptibly impelled by the awakening of
this thinking principle within us—we no sooner get into the
second Chamber, which I call the Chamber of Maiden-
Thought, than we become intoxicated with the light and
atmosphere, we see nothing but pleasant wonders, and think
of delaying there for ever in delight: However among the
effects this breathing is father of is that tremendous one of
sharpening one's vision into the heart and nature of Man—
of convincing one's nerves that the world is full of Misery and
Heartbreak, Pain, Sickness and oppression—whereby this
Chamber of Maiden Thought becomes gradually darken'd
and at the same time on all sides of it many *doors* are set open
—but all dark—all leading to dark passages—We see not
the balance of good and evil. We are in a Mist. *We* are now
in that state—We feel the 'burden of the Mystery'. To this
Point was Wordsworth come, as far as I can conceive when he
wrote *Tintern Abbey* and it seems to me that his genius is
explorative of those dark Passages. Now if we live, and go on
thinking, we too shall explore them—he is a Genius and
superior to us, in so far as he can, more than we, make discoveries, and shed a light in them—Here I must think Wordsworth is deeper than Milton—though I think it has depended
more upon the general and gregarious advance of intellect,
than individual greatness of Mind.

Letter to Reynolds   May 1818

I begin to get a little acquainted with my own strength and
weakness.—Praise or blame has but a momentary effect on
the man whose love of beauty in the abstract makes him a
severe critic on his own Works. My own domestic criticism
has given me pain without comparison beyond what *Blackwood* or the *Quarterly* could possibly inflict, and also when
I feel I am right, no external praise can give me such a glow
as my own solitary reperception & ratification of what is fine.

J.S. is perfectly right in regard to the slip-shod *Endymion.*
That it is so is no fault of mine.—No!—though it may sound a
little paradoxical. It is as good as I had power to make it—
by myself. Had I been nervous about its being a perfect piece,
& with that view asked advice, & trembled over every page,
it would not have been written; for it is not in my nature to
fumble—I will write independently.—I have written independently *without Judgment.*—I may write independently, &
with Judgment hereafter. The Genius of Poetry must work out
its own salvation in a man: It cannot be matured by law and
precept, but by sensation and watchfulness in itself. That
which is creative must create itself—In *Endymion,* I leaped
headlong into the Sea, and thereby have become better
aquainted with the Soundings, the quicksands, & the rocks,
than if I had stayed upon the green shore, and piped a silly
pipe, and took tea & comfortable advice.—I was never afraid
of failure; for I would sooner fail than not be among the
greatest. But I am nigh getting into a rant.

Letter to Hessey   October 1818

I will give you a few reasons why I shall persist in not
publishing *The Pot of Basil.* It is too smokeable! (9) I can get
it smoak'd at the Carpenters shaving chimney much more
cheaply—There is too much inexperience of life, and simplicity
of knowledge in it—which might do very well after one's
death—but not while one is alive. There are very few would
look to the reality. I intend to use more finesse with the Public.
It is possible to write fine things which cannot be laugh'd at in
any way. Isabella is what I should call were I a reviewer 'A
weak-sided Poem' with an amusing sober-sadness about it. . . .
If I may so say, in my dramatic capacity I enter fully into the
feeling: but in Propria Persona I should be apt to quiz it
myself—There is no objection of this kind to *Lamia*—A good
deal to *St Agnes Eve*—only not so glaring.

Letter to Woodhouse   September 1819

I have given up *Hyperion*—there were too many Miltonic
inversions in it—Miltonic verse cannot be written but in an

artful or rather artist's humour. I wish to give myself up to other sensations. English ought to be kept up. It may be interesting to you to pick out some lines from *Hyperion* and put a mark X to the false beauty proceeding from art, and one ‖ to the true voice of feeling. Upon my soul 'twas imagination I cannot make the distinction—Every now and then there is a Miltonic intonation.

Letter to Reynolds   September 1819

[See also the passage given on pp. 125–6 of Volume I, *The Poets and their Critics*. It is from a letter to George Keats written at the same time as the above]

LEIGH HUNT

. . . here is a young poet giving himself up to his own impressions, and revelling in real poetry for its own sake. . . . We do not, of course, mean to say that Mr Keats has as much talent as he will have ten years hence, or that there are no imitations in his book, or that he does not make mistakes common to inexperience; the reverse is inevitable at his time of life. In proportion to our ideas, or impressions of the images of things, must be our acquaintance with the things themselves. But our author has all the sensitiveness of temperament requisite to receive these impressions; and wherever he has turned hitherto, he has evidently felt them deeply.

The very faults of Mr Keats arise from a passion for beauties, and a young impatience to vindicate them; and as we have mentioned these, we shall refer to them at once. They may be comprised in two; first, a tendency to notice every thing too indiscriminately and without an eye to natural proportion and effect; and second, a sense of the proper variety of versification without a due consideration of its principles.

Examiner   1817

Mr Keats' versification sometimes reminds us of Milton in his blank verse, and sometimes of Chapman both in his blank verse and rhyme; but his faculties, essentially speaking, though partaking of the unearthly aspirations and abstract yearnings of both these poets, are altogether his own. They are ambitious, but less directly so. They are more social, and in the finer sense of the word, sensual than either. They are more coloured by the modern philosophy of sympathy and natural justice. *Endymion*, with all its extraordinary powers, partook of the faults of youth, though the best ones; but the reader of *Hyperion* and these other stories would never guess that they were written at twenty. The author's versification is now perfected, the exuberances of his imagination restrained, and a calm power, the surest and loftiest of all power, takes the place of the impatient workings of the younger god within him. The character of his genius is that of energy and voluptuousness, each able at will to take leave of the other, and possessing, in their union, a high feeling of humanity not common to the best authors who can less combine them. Mr Keats undoubtedly takes his seat with the oldest and best of our living poets.

Indicator 1820

Keats' early poetry, indeed, partook plentifully of the exuberance of youth; and even in most of his later, his sensibility, sharpened by mortal illness, tended to a morbid excess. His region is 'a wilderness of sweets,'—flowers of all hue, and 'weeds of glorious feature,'—where, as he says, the luxuriant soil brings

The pipy hemlock to strange overgrowth.

But there also is the 'rain-scented eglantine,' and bushes of May-flowers, with bees, and myrtle, and bay,—and endless paths into forests haunted with the loveliest as well as the gentlest beings; and the gods live in the distance, amid notes of majestic thunder. I do not say that no 'surfeit' is ever there; but I do, that there is no end of the 'nectared sweets'. In what other English poet (however superior to him in other respects) are you so *certain* of never opening a page without lighting upon the loveliest imagery and the most eloquent expressions?

Name one. Compare any succession of their pages at random, and see if the young poet is not sure to present his stock of beauty; crude it may be, in many instances; too indiscriminate in general; never, perhaps, thoroughly perfect in cultivation; but there it is, exquisite of its kind, and filling envy with despair. He died at five-and-twenty; he had not revised his earlier works, nor given his genius its last pruning. His *Endymion*, in resolving to be free from all critical trammels, had no versification; and his last noble fragment, *Hyperion*, is not faultless,— but it is nearly so.

Imagination and Fancy   1844

CROKER

Reviewers have been sometimes accused of not reading the works which they affect to criticise. On the present occasion we shall anticipate the author's complaint, and honestly confess that we have not read his work. Not that we have been wanting in our duty—far from it—indeed, we have made efforts almost as superhuman as the story itself appears to be to get through it; but with the fullest stretch of our perseverance, we are forced to confess that we have not been able to struggle beyond the first of the four books of which this Poetic Romance [*Endymion*] consists. We should extremely lament this want of energy, or whatever it may be, on our parts, were it not for one consolation—namely, that we are no better acquainted with the meaning of the book through which we have so painfully toiled, than we are with that of the three which we have not looked into.

It is not that Mr Keats, (if that is his real name, for we almost doubt that any man in his senses would put his real name to such a rhapsody), it is not, we say, that the author has not powers of language, rays of fancy, and gleams of genius— he has all these; but he is unhappily a disciple of the new school of what has been somewhere called Cockney poetry; which may be defined to consist of the most incongruous ideas in the most uncouth language. . . .

. . . we confess that we should have abstained from inflicting upon him any of the tortures of the 'fierce hell' of criticism, which terrify his imagination, if he had not begged to be spared in order that he might write more; if we had not observed in him a certain degree of talent which deserves to be put in the right way, or which, at least, ought to be warned of the wrong; and if, finally, he had not told us that he is of an age and temper which imperiously require mental discipline.

Of the story we have been able to make out but little; it seems to be mythological, and probably relates to the loves of Diana and Endymion; but of this, as the scope of the work has altogether escaped us, we cannot speak with any degree of certainty; and must therefore content ourselves with giving some instances of its diction and versification:—and here again we are perplexed and puzzled.—At first it appeared to us that Mr Keats had been amusing himself and wearying his readers with an immeasurable game at *bouts-rimés*; but, if we recollect rightly, it is an indispensable condition at this play that the rhymes when filled up shall have a meaning; and our author, as we have already hinted, has no meaning. He seems to us to write a line at random, and then he follows not the thought excited by this line, but that suggested by the *rhyme* with which it concludes. There is hardly a complete couplet inclosing a complete idea in the whole book. He wanders from one subject to another, from the association, not of ideas but of sounds, and the work is composed of hemistichs which, it is quite evident, have forced themselves upon the author by the mere force of the catchwords on which they turn.

We shall select, not as the most striking instance, but as that least liable to suspicion, a passage from the opening of the poem.

> —Such the sun, the moon,
> Trees old and young, sprouting a shady boon
> For simple sheep; and such are daffodils
> With the green world they live in; and clear rills
> That for themselves a cooling covert make
> 'Gainst the hot season; the mid forest brake,
> Rich with a sprinkling of fair musk-rose blooms:
> And such too is the grandeur of the dooms
> We have imagined for the mighty dead; &c. &c.

Here it is clear that the word, and not the idea, *moon* produces the simple sheep and their shady *boon*, and that 'the *dooms* of the mighty dead' would never have intruded themselves but for the 'fair musk-rose *blooms*'. . . .

We come now to the author's taste in versification. He cannot indeed write a sentence, but perhaps he may be able to spin a line. Let us see. The following are specimens of his prosodial notions of our English heroic metre.

> Dear as the temple's self, so does the moon,
> The passion poesy, glories infinite.

> So plenteously all weed-hidden roots.

> Of some strange history, potent to send.

> The stubborn canvas for my voyage prepared. . . .

By this time our readers must be pretty well satisfied as to the meaning of his sentences and the structure of his lines: we now present them with some of the new words with which, in imitation of Mr Leigh Hunt, he adorns our language.

We are told that 'turtles *passion* their voices,' that 'an arbour was *nested*,' and a lady's locks '*gordian'd* up'; and to supply the place of the nouns thus verbalized Mr Keats, with great fecundity, spawns new ones; such as 'men-slugs and human *serpentry*,' the '*honey-feel* of bliss,' 'wives prepare *needments*,' and so forth.

Then he has formed new verbs by the process of cutting off their natural tails, the adverbs, and affixing them to their foreheads; thus 'the wine out-sparkled,' the 'multitude up-followed,' and 'night up-took'. 'The wind up-blows,' and the 'hours are down-sunken'.

But if he sinks some adverbs in the verbs he compensates the language with adverbs and adjectives which he separates from the parent stock. Thus, a lady 'whispers *pantingly* and close,' makes '*hushing* signs,' and steers her skiff into a '*ripply* cove'; a shower falls '*refreshfully*,' and a vulture has a '*spreaded* tail'.

But enough of Mr Leigh Hunt and his simple neophyte. If any one should be bold enough to purchase this 'Poetic

Romance,' and so much more patient, than ourselves, as to get beyond the first book, and so much more fortunate as to find a meaning, we entreat him to make us acquainted with his success; we shall then return to the task which we now abandon in despair, and endeavour to make all due amends to Mr Keats and to our readers.

The Quarterly Review 1818

[This was the review which passed into literary history—or mythology—as one of the causes of Keats' illness and death. It strikes one as being on the whole less virulent than the attacks in *Blackwood*, from which it borrowed the notion of the 'Cockney poets'. But perhaps the point was that the *Blackwood* reviewers were well understood to be merely scurrilous, while the *Quarterly* was a sober and very influential Tory journal]

LOCKHART

Of all the manias of this mad age, the most incurable as well as the most common, seems to be no other than the *Metromanie*. The just celebrity of Robert Burns and Miss Baillie has had the melancholy effect of turning the heads of we know not how many farm-servants and unmarried ladies; our very footmen compose tragedies, and there is scarcely a superannuated governess in the island that does not leave a roll of lyrics behind her in her band-box. To witness the disease of any human understanding, however feeble, is distressing; but the spectacle of an able mind reduced to a state of insanity is of course ten times more afflicting. It is with such sorrow as this that we have contemplated the case of Mr John Keats. This young man appears to have received from nature talents of an excellent, perhaps even of a superior order—talents which, devoted to the purposes of any useful profession, must have rendered him a respectable, if not an eminent citizen. His friends, we understand, destined him to the career of medicine, and he was bound apprentice some years ago to a worthy apothecary in town. But all has been undone by a sudden attack of the malady to which we have alluded. Whether Mr John had been sent home with a diuretic or composing draught to some patient far gone in the poetical mania, we have not heard. This much is certain, that he has caught the infection, and that thoroughly. For some time we were in hopes that he might get off with a violent fit or two; but of late the symptoms are terrible. The phrenzy of the *Poems* was bad enough in its way; but it did not alarm us half so seriously as the calm, settled, imperturbable drivelling idiocy of *Endymion*.

. . . our youthful poet passes . . . into a long strain of foaming abuse against a certain class of English Poets, whom, with Pope at their head, it is much the fashion with the ignorant unsettled pretenders of the present time to undervalue . . . fanciful dreaming tea-drinkers, who, without logic enough to analyse a single idea, or imagination enough to form one original image, or learning enough to distinguish between the written language of Englishmen and the spoken jargon of Cockneys, presume to talk with contempt of some of the most exquisite spirits the world ever produced, merely because they did not happen to exert their faculties in laborious affected descriptions of flowers seen in window-pots, or cascades heard at Vauxhall; in short, because they chose to be wits, philosophers, patriots, and poets, rather than to found the Cockney school of versification, morality, and politics, a century before its time. . . .

Mr Keats has adopted the loose, nerveless versification and Cockney rhymes of the poet of Rimini; but in fairness to that gentleman, we must add, that the defects of the system are tenfold more conspicuous in his disciple's work than in his own. Mr Hunt is a small poet, but he is a clever man. Mr Keats is a still smaller poet, and he is a boy of pretty abilities, which he has done everything in his power to spoil. . . .

From some verses addressed to various amiable individuals of the other sex, it appears, notwithstanding all this gossamerwork, that Johnny's affections are not entirely confined to objects purely etherial. Take, by way of specimen, the following prurient and vulgar lines, evidently meant for some young lady east of Temple-bar.

Add too, the sweetness
Of thy honied voice . . .
Will I call Graces four.

Who will dispute that our poet, to use his own phrase (and rhyme),

Can mingle music fit for the soft *ear*
Of Lady *Cytherea*. . . .

And now, good-morrow to 'the Muses' son of Promise;' as for 'the feats he yet may do,' as we do not pretend to say, like himself, 'Muse of my native land am I inspired,' we shall adhere to the safe old rule of *pauca verba*. We venture to make one small prophecy, that his bookseller will not a second time venture £50 upon any thing he can write. It is a better and a wiser thing to be a starved apothecary than a starved poet; so back to the shop Mr John, back to 'plasters, pills, and ointment boxes,' &c. But, for Heaven's sake, young Sangrado, be a little more sparing of extenuatives and soporifics in your practice than you have been in your poetry.

Blackwood's Magazine 1818

[That Lockhart continued to be proud—if perhaps defiantly proud—of this unspeakably mean attack may be seen from his comments a decade later, given on p. 247–8.

The point he raises about the rhyme of *ear* and *Cytherea* is perhaps a more interesting one than he was able to perceive —fortunately. In modern standard English, there is no difference in the pronunciation; both sounds are represented by the phonetic symbols iə in authorities such as Daniel Jones. But Hopkins, in his comment on rhymes of this kind in Keats, quoted on p. 230, says that the *r* was still pronounced by quite a number of people. It seems very possible that Keats' English may have been 'cockney' in just this way: that he actually spoke both words the same. Moreover, he may not have *felt* the end of the word *Cytherea* as it would have been felt by someone who knew Latin, and had been taught to count it as two syllables for the purpose of Latin verses. Similar differences may account for the specimens of bad versification pointed out by

Croker in the preceding review. Thus if *poesy* in the first is spoken as two syllables (again disregarding the reminiscence of the long *e* in the Greek word) the line runs safely; in the second, *plenteously* needs to be four syllables for the line to run smooth, and can be made so if the second *e* is pronounced; in the third, the scansion depends upon making *history* fill out only two syllables, which might perhaps come a little easier to an ear not familiar with the Latin *historia*; and in the fourth, all goes well if *voyage* is read as only one syllable, but such a pronunciation might be less likely in an ear familiar with French. It is often upon such differences as these that standard English can be distinguished from its not-quite-U variants, and it is quite possible that in uses such as these, Keats was indeed not quite U. Perhaps it was fortunate that the Tory reviewers were stupid as well as mean]

JEFFREY

We had never happened to see either of these volumes till very lately—and have been exceedingly struck with the genius they display, and the spirit of poetry which breathes through all their extravagance. That imitation of our old writers, and especially of our older dramatists, to which we cannot help flattering ourselves that we have somewhat contributed, has brought on, as it were, a second spring in our poetry;—and few of its blossoms are either more profuse of sweetness, or richer in promise, than this which is now before us. Mr Keats, we understand, is still a very young man; and his whole works, indeed, bear evidence enough of the fact. They are full of extravagance and irregularity, rash attempts at originality, interminable wanderings, and excessive obscurity. They manifestly require, therefore, all the indulgence that can be claimed for a first attempt. But we think it no less plain that they deserve it: for they are flushed all over with the rich lights of fancy; and so coloured and bestrewn with the flowers of poetry, that even while perplexed and bewildered in their labyrinths, it is impossible to resist the intoxication of their sweetness, or to shut our hearts to the enchantments they so lavishly present. The models upon which he has formed himself, in the

Endymion, the earliest and by much the most considerable of his poems, are obviously *The Faithful Shepherdess* of Fletcher, and *The Sad Shepherd* of Ben Jonson;—the exquisite metres and inspired diction of which he has copied with great boldness and fidelity—and, like his great originals, has also contrived to impart to the whole piece that true rural and poetical air—which breathes only in them and in Theocritus—which is at once homely and majestic, luxurious and rude, and sets before us the genuine sights and sounds and smells of the country, with all the magic and grace of Elysium. . . . A great part of the work, indeed, is written in the strangest and most fantastical manner that can be imagined. It seems as if the author had ventured every thing that occurred to him in the shape of a glittering image or striking expression—taken the first word that presented itself to make up a rhyme, and then made that word the germ of a new cluster of images—a hint for a new excursion of the fancy—and so wandered on, equally forgetful whence he came, and heedless whither he was going, till he had covered his pages with an interminable arabesque of connected and incongruous figures, that multiplied as they extended, and were only harmonized by the brightness of their tints, and the graces of their forms. In this rash and headlong career he has of course many lapses and failures. There is no work, accordingly, from which a malicious critic could cull more matter for ridicule, or select more obscure, unnatural, or absurd passages. But we do not take *that* to be our office; and must beg leave, on the contrary, to say that any one who, on this account, would represent the whole poem as despicable, must either have no notion of poetry, or no regard to truth.

It is, in truth, at least as full of genius as of absurdity; and he who does not find a great deal in it to admire and give delight, cannot in his heart see much beauty in the two exquisite dramas to which we have already alluded; or find any great pleasure in some of the finest creations of Milton and Shakespeare. There are very many such persons, we verily believe, even among the reading and judicious part of the community—correct scholars, we have no doubt, many of them, and, it may be, very classical composers in prose and in verse—but utterly ignorant, in our view of the matter, of the true genius of English poetry, and incapable of estimating its appropriate and most exquisite beauties. With that spirit we have no hesitation in saying that Mr Keats is deeply imbued—and of those beauties he has presented us with many striking examples. We are very much inclined indeed to add that we do not know any book which we would sooner employ as a test to ascertain whether any one had in him a native relish for poetry, and a genuine sensibility to its intrinsic charm . . . it must, we fear, be admitted, that, besides the riot and extravagance of his fancy, the scope and substance of Mr Keats' poetry is rather too dreamy and abstracted to excite the strongest interest, or to sustain the attention through a work of any great compass or extent. He deals too much with shadowy and incomprehensible beings, and is too constantly rapt into an extra-mundane Elysium, to command a lasting interest with ordinary mortals and must employ the agency of more varied and coarser emotions, if he wishes to take rank with the enduring poets of this or of former generations. . . .

Mr Keats has unquestionably a very beautiful imagination, a perfect ear for harmony, and a great familiarity with the finest diction of English poetry; but he must learn not to misuse or misapply these advantages; and neither to waste the good gifts of Nature and study on intractable themes, nor to luxuriate too recklessly on such as are more suitable.

Review of Endymion *and* Lamia *etc.*   1820

JOHN SCOTT [?]

We opened this volume with very considerable anxiety:—an anxiety partly occasioned by the unqualified praises of which the author has been the object,—but more owing to the abuse by which he has been assailed. Perhaps from the whole history of criticism, real and pretended, nothing more truly unprincipled than that abuse can be quoted; nothing more heartless, more vindictive,—more nefarious in design, more pitiful and paltry in spirit. We consider it one of the worst signs of these, the worst times which England, we are afraid, has ever seen, that the miserable selfishness of political party has erected itself into a literary authority, and established, by means of popular channels, the most direct and easy access to the public ear on literary questions. The provocation, we allow, is reciprocal: the vanity of the *Examiner* manifests just as great a deficiency in real candour as is apparent in the bitter spite of the *Quarterly*, or the merry ruffianism of *Blackwood*. But the distinct consciousness of depravity in the two latter, which must accompany them in many of their lucubrations, gives a blacker feature to their conduct. . . .

Mr Keats, though not a political writer, plunged at once, with what we shall take the liberty of calling a boyish petulance, and with an air of rather insulting bravado, into some very delicate subjects;—subjects on which, we have no hesitation to say, those very qualities of his mind which confer on his poetry its most characteristic beauties, incapacitate him fairly to pronounce. There have been, and it is possible there may be even now, great comprehensive intellects, which, to wealthy and voluptuous imaginations, add a far-sightedness sufficient to discern, and a magnanimity inducing them to acknowledge, the deep, internal, and inextricable connection between the pains and penalties of human nature, and its hopes and enjoyments: whose spirits dwell and play in 'the plighted clouds,'— but who understand enough of the philosophy of earthly existence to know, that, as man must cultivate the ground by the sweat of his brow, so he must cultivate his faculties by self-denials and struggles of soul—who perceive lurking in the common restraints of society, eternal principles of human nature. . . . A man may smell to a rose, or walk out to admire an effect of sunset, and yet not have half that complication of the warmer affections stirring within him which shall move a tradesman of the Strand, seated with his wife, children, and shopman, in his back parlour. . . . It may be allowable in poetry to treat ancient thieves with the respect due to true men; but the poet has no business, more than the police officer, to treat true men, his neighbours, as thieves. . . . Mr Keats' sensibility is diseased in this respect . . . his spirit is impregnated with a flippant impatience (irritated and justified by a false philosophy), of the great phenomena of society, and the varieties of human nature, which hurts his poetry quite as much as it corrupts his sentiments—and which is altogether unworthy of the grandeur of his powers. There are some stanzas introduced into his delicious tale of 'Isabel—poor simple Isabel,' in this volume which, we think, dreadfully mar the musical tenderness of its general strain. They are no better than an extravagant schoolboy vituperation of trade and traders; just as if lovers did not trade,—and that, often, in stolen goods—or had in general any higher object than a barter of enjoyment! These stanzas in Mr Keats' poem, when contrasted with the larger philosophy of Boccaccio, and his more genial spirit, as exemplified with reference to the very circumstances in question, are additionally offensive. Instead of tirading against the brothers as 'money-bags,' 'Baalites of pelf,' 'ledger-men,'—and asking, 'why, in the name of glory, were they proud?' Boccaccio describes the honour of the family as actually injured by Lorenzo, whom they employed—he shows us the elder brother, on discovering his sister's dishonour, afflicted with grief and perplexity, and passing a sleepless night on his bed—he even compliments the discretion of this member of the family—and it is thus naturally, and faithfully, and feelingly introduced, that he leads up the dreadful catastrophe to its consummation in Italian revenge, and the broken-heartedness of widowed love. . . . Mr Keats, we are sure, has a sensibility sufficiently delicate to feel this beauty in Boccaccio: why then has he substituted for it, in his own composition, a boisterous rhapsody, which interrupts the harmony of the sorrowful tale,—repels sympathy by the introduction of caricature,—and suggests all sorts of dissenting, and altercating prejudices and opinions? His device is a clumsy one: Boccaccio's delicate and true. . . . (10)

From what we have said, in the way of objection to the fashion of Mr Keats' thinking, on certain important questions, it will easily be seen that he has very much, and very incautiously exposed himself to attack. . . . His delusion, however, is the offspring of a romantic temperament; whereas his maulers are but things of brute matter, machines for grinding grist. . . .

The injustice which has been done to our author's works, in estimating their poetical merit, rendered us doubly anxious, on opening his last volume, to find it likely to seize fast hold of general sympathy, and thus turn an overwhelming power against the paltry traducers of a talent, more eminently promising in many respects, than any that the present age has been called upon to encourage. We have not found it to be quite all that we had wished in this respect—and it would have been very extraordinary if we had, for our wishes went far beyond reasonable expectations. But we have found it of a nature to present to common understandings the poetical power with which the author's mind is gifted, in a more tangible and intelligible shape than that in which it has appeared in any of his former compositions. . . . Take, for instance, as a proof of the justice of our praise, the following passage from an *Ode to the Nightingale*:—it is distinct, noble, pathetic, and true; the thoughts have all chords of direct communication with naturally-constituted hearts: the echoes of the strain linger about the depths of human bosoms. . . .

One more extract,—again varying entirely the style of the composition. It shall be taken from a piece called *Hyperion*; one of the most extraordinary creations of any modern imagination. Its 'woods are ruthless, dreadful, deaf, and dull:' the soul of dim antiquity hovers, like a mountain-cloud, over its vast and gloomy grandeur: it carries us back in spirit beyond the classical age; earlier than 'the gods of the Greeks;' when the powers of creation were to be met with visible about the young earth, shouldering the mountains, and with their huge forms filling the vallies. The sorrows of this piece are 'huge;' its utterance 'large;' its tears 'big.'—Alas, centuries have brought littleness since then,—otherwise a crawling reptile of office, with just strength enough to leave its slimy traces on the pages of a fashionable Review, could never have done a real mischief to the poet of the Titans! It is but a fragment we have of *Hyperion*: an advertisement tells us that 'the poem was intended to have been of equal length with *Endymion but the reception given to that work discouraged the author from proceeding.*' Let Mr Croker read the sublime and gorgeous personification of Asia, and be proud of the information thus given him—and of that superior encouragement to which it is owing that we have his *Talavera* in a complete state! . . .

Will not our readers feel it as a disgrace attaching to the

character of the period, that a dastardly attempt should have been made to assassinate a poet of power equal to these passages? . . . Cold-blooded conscious dishonesty, we have no hesitation to say, must have directed the pen of the critic of *Endymion* in the *Quarterly Review*: making every allowance for the callousness of a worldly spirit, it is impossible to conceive a total insensibility to the vast beauties scattered profusely over that disordered, ill-digested work. The author provokes opposition, as we have already fully said: not un-frequently he even suggests angry censure. We cannot help applying the word *insolent*, in a literary sense, to some in-stances of his neglectfulness, to the random swagger of occa-sional expressions, to the bravado style of many of his senti-ments. But, coupling these great faults with his still greater merits, what a fine, what an interesting subject did he offer for perspicacious, honourable criticism! But he was beset by a very dog-kennel; and he must be more than human if he has not had his erroneous tendencies hardened in him in consequence.

The London Magazine 1820

[This generous defence was probably written by the Editor, John Scott. In following numbers, he launched an attack on the scurrilous criticism of *Blackwood's Magazine*, was chal-lenged to a duel by one of its agents, and died of his wounds, within a week or so of Keats' own death]

CRABB ROBINSON

The beginning of the *Hyperion*—really a piece of great promise. There is a force, wildness, and originality in the works of this young poet which, if his perilous journey to Italy does not destroy him, promise to place him at the head of the next generation of poets. Lamb places him next to Wordsworth —not meaning any comparison, for they are dissimilar.

Diary 1820

Keats was a promising young man, but a great deal of fuss was made about his death which Lord Byron unjustly ridiculed as if he were killed by 'an article.' Keats had probably as few enemies as any young poet. Through bad taste his genius was not appreciated, and from party spirit, he being a friend of persons who were proud in rendering themselves odious, his works were treated with unjust and stupid contempt in the *Quarterly Review. Voilá tout.*

Diary 1831

HAZLITT

Mr Keats is also dead. He gave the greatest promise of genius of any poet of his day. He displayed extreme tenderness, beauty, originality and delicacy of fancy; all he wanted was manly strength and fortitude to reject the temptations of singularity in sentiment and expression. Some of his shorter and later pieces are, however, as free from faults as they are full of beauties.

Select British Poets 1824

LANDOR

... the animated and pathetic Keats in his *Endymion* is richer in imagery than either [Chaucer or Burns]: and there are passages in which no poet has arrived at the same excellence on the same ground. Time alone was wanting to complete a poet, who already far surpassed all his contemporaries in this country in the poet's most noble attributes. ...

In Keats, I acknowledge, there are many wild thoughts, and there are expressions which even outstrip them in extravagance: but in none of our poets, with the sole exception of Shakespeare, do we find so many phrases so happy in their boldness.

Imaginary Conversations: Landor, English Visitor, and
Florentine 1828

ANON

This little book [Tennyson's *Poems*] ... is full of precisely the kind of poetry for which Mr Keats was assailed, and for which the world is already beginning to admire him. We do

not mean that it contains any thing equal, or nearly equal, to
the *Hyperion*, the *Ode to the Nightingale*, or *The Eve of St
Agnes*. But it does contain many indications of a similar
genius; and this assurance will, we are convinced, by such a
mind as Mr Tennyson's, be accepted as a grateful and delicate
compliment. Such we intend it to be. There is the same fulness
of thoughts and fervour of feeling, with much of the same
quaintness of expression,—an equal degree of idolatry of the
old writers, mixed with a somewhat more apparent reverence
for the moderns,—fewer faults, perhaps, and certainly fewer
dazzling and bewildering beauties. But Nature is the same in
both, and her rich and golden gifts will not be lavished in vain.

The New Monthly Magazine 1831

HORNE

A very striking remark was made in the *Times* (December
26, 1842) with reference to the fate and progress of true poets
in the mind of the public. Alluding to 'the noble fragment of
Hyperion,' the writer says, 'Strange as it may appear, it is
no less certain that the half-finished works of this young,
miseducated, and unripe genius have had the greatest influence
on that which is now the popular poetry. In the eyes of the
"young England" of poets, as in those of Shelley—

The soul of Adonais, like a star,
Beacons from the abode where the immortals are.' (11)

'What a text,' pursues the same writer, 'for a dissertation
on the mutability of popular taste!' True indeed; but we must
not be tempted into it, at present. Objecting to the expressions of 'miseducated' and 'unripe', as only applicable to
the errors in *Endymion* and his earlier poems; and to 'half-
finished' as only applicable (we believe this is correct?) to
Hyperion, there can be no sort of doubt of the influence. But
there is this peculiarity attached to it, one which stands alone
in the history, certainly of all modern influences. It is, that he
has not had a single mechanical imitator. There is an excellent
reason for this. A mechanical imitation of style, or by choice

of similar subjects, would not bear any resemblance to Keats; no one would recognize the intended imitation. When somebody expressed his surprise to Shelley that Keats, who was not very conversant with the Greek language, could write so finely and classically of their gods and goddesses, Shelley replied 'He *was* a Greek'. We may also refer to what Landor has said of him, in the paper headed with that gentleman's name earlier in the present work. The writings of Keats are saturated and instinct with the purest inspiration of poetry; his mythology is full of ideal passion; his divinities are drawn as from 'the life', nay, from their inner and essential life; his enchantments and his 'faery land' are exactly like the most lovely and truthful records of one who has been a dweller among them and a participator in their mysteries; and his descriptions of pastoral scenery are often as natural and simple as they are romantic, and tinged all over with ideal beauty. Admitting all the faults, errors in taste, and want of design in his earliest works, but laying our hands with full faith upon his *Lamia, Isabella, The Eve of St Agnes*, the four *Odes* in the same collection, and the fragment of *Hyperion*, we unhesitatingly say that there is no poet, ancient or modern, upon whom the title of 'Divine' can be more appropriately conferred than upon Keats. While the 'Byron School' was in its glory, it is no great wonder that Wordsworth should have been a constant laughing-stock, and Keats an object of contemptuous dismissal to the tomb. It must, however, be added that the marked neglect of the public towards the latter has continued down to the present day. The pure Greek wine of Keats has been set aside for the thin gruel of Kirk White. But if there be faith in the pure Ideal, and in the progress of intelligence and refinement, the ultimate recognition of Keats by the public will certainly follow that of the 'fit audience' which he will ever continue to possess. Of all the numerous imitators of Lord Byron, not one now remains. And this may be mentioned as a quiet commentary upon his supercilious fling at the superior genius of John Keats.

How it should happen that the influencer of so many spirits of the present time should himself have been left to the ecstatic solitude of his own charmed shores and 'faery lands forlorn', while those very spirits have each and all of them made some passage for themselves into the public mind, is one of those problems to which neither the common fate of originators, the obduracy or caprice of the public, the clinging poison of bygone malice and depreciation, nor the want of sufficient introduction and championship on the part of the living appreciators, can furnish a perfectly satisfactory solution. Such, however, is the fact at this very time. Against this we have only to place a cheap 'popular' reprint of his poems, and his admission into Galignani's collection.

A New Spirit of the Age   1844

MILNES

Let any man of literary accomplishment, though without the habit of writing poetry, or even much taste for reading it, open *Endymion* at random (to say nothing of the later and more perfect poems), and examine the characteristics of the page before him, and I shall be surprised if he does not feel that the whole range of literature hardly supplies a parallel phenomenon. As a psychological curiosity, perhaps Chatterton is more wonderful; but in him the immediate ability displayed is rather the full comprehension of and identification with the old model, than the effluence of creative genius. In Keats, on the contrary, the originality in the use of his scanty materials, his expansion of them to the proportions of his own imagination and above all, his field of diction and expression extending so far beyond his knowledge of literature, is quite inexplicable by any of the ordinary processes of mental education. If his classical learning had been deeper, his seizure of the full spirit of Grecian beauty would have been less surprising; if his English reading had been more extensive, his inexhaustible vocabulary of picturesque and mimetic words could more easily be accounted for; but here is a surgeon's apprentice, with the ordinary culture of the middle classes, rivalling in aesthetic perceptions of antique life and thought the most careful scholars of his time and country, and reproducing these impressions in a phraseology as complete and unconventional as if he had mastered the whole history and the frequent variations of the English tongue, and elaborated a mode of utterance commensurate with his vast ideas.

Life, Letters, and Literary Remains of John Keats   1848

ARNOLD

My dearest Clough

What a brute you were to tell me to read Keats' Letters. However it is over now: and reflexion resumes her power over agitation.

What harm he has done in English Poetry. As Browning is a man with a moderate gift passionately desiring movement and fulness, and obtaining but a confused multitudinousness, so Keats with a very high gift, is yet also consumed by this desire: and cannot produce the truly living and moving, as his conscience keeps telling him. They will not be patient neither understand that they must begin with an Idea of the world in order not to be prevailed over by the world's multitudinousness: or if they cannot get that, at least with isolated ideas: and all other things shall (perhaps) be added unto them.

—I recommend you to follow up these letters with the *Laocoön* of Lessing: it is not quite satisfactory, and a little mare's nesty—but very searching.

—I have had that desire of fulness without respect of the means, which may become almost maniacal: but nature had placed a bar thereto not only in the conscience (as with all men) but in a great numbness in that direction. But what perplexity Keats Tennyson et id genus omne must occasion to young writers of the ὁπλίτης[1] sort: yes and those d——d Elizabethan poets generally. Those who cannot read Greek shld read nothing but Milton and parts of Wordsworth: the state should see to it: for the failures of the σταθμοί[2] may leave them good citizens enough, as Trench: but the others go to the dogs failing or succeeding.

Letter to Clough   1848-9

---

[1] Heavily armed foot-soldier.
[2] Stages along the road of royalty or important persons.

What is Keats? A style and form seeker, and this with an impetuosity that heightens the effect of his style almost painfully.

Letter to Clough 1849

More and more I feel that the difference between a mature and a youthful age of the world compels the poetry of the former to use great plainness of speech as compared with that of the latter: and that Keats and Shelley were on a false track when they set themselves to reproduce the exuberance of expression, the charm, the richness of images, and the felicity of the Elizabethan poets. Yet critics cannot get to learn this, because the Elizabethan poets are our greatest, and our canons of poetry are founded on their works. They still think that the object of poetry is to produce exquisite bits and images—such as Shelley's *clouds shepherded by the slow unwilling wind,* and Keats passim: whereas modern poetry can only subsist by its *contents*: by becoming a complete magister vitae as the poetry of the ancients did: by including, as theirs did, religion with poetry, instead of existing as poetry only, and leaving religious wants to be supplied by the Christian religion, as a power existing independent of poetical power. But the language, style and general proceedings of a poetry which has such an immense task to perform, must be very plain direct and severe: and it must not lose itself in parts and episodes and ornamental work, but must press forwards to the whole.

Letter to Clough 1852

... there is the conventional way of handling nature, there is the faithful way of handling nature, there is the Greek way of handling nature, there is the magical way of handling nature. In all these three last the eye is on the object, but with a difference; in the faithful way of handling nature, the eye is on the object, and that is all you can say; in the Greek, the eye is on the object, but lightness and brightness are added; in the magical, the eye is on the object, but charm and magic are added. In the conventional way of handling nature, the eye is not on the object; what that means we all know, we have only to think of our eighteenth-century poetry:—

> As when the moon, refulgent lamp of night—

to call up any number of instances. . . . But from our own poetry we may get specimens of the Greek way of handling nature, as well as of the conventional: for instance, Keats':

> What little town by river or seashore,
> Or mountain-built with quiet citadel,
> Is emptied of its folk, this pious morn?

is Greek, as Greek as a thing from Homer or Theocritus; it is composed with the eye on the object, a radiancy and light clearness being added. German poetry abounds in specimens of the faithful way of handling nature. . . . Only the power of natural magic Goethe does not, I think, give; whereas Keats passes at will from the Greek power to that power which is, I say, Celtic; from his:

> What little town by river or seashore—

to his:

> White hawthorn and the pastoral eglantine,
> Fast-fading violets cover'd up in leaves—

or his:

> . . . magic casements, opening on the foam
> Of perilous seas, in fairy lands forlorn—

in which the very same note is struck as in those extracts which I quoted from Celtic romance, and struck with authentic and unmistakeable power.

On the Study of Celtic Literature 1867

So baffled and so sorely tried,—while laden, at the same time, with a mighty formative thought requiring health, and

many days, and favouring circumstances, for its adequate
manifestation,—what wonder if the achievement of Keats be
partial and incomplete?

Nevertheless, let and hindered as he was, and with a short
term and imperfect experience,—'young', as he says of himself,
'and writing at random, straining after particles of light in the
midst of a great darkness, without knowing the bearing of any
one assertion, of any one opinion,'—notwithstanding all
this, by virtue of his feeling for beauty and of his perception
of the vital connection of beauty with truth, Keats accomplished so much in poetry, that in one of the two great modes
by which poetry interprets, in the faculty of naturalistic interpretation, in what we call natural magic, he ranks with Shakespeare. 'The tongue of Kean,' he says in an admirable criticism
of that great actor and of his enchanting elocution, 'the tongue
of Kean must seem to have robbed the Hybla bees and left
them honeyless. There is an indescribable *gusto* in his voice;—
in *Richard*, "Be stirring with the lark to-morrow, gentle
Norfolk!" comes from him as through the morning atmosphere
towards which he yearns.' This magic, this 'indescribable *gusto*
in the voice,' Keats himself, too, exhibits in his poetic expression. No one else in English poetry, save Shakespeare,
has in expression quite the fascinating felicity of Keats, his
perfection of loveliness. 'I think,' he said humbly, 'I shall be
among the English poets after my death.' He is; he is with
Shakespeare.

For the second great half of poetic interpretation, for that
faculty of moral interpretation which is in Shakespeare, and is
informed by him with the same power of beauty as his naturalistic interpretation, Keats was not ripe. For the architectonics
of poetry, the faculty which presides at the evolution of works
like the *Agamemnon* or *Lear*, he was not ripe. His *Endymion*,
as he himself well saw, is a failure, and his *Hyperion*, fine
things as it contains, is not a success. But in shorter things,
where the matured power of moral interpretation, and the
high architectonics which go with complete poetic development, are not required, he is perfect.

John Keats   1880

H

FITZGERALD

I heard Alfred [Tennyson] had been seen flying through town to the Lushingtons: but I did not see him. He is said to be still busy about that accursed *Princess*. By the by, beg, borrow, steal, or buy Keats' *Letters* and *Poems*; most wonderful bits of *Poems*, written off hand at a sitting, most of them: I only wonder they do not make more noise in the world.

Letter to Frederick Tennyson 1849

MASSON

When critics or poets themselves speak of the love of nature or the perception of natural beauty as essential in the constitution of the poet, it will often be found that what they chiefly mean is an unusual sensibility to the pleasures of one of the senses—the sense of sight. What they mean is chiefly a fine sense of form, colour, lustre, and the like. Now, though it may be admitted that in so far as ministration of material for the intellect is concerned, sight is the most important of the senses, yet this all but absolute identification of love of nature with sensibility to visual pleasures seems erroneous. It is a kind of treason to the other senses, all of which are avenues of communication between nature and the mind, though sight may be the main avenue. In this respect I believe that one of the most remarkable characteristics of Keats is the universality of his sensuousness.

But farther. Not only, in popular language, does the love of nature seem to be identified with a sensibility to the pleasures of the one sense of sight; but, by a more injurious restriction still, this love of nature or perception of natural beauty seems to have been identified, especially of late, with one class of the pleasures of this one sense of sight—to wit, the pleasures derived from the contemplation of vegetation. Roses, lilies, grass, trees, cornfields, ferns, heaths, and poppies: these are what pass for 'nature' with not a few modern poets and critics of poetry. It seems as if, since Wordsworth fulminated the advice to poets to go back to nature and to study nature, it had been the impression of many that the proper way to comply with the advice was to walk out in the fields to some spot where the grass was thick and the weeds and wild-flowers plentiful, and there lie flat upon the turf, chins downwards, peering into grasses and flowers, and inhaling their breath. Now, it ought to be distinctly represented, in correction of this, that ever so minute and loving a study of vegetation, though laudable and delightful in itself, does not amount to a study of nature—that, in fact, vegetation, though a very respectable part of visible nature, is not the whole of it. When night comes, for example, where or how much is your vegetation then? Vegetation is *not* nature: I know no proposition that should be more frequently dinned in the ears of our young poets than this. The peculiar notion of natural beauty involved in the habit spoken of may be said to have come in with the microscope. In the ancient Greek poets we have very little of it. They give us trees and grass and flowers, but they give them more by mere suggestion; and, so far as they introduce physical nature at all (which is chiefly by way of a platform for human action), it is with the larger forms and aspects of nature that they deal, the wide and simple modifications of the great natural elements. Shakespeare, when he chooses, is minutely and lusciously rich in his scenes of vegetation (and, indeed, in comparing modern and romantic with ancient and classical poets generally, it is clear that, in this respect, there has been a gradual development of literary tendency); but no man more signally than Shakespeare keeps the just proportion. Wordsworth himself, when he called out for the study of nature, and set the example in his own case by retiring to the Lakes, did not commit the error of confounding nature with vegetation. In that district, indeed, where there are mountains and tarns, incessant cloud-variations, and other forms of nature on the great scale, to employ the eye, it was not likely that it would disproportionately exercise itself on particular banks and gardens or individual herbs and flowers. Such an affection for the minutiae of vegetation was reserved perhaps for the so-called Cockney poets; and one can see that, if it were once supposed that they introduced the taste, the fact might be humorously explained by recollecting that nature to most of them was nature as seen from Hampstead Heath.

Now, undoubtedly, Keats is great in botanical circumstance. . . .

But, though Keats did 'joy in all that is bloomy,' I do not
know that he joyed 'too much'. Though luscious vegetation was
one of his delights, I do not think that in him there is such a
disproportion between this and other kinds of imagery as
there has been in other and inferior poets. There are sea and
cloud in his poetry, as well as herbage and turf; he is as rich
in mineralogical and zoological circumstance as in that of
botany. His most obvious characteristic, I repeat, is the
universality of his sensuousness. And this it is, added to his
exquisite mastery in language and verse, that makes it such a
luxury to read him. In reading Shelley, even when we admire
him most, there is always a sense of pain; the influence of
Keats is uniformly soothing. In part, as I have said, this arises
from his exquisite mastery in language and verse—which, in
itself, is one form or result of his sensuousness. . . .

Neither sensuousness alone, however, nor sensuousness
governed by a reflective and fanciful intellect, will constitute
a great poet. However highly endowed a youthful poet may
be in these, his only chance of real greatness is in passing on,
by due transition and gradation, to that more matured state
of mind in which, though the sensuous may remain and the
cool fancy may weave its tissues as before, human interest and
sympathy with the human heart and grand human action
shall predominate in all. Now, in the case of Keats, there is
evidence of the fact of this gradation. There is evidence of a
progress both intellectually and morally; of a disposition,
already consciously known to himself, to move forward out
of the sensuous or merely sensuous-ideal mood, into the mood
of the truly epic poet, the poet of life, sublimity and action.
Thus, in one of his prose letters, he says, 'Although I take
poetry to be the chief, yet there is something else wanting to
one who passes his life among books and thoughts of books.'
And again, 'I find earlier days are gone by; I find that I can
have no enjoyment in the world but continual drinking of
knowledge. I find there is no worthy pursuit but the idea of
doing some good to the world. Some do it with their society;
some with their art; some with their benevolence; some with

a sort of power of conferring pleasure and good humour on all they meet—and, in a thousand ways, all dutiful to the command of nature. There is but one way for me. The road lies through application, study and thought. I will pursue it. I have been hovering for some time between an exquisite sense of the luxurious and a love for philosophy. Were I calculated for the former, I should be glad; but, as I am not, I shall turn all my soul to the latter.' In his poetry we have similar evidence. Even in his earlier poems one is struck not only by the steady presence of a keen and subtle intellect, but also by frequent flashes of permanently deep meaning, frequent lines of lyric thoughtfulness, and occasional maxims of weighty and historic generality. What we have quoted for our special purpose would fail utterly to convey the proper impression of the merits of Keats in these respects, or indeed of his poetic genius generally, unless the memory of the reader were to suggest the necessary supplement. From *Endymion* itself, sensuous to very wildness as the poem is considered, scores of passages might be quoted to prove that already, while it was being written, intellect, feeling, and experience were doing their work with Keats—that, to use his own figure, he had then already advanced for some time out of the Infant Chamber, or Chamber of mere Sensation, into the Chamber of Maiden Thought, and had even there begun to distinguish the openings of the dark passages beyond and around, and to be seized with the longing to explore them. Seeing this, looking then at such of his later poems as *Lamia* and *The Eve of St Agnes*, and contemplating last of all that wonderful fragment of *Hyperion* which he hurled into the world as he was leaving it, and of which Byron but expressed the common opinion when he said 'It seems actually inspired by the Titans, and is as sublime as Æschylus,' we can hardly be wrong in believing that, had Keats lived to the ordinary age of man, he would have been one of the greatest of all our poets. As it is, though he died at the age of twenty-five, and left only what in all does not amount to much more than a day's leisurely reading, I believe we shall all be disposed to place him very near indeed to our very best.

The Life and Poetry of Keats   Macmillan's Magazine   1860

HOPKINS

Keats' genius was so astonishing, unequalled at his age and scarcely surpassed at any, that one may surmise whether if he had lived he would not have rivalled Shakespere.

Letter to R. W. Dixon 1878

. . . imagery inheriting Keats' mantle, the other-world of imagination (constructive imagination is rare even among poets), the 'instress' of feeling, and a pathos the deepest, I think, that I have anywhere found. (By the by there is one thing that Keats' authority can never excuse, and that is rhyming open vowels to silent *rs*, as *higher* to *Thalia*: as long as the *r* is pronounced by anybody, and it is by a good many yet, the feeling that it is there makes this rhyme most offensive, not indeed to the ear, but to the mind.)

Letter to R. W. Dixon 1880

TENNYSON

Tennyson: 'But the man I count greater than them all—Wordsworth, Coleridge, Byron, Shelley, every one of 'em—is Keats, who died at twenty-five—thousands of faults! (twiddling the fingers of one hand in the air)—but he's wonderful!'

De Vere: 'He doesn't pall upon you?'

Tennyson: 'No.'

De Vere: 'Shelley used to be a great idol of yours.'

Tennyson: 'O yes. We lived near the most prosaic village in the world, a little beast! where they had never heard of anything. One day we went there to meet my brother Frederick, who was coming back from somewhere, and as we were driving home he whispered, "I've got a poet who's much grander than Byron," and repeated one line—

Waterfalls leap among wild islands green,

which I thought delicious.

'*Alastor* was the first poem of his I read. I said, "This is

what I want!"—and still I like it the best, though one can't
tell how much these first loves are to be trusted. *The Revolt of
Islam* is splendid but gives me a headache—it's fatiguing—all
mountain tops and glories.'

De Vere agreed, and named as his favourites *The Ode to
the West Wind—Ode to Naples*—(of which he recited some
lines, and another piece).

Tennyson quoted a passage from Shelley and said 'what can
you do with a man who has such command of language? But
Keats was not wild and wilful, he had always an intention.
At the same time he was *daimonish*,—he had a touch (he was
a livery-stable keeper's son—I don't know where he got it
from, unless from Heaven).

> Perhaps the self-same song that found a path
>   Through the sad heart of Ruth when, sick for home,
>   She stood in tears amid the alien corn;
> The same that oft-times hath
>   Charm'd magic casements opening on the foam
>   Of perilous seas, in faery lands forlorn. (12)

'What can be lovelier? (He said the last two lines again.)
I once saw it printed "In fairyland forlorn," which totally
ruined it—one doesn't know why.'

William Allingham: ' "Fairyland" has been much used.'

William Allingham: A Diary   1880

SWINBURNE

Two or three phrases cancelled, two or three lines erased,
would have left us in *Lamia* one of the most faultless as surely
one of the most brilliant jewels in the crown of English poetry.
Isabella, feeble and awkward in narrative to a degree almost
incredible in a student of Dryden and a pupil of Leigh Hunt,
is overcharged with episodical effects of splendid and pathetic
expression beyond the reach of either. *The Eve of St Agnes*,
aiming at no doubtful success, succeeds in evading all casual
difficulty in the line of narrative; with no shadow of pretence

to such interest as may be derived from stress of incident or depth of sentiment, it stands out among all other famous poems as a perfect and unsurpassable study in pure colour and clear melody. . . . The triumph of *Hyperion* is as nearly complete as the failure of *Endymion*; yet Keats never gave such proof of a manly devotion and rational sense of duty to his art as in his resolution to leave this great poem unfinished; not, as we may gather from his correspondence on the subject, for the pitiful reason assigned by his publishers, that of discouragement at the reception given to his former work, but on the solid and reasonable ground that a Miltonic study had something in its very scheme and nature too artificial, too studious of a foreign influence, to be carried on and carried out at such length as was implied by his original design. . . .

Keats, on a high and recent authority, has been promoted to a place beside Shakespeare; and it was long since remarked by some earlier critic of less note that as a painter of flowers his touch had almost a Shakespearean felicity. . . . The faultless force and profound subtlety of this deep and cunning instinct for the absolute expression of absolute natural beauty can hardly be questioned or overlooked; and this is doubtless the one main distinctive gift or power which denotes him as a poet among all his equals, and gives him right to a station near that of Coleridge and Shelley.

Encyclopedia Britannica 1882

That exquisite and epicurean subtlety in expression of sensations impressed upon an exceptionally sensitive temper of mind and body, which was so specially characteristic of Keats as a student of nature, might have been supposed impossible of attainment without some sacrifice of simplicity and straightforwardness: yet, if the secrets of his workshop had never been made public, we could no more have felt certain that his work had not been thrown off at a jet, like Shakespeare's and Hugo's, than we should have dreamed of looking for the traces of the file on Wordsworth's.

Wordsworth and Byron 1884

OSCAR WILDE

It is in Keats that one observes the beginning of the artistic renaissance of England. Byron was a rebel, and Shelley a dreamer; but in the calmness and clearness of his vision, his self-control, his unerring sense of beauty, and his recognition of a separate realm for the imagination, Keats was the pure and serene artist, the forerunner of the Pre-Raphaelite school. . . .

Report of Oscar Wilde's first lecture in The New York World 1882

W. M. ROSSETTI

Sensuousness has been frequently defined as the paramount bias of Keats' poetic genius. This is, in large measure, unassailably true. He was a man of perception rather than of contemplation or speculation. Perception has to do with perceptible things; perceptible things must be objects of sense, and the mind which dwells on objects of sense must *ipso facto* be a mind of the sensuous order. But the mind which is mainly sensuous by direct action may also work by reflex action, and pass from sensuousness into sentiment. It cannot fairly be denied that Keats' mind continually did this; it had direct action potently, and reflex action amply. He saw so far and so keenly into the sensuous as to be penetrated with the sentiment which, to a healthy and large nature, is its inseparable outcome. We might say that, if the sensuous was his atmosphere, the breathing apparatus with which he respired it was sentiment. In his best work—for instance, in all the great odes—the two things are so intimately combined that the reader can only savour the sensuous nucleus through the sentiment, its medium or vehicle. One of the most compendious and elegant phrases in which the genius of Keats has been defined is that of Leigh Hunt: 'He never beheld an oak tree without seeing the Dryad.' In immediate meaning Hunt glances here at the mythical sympathy or personifying imagination of the poet; but, if we accept the phrase as applying to the sensuous object-painting, along with its ideal aroma or suggestion in his finest work, we shall still find it full of right significance. We need not dwell upon other less mature performances in which the two things are less closely interfused. Certainly some of his work is merely, and some even crudely, sensuous: but this is work in which the poet was trying his materials and his powers, and rising towards mastery of his real faculty and ultimate function.

While discriminating between what was excellent in Keats, and what was not excellent, or was merely tentative in the direction of final excellence, we must not confuse endowments, or the homage which is due to endowments, of a radically different order. Many readers, and there have been among them several men highly qualified to pronounce, have set Keats beside his great contemporary Shelley, and indeed above him. I cannot do this. To me it seems that the primary gift of Shelley, the spirit in which he exercised it, the detail and the sum of his achievement, the actual produce in appraisable work done, the influence and energy of the work in the future, were all superior to those of Keats, and even superior beyond any reasonable terms of comparison. If Shelley's poems had defects—which they indisputably had—Keats' poems also had defects. After all that can be said in their praise—and this should be said in the most generous or rather grateful and thankful spirit—it seems to me true that not many of Keats' poems are highly admirable; that most of them, amid all their beauty, have an adolescent and frequently a morbid tone, marking want of manful thew and sinew and of mental balance; that he is not seldom obscure, chiefly through indifference to the thought itself and its necessary means of development; that he is emotional without substance, and beautiful without control; and that personalism of a wilful and fitful kind pervades the mass of his handiwork. We have already seen, however, that there is a certain not inconsiderable proportion of his poems to which these exceptions do not apply, or apply only with greatly diminished force; and, as a last expression of our large and abiding debt to him and his well-loved memory, we recur to his own words,

and say that he has given us many a 'thing of beauty,' which
will remain 'a joy for ever'. By his early death he was doomed
to be the poet of youthfulness; by being the poet of youthfulness he was privileged to become and to remain enduringly
the poet of rapt expectation and passionate delight.

Life of Keats   1886

MIDDLETON MURRY

The relation between Beauty and Truth was one which
exercised the mind and heart of Keats throughout his life.
This was the chief form into which his search for a purpose in
life was cast. The words recur constantly, and always signi-
ficantly, in his Letters. They are at the core of his famous
definition: 'The excellence of every art is its intensity, capable
of making all disagreeables evaporate from their being in
close relationship to Beauty and Truth.'

The bearing of this statement on the last stanza of the
Ode on a Grecian Urn, and upon the whole poem, is immediate.
The statement was made long before the *Ode* was written,
while Keats was still comparatively a happy man. In the
ensuing time the 'disagreeables' which his art had to 'evaporate' had come to deserve a harsher name. He had been 'convinced on his nerves that the world is full of heart-break,
misery, pain and oppression'. The evaporating of disagreeables
had passed into the lifting of the burden of misery. The tone
is deeper, as the experience is more profound. Nevertheless,
the words are, as continually in Keats, perfectly prophetic of
the last stanza of *The Grecian Urn*.

The Urn is such a work of art; it is capable of making
'all disagreeables evaporate from their being in close relationship to Beauty and Truth'. The thought came to Keats as he
was meditating on the effect of a painting; it was exemplified,
he said, throughout *King Lear*—a dramatic poem. And the
Grecian Urn, as it is depicted in Keats' Ode, is something
between a painting and a dramatic poem. It is a sculptured
drama. And this is as important to remember as it is readily
forgotten. The Grecian Urn of Keats' poem is not some
hypothetical actual vase, but the Urn of his imagination. To

know what it was, we are not to conceive some hypothetical original, but simply to read his poem.

No doubt, at some time or other, Keats had actually seen and delighted in the beauty of a Greek vase. But that may have been long before he wrote his poem. It was probably long before. The vision lay somewhere in the deeps of his being, to appear at moments before his conscious imagination. In the Third Book of *Endymion* (11. 29–32) we read:

> Aye, 'bove the withering of old-lipped Fate
> A thousand Powers keep religious state,
> In water, fiery realm, and airy bourne;
> And, *silent as a consecrated urn*,
> Hold sphery sessions for a season due.

It appeared more visibly, a year before he actually wrote *The Grecian Urn*, in a letter to Reynolds, where he complained of the ugly visions which haunted him when he lay sleepless. Perhaps, he said, some were more fortunate than himself, and escaped these evil visitations. What these fortunate ones would see, in their happier visions, would be:

> Some Titian colours touch'd into real life,—
> The sacrifice goes on; the pontiff knife
> Gleams in the sun, the milk-white heifer lows,
> The pipe goes shrilly; the libation flows:
> A white sail shows above the green-head cliff,
> Moves round the point, and throws her anchor stiff;
> The mariners join hymn with those on land.

There is the frieze of another Grecian Urn—manifestly no real one, in the practical and tangible sense, but as beautiful and of the same kind as the vase of the *Ode*. The Greek vase was a form into which Keats' sensuous imagination could naturally be cast.

Later, and near to the time of writing the *Ode*, the vision came again—On the morning when, he said, 'the fibres of the brain were relaxed in common with the rest of his body, and to such a happy degree that pleasure had no show of enticement nor pain no unbearable power'. 'Neither Poetry, nor Ambition, nor Love,' he wrote, 'have any alertness of countenance as they pass by me; they seem rather like figures on a Greek vase—a Man and two women whom no one but myself could distinguish in their disguisements.' This vision formed the whole theme of the *Ode on Indolence*. The Greek vase, with its surrounding frieze, was a form congenial to Keats' richly plastic imagination; it was a means by which he could immobilize, in 'a frozen moment', the beauty of an imagined action.

The Grecian Urn may have been in part actual, or wholly an imaginative creation; that is indifferent. The important thing is the action depicted upon it—the drama, the thing doing, in the actual sense of the Greek word. That is evident enough to any one who simply reads the poem; the vase is primarily a sculptured frieze, an arrested action, of the same kind as the Parthenon pediment.

It is on this arrested action that Keats' imagination intensely plays. He envies the felicity of the participants who are immune from mortality and decay. But they are human still. Mortality and decay have slipped from them, like a garment; but that is all. They are mortals as we are; who have wandered unawares into an enchanted land, whence they can never return. Their felicity has its tinge of sorrow; the poet who began by envying, ends almost by pitying. They are, as it were, lost to humanity.

> And, little town, thy streets for evermore
> Will silent be; and not a soul to tell
> Why thou art desolate, can e'er return.

The happening is utterly human. It is to misconceive the poem completely to conceive it as a theorizing on some exquisite piece of decorative art. It is a drama of the pure imagination. A destiny falls upon some human beings; they pass into the spell-bound land of eternity,

> All breathing human passion far above

and the poet who watches them, who indeed himself has cast the spell of eternal immobility upon them, envies and grieves for them. The Urn is the record of the lovely and yet fatal enchantment.

More exactly, the Grecian Urn is the symbol of a possibility of vision. All human action, all human experience, can be thus arrested in enchantment. All the visible and invisible drama of human life can be thus seen, or imagined, under the aspect of eternity, *sub specie aeternitatis*. That is why the 'silent form doth tease us out of thought as doth eternity'. It is not that it is incomprehensible as the abstract concept of eternity; but that it is terribly simple and lucid as is the eternal aspect of things of which it is a symbol. This aspect of things is beyond thought, because it is prior to thought; and beyond thought because it is the end of thinking. Under this aspect the innocent vision of the child doubtless beholds existence; the grown man can recapture it only when he has struggled onwards towards a second innocence. And then he is unable to declare what it is that he sees; it is too simple for speech. What words can there be to describe this seeing of the world and of ourselves with a vision from which all passion has been dissolved away; with a vision which is unclouded by any desire or any regret; by any belief or any anxiety: this moment of untroubled lucidity in which we are unmoved spectators of the great drama of human destiny?

Studies in Keats 1930

LEAVIS

In fact, the main impulsion of the *Ode to a Nightingale* is essentially of the same order as that exhibited more simply by the *Ode on a Grecian Urn*. The urn, with its 'leaf-fringed legend', gives a firmer stay to fancy than Keats could make of his imagined light-winged Dryad of the trees in its melodious plot of beechen green:

> Heard melodies are sweet, but those unheard
> Are sweeter. . . .

—They are less disturbing, if less intensely felt. The compensation for the lack of rich immediacy is the idyllic serenity of the

fourth stanza, with its 'green altar' and its 'peaceful citadel'.
But even here we are made aware of a price to be paid. The
serenity, before the end of the stanza, takes on another quality:

> Who are these coming to the sacrifice?
>   To what green altar, O mysterious priest,
> Lead'st thou that heifer lowing at the skies,
>   And all her silken flanks with garlands drest?
> What little town by river or sea shore,
>   Or mountain-built with peaceful citadel,
>   Is emptied of this folk this pious morn?

That 'emptied' is a key-word: we end the stanza contemplating,
not the scene of ideally happy life, but the idea of streets that

> for evermore
> Will silent be;

and of a town to which

> not a soul to tell
> Why thou art desolate, can e'er return.

The victory over time seems an equivocal one. The attempt to
get it both ways could, in the nature of things, have only a
very qualified success.

Getting it both ways—the poem essentially *is* that. The
bargain with life and time proposed in the second stanza—

> those unheard
> Are sweeter

and

> Bold lover, never, never canst thou kiss,
> Though winning near the goal—yet do not grieve:
> She cannot fade, though thou hast not thy bliss,
> For ever wilt thou love and she be fair!

—the implicit bargain is within a dozen lines of this forgotten:

More happy love! More happy, happy love!
 For ever warm and still to be enjoyed,
  For ever panting, and for ever young;
All breathing human passion far above,
 That leaves a heart high-sorrowful and cloyed,
  A burning forehead and a parching tongue.

—In what way 'All breathing human passion far above'?
'Warm' and 'panting'—the accordant ditty would be very
decidedly to the 'sensual ear'. Clearly, the urn for Keats is the
incitement and support to a day-dream; the dream of a life
that, without any drawbacks, shall give him all he desires—
shall be for ever warm and still be enjoyed, remaining, 'among
the leaves', free from all the inevitable limitations that the
nightingale, the light-winged Dryad, has never known.

These observations are not offered as proof of any remarkable percipience. The excuse for them is the puzzled, awed or
Delphic attention that, in spite of their obviousness, has been
paid to the famous concluding pronouncement of the Ode—
the subtleties and profundities it still provides occasion for.

 'Beauty is truth, truth beauty'—that is all
  Ye know on earth, and all ye need to know.

This surely, in the context just examined, should cause no
metaphysical tremors of excitement or illumination, and need
no great profundity or ingenuity of any kind to elucidate it.
The proposition is strictly in keeping with the attitude con-
cretely embodied in the poem. The use of the word 'truth'
corresponds strictly to the attitude towards reality analysed
above. Life, alas! is not as we would have it; but it ought to
be, and, with the aid of the Grecian urn, can be felt for a
moment to be: imagination, concentrating on the beauty of
the urn and ignoring the discordant and indocile facts, attains
a higher reality, compared with which actual life seems thin
and unreal. By the last stanza imagination in Keats has
flagged, has relapsed from its inspired dream, the enchantment has waned and the actual has reasserted itself; but
although the 'leaf-fringed legend' is now a 'Cold Pastoral',

it remains there, a permanent incitement to warm imaginings of an ideal life, a purely beautiful reality. . . .

The relation between the firmness of the art and the firm grasp on the outer world appears most plainly in the Ode *To Autumn*. Of this Mr Middleton Murry says:

> It is the perfect and unforced utterance of the truth contained
> In the magic words: 'Ripeness is all.'

Such talk is extravagant, and does not further the appreciation of Keats. No one could have found that order of significance in the Ode merely by inspecting the Ode itself. The ripeness with which Keats is concerned is the physical ripeness of autumn, and his genius manifests itself in the sensuous richness with which he renders this in poetry, without the least touch of artistic over-ripeness.

If one might justifiably call the poem Shakespearian, it would be in emphasizing how un-Tennysonian it is—how different from the decorative-descriptive verse to which we see it as pointing forward. The explicit richness of detail has its life in the vigour of the medium:

> To bend with apples the moss'd cottage-trees,
>   And fill all fruit with ripeness to the core;
>   To swell the gourd, and plump the hazel shells
> With a sweet kernel. . . .

That 'moss'd cottage-trees' represents the strength—a native English strength—lying beyond the scope of the poet who aimed to make English as like Italian as possible. So too with the unpoetical 'plump': its sensuous firmness—it introduces a tactual image—represents a general concrete vigour such as is alien to the Tennysonian habit, and such as a Tennysonian handling of the medium cannot breed. This English strength pervades the Ode; in another of its forms it is notably exemplified by this, from the second stanza:

> And sometimes like a gleaner thou dost keep
>   Steady thy laden head across a brook. . . .

In the step from the rime-word 'keep', across (so to speak) the pause enforced by the line-division, to 'Steady' the balancing movement of the gleaner is enacted.

The warm richness of the poem is qualified, as with the autumnal hint of sharpness in the air, by the last stanza, which, from 'the stubble plains' (appropriately unvoluptuous in suggestion) onward, is full of the evocation of thin sounds— the gnats 'mourn' in a 'wailful choir', the lambs bleat, hedge-crickets sing, the redbreast 'with treble soft' whistles, and gathering swallows twitter in the skies.

If, then, in Keats' development from *Endymion* to the Ode *To Autumn* we see, as we may (leaving aside for a moment the *Hyperions*), the promise of greatness, it does not lie in any effective presence of the kind of seriousness aspired to in *Sleep and Poetry*:

> And can I ever bid these joys farewell?
> Yes, I must pass them for a nobler life,
> Where I may find the agonies, the strife
> Of human hearts. . . .

It lies rather in the marvellous vitality of the art that celebrates 'these joys'—in the perfection attained within a limiting aestheticism. Remarkable intelligence and character are implied in that attainment, especially when we consider the starting-point and the surrounding influences: the beginning in 'pleasant smotherings', with, as the incitement towards discipline, such poetic models as are represented by Leigh Hunt and the Cockney taste (at the highest level:

> Spenserian vowels that elope with ease
> And float along like birds o'er summer seas).

Revaluation 1936

Lord Tennyson

The chief Reviews, the Quarterly, Blackwood's, *the* Edinburgh, *can justly be blamed for much folly, meanness, and even damage done to letters in the first quarter of the nineteenth century. But one thing they had achieved of potentially positive value. They had accustomed their readers to the idea that a nation with any pretensions to greatness ought to have some poetry about the place, not necessarily to be read much, but simply for the look of the thing. And as the Victorian age moved to its first climax, in the Great Exhibition of 1851, it was very generally felt that Britain must have its Bards, together with its navy and its modern sanitation.*

Poetry, however, proved somewhat harder to run up than sewers and battleships, largely because, when the matter came to be looked into, the engineers of the time turned out on the whole to be a cleverer lot than the poets, and much easier to manage. The choice finally fell upon Tennyson, and it is difficult to see now that the age could have done much better. He was made Poet Laureate a few months before the Great Exhibition opened, mainly by the influence of the chief promoter of the Exhibition, the Prince Consort. It was not entirely for nothing that Tennyson so presciently dreamed, the night before the arrival of the sacred letter from Windsor, 'that Prince Albert came and kissed him on the cheek, and that he said in his dream, "Very kind, but very German".' The efforts made by his friends for some time past to turn him into a Bardic Sage were now seconded from all sides. The other Sages joined in, not least Carlyle: 'he used to tell me "you must do this—You mustn't do that",' his pupil later blabbed. The reviewers, public opinion, the Queen, Mr Gladstone—all took a hand in the attempt to make the Palace of Art into something more like the Crystal Palace. And with fair success, for Tennyson was as devoid of inward privacy as that translucent edifice, and as helplessly pervious to the glances, admiring or critical, of every one who passed by. Many of the following passages illustrate how he was groomed for his great office; and most of his poems show how pathetically, how comically, groomable he was.

The quality which made him so well suited to the purposes of the age was precisely his own uncertainty about what poetry should be, and should be about, and the morbid sensitiveness to criticism which naturally resulted from this inner uncertainty. That he had a notable knack for verses, and no little industry, was obvious from his earliest writings; and no less obvious was the floundering round for a subject, a direction, a kind of attempt which he might make his own. No wonder that he looked so much like a Bard going begging, a mouthpiece waiting to be filled by the age. And no wonder, either, that he never became anything more than a Bard going begging, that his promise and his abilities never filled themselves up, as it were, with anything much of his own. A generation later, even his age had given him up, for all serious purposes. He was read, of course; at least his poetry sold, richly. Loyalty to the Age and to the Queen demanded it. But no sensible or sensitive critic could be found to say that it had been one of the great Victorian successes. By 1886 it was no treason to call his verses 'glorified music-hall songs'; and it was not, for much of them, at all a bad description.

But it was not the right description for quite all of them. There was, in the early poems, a thin but personal note occasionally heard, one of languid and musical nostalgia which would not be bearable for long, but is all very well for a line or two; and in the later poems its echoes can now and then be picked out from the surrounding din, like the notes of a flute in the crevices of some turgid Romantic orchestration. There are, too, those few occasions when he rounded on his pursuers, and snarled; as he did in the two Locksley Halls *and in* Maud. *The snarl has a certain human dignity, if not much poetry, and it helps one's sense of decency to see the thing done at all.*

Finally, he deserves preserving, even deserves some closer study, because his personal predicament illustrates so fully the predicament of poetry in his time. It would be unfair, and unwise, to blame his perviousness to criticism upon some purely private

*weakness in the man himself; it was something much larger, a
hesitation, a bewilderment as to the true nature of poetry in the
whole age. Other, though much stronger and more manly, expressions of it may be found in Taylor's* Artevelde *Preface of
1834, and in Arnold's very similar pronouncements in his Preface
to the* Poems *of 1853. Somehow or other, they all felt, the
subject, the serious and workable and worthwhile subject, had
slipped out of their grasp. What seems not to have occurred to
any of them was that it had not just dropped from their hands,
but had been very forcibly taken out of them by the rise of the
novel, the form of literature which was so naturally and suitably
the product of the age. It is no accident that the most penetrating,
the most kindly and subtly patronizing of all the extracts which
follow, that by Henry James, is by a novelist, not by a poet or a
critic of poetry. The novel had come of age, without the poets
really noticing what had happened; and a literary perception
trained in the field of fiction was already a good long way ahead
of one exercised only in the silver age of poetry.*

*The last extract briefly adumbrates Professor Auden's
attempt to resuscitate Tennyson's poetry by comparing it with
that of Baudelaire; a sporting attempt, if ever there was one.
No doubt there will be another attempt—a desperate one. And
the attempt after that will be merely foolhardy. Probably the
kindest, the most humane way of dealing with a reputation that
is plainly drowning, and has already come to the surface for the
second time, would be to accept, without more ado, Hopkins'
splendid epithet—'chryselephantine'. Like so much of Hopkins,
it sounds wonderful; and unlike much that he wrote, it can do
no great harm.*

HALLAM

One of the faithful Islâm, a poet in the truest and highest
sense, we are anxious to present to our readers. He has yet
written little and published less; but in these 'preludes of a
loftier strain' we recognize the inspiring god. Mr Tennyson
belongs decidedly to the class we have already described as
Poets of Sensation. He sees all the forms of nature with the
eruditus oculus, and his ear has a fairy fineness. There is a

strange earnestness in his worship of beauty which throws a
charm over his impassioned song, more easily felt than described, and not to be escaped by those who have once felt it.
We think he has more definiteness and roundness of general
conception than the late Mr Keats, and is much more free from
blemishes of diction and hasty capriccios of fancy. He has
also this advantage over that poet and his friend Shelley, that
he comes before the public unconnected with any political
party or peculiar system of opinions. Nevertheless, true to the
theory we have stated, we believe his participation in their
characteristic excellences is sufficient to secure him a share of
their unpopularity.

The volume of *Poems, chiefly Lyrical*, does not contain
above 154 pages; but it shews us much more of the character
of its parent mind than many books we have known of much
larger compass and more boastful pretensions. The features of
original genius are clearly and strongly marked. The author
imitates nobody; we recognize the spirit of his age, but not
the individual form of this or that writer. His thoughts bear
no more resemblance to Byron or Scott, Shelley or Coleridge,
than to Homer or Calderon, Firdusi or Calidasa.

We have remarked five distinctive excellencies of his own
manner. First, his luxuriance of imagination, and at the same
time his control over it. Secondly his power of embodying
himself in ideal characters, or rather moods of character, with
such extreme accuracy of adjustment, that the circumstances
of the narration seem to have a natural correspondence with
the predominant feeling, and, as it were, to be evolved from
it by assimilative force. Thirdly his vivid, picturesque delineation of objects, and the peculiar skill with which he holds all
of them *fused*, to borrow a metaphor from science, in a medium
of strong emotion. Fourthly, the variety of his lyrical measures,
and exquisite modulation of harmonious words and cadences
to the swell and fall of the feelings expressed. Fifthly, the
elevated habits of thought, implied in these compositions, and
imparting a mellow soberness of tone, more impressive, to our
minds, than if the author had drawn up a set of opinions in
verse, and sought to instruct the understanding rather than to
communicate the love of beauty to the heart. . . .

A considerable portion of this book is taken up with a very singular and very beautiful class of poems on which the author has evidently bestowed much thought and elaboration. We allude to the female characters, every trait of which presumes an uncommon degree of observation and reflection. Mr Tennyson's way of proceeding seems to be this. He collects the most striking phenomena of individual minds until he arrives at some leading fact, which allows him to lay down an axiom or law; and then, working on the law thus attained, he clearly discerns the tendency of what new particulars his imagination suggests, and is enabled to impress an individual freshness and unity on ideal combinations. These expressions of character are brief and coherent; nothing extraneous to the dominant fact is admitted, nothing illustrative of it, and, as it were, growing out of it, is rejected. They are like summaries of mighty dramas. We do not say this method admits of such large luxuriance of power as that of our real dramatists; but we contend that it is a new species of poetry, a graft of the lyric on the dramatic, and Mr Tennyson deserves the laurel of an inventor, an enlarger of our modes of knowledge and power.

The Englishman's Magazine 1831

LOCKHART

This is, as some of his marginal notes intimate, Mr Tennyson's second appearance. By some strange chance we have never seen his first publication, which, if it at all resembles its younger brother, must be by this time so popular that any notice of it on our part would seem idle and presumptuous; but we gladly seize this opportunity of repairing an unintentional neglect, and of introducing to the admiration of our more sequestered readers a new prodigy of genius—another and a brighter star of that galaxy or *milky way* of poetry of which the lamented Keats was the harbinger; and let us take this occasion to sing our palinode on the subject of *Endymion*. We certainly did not discover in that poem the same degree of merit that its more clear-sighted and prophetic admirers did. We did not see the unbounded popularity which has carried

it through we know not how many editions; which has placed
it on every table; and, what is still more unequivocal, familiar-
ized it in every mouth. All this splendour of fame, however,
though we had not the sagacity to anticipate, we have the
candour to acknowledge. . . . (13)

Warned by our former mishap, wiser by experience, and
improved, as we hope, in taste, we have to offer Mr Tennyson
our tribute of unmingled approbation, and it is very agreeable
to us, as well as to our readers, that our present task will be
little more than the selection, for their delight, of a few specimens of Mr Tennyson's singular genius, and the venturing to
point out, now and then, the peculiar brilliancy of some of
the gems that irradiate his poetical crown.

A prefatory sonnet opens to the reader the aspirations of
the young author, in which, after the manner of sundry poets,
ancient and modern, he expresses his own peculiar character,
by wishing himself to be something that he is not. The amorous
Catullus aspired to be a sparrow; the tuneful and convivial
Anacreon . . . wished to be a lyre and a great drinking cup; a
crowd of more modern sentimentalists have desired to approach
their mistresses as flowers, tunicks, sandals, birds, breezes, and
butterflies;—all poor conceits of narrow-minded poetasters!
Mr Tennyson (though he, too, would, as far as his true-love
is concerned, not unwillingly be 'an earring,' 'a girdle,' and
'a necklace,') in the more serious and solemn exordium of his
works ambitions a bolder metamorphosis—he wishes to be—
a river!

Sonnet

Mine be the strength of spirit fierce and free,
  Like some broad river rushing down *alone*—

rivers that travel in company are too common for his taste—

With the self-same impulse wherewith he was thrown—

a beautiful and harmonious line—

From his loud fount upon the echoing lea:—
  Which, with *increasing might*, doth *forward flee*—

Every word of this line is valuable—the natural progress of human ambition is here strongly characterised—two lines ago he would have been satisfied with the *self-same* impulse—but now he must have *increasing might*; and indeed he would require all his might to accomplish his object of *fleeing forward*, that is, going backwards and forwards at the same time. Perhaps he uses the word *flee* for *flow*; which latter he could not well employ in *this* place, it being, as we shall see, essentially necessary to rhyme to *Mexico* towards the end of the sonnet— as an equivalent to *flow* he has, therefore, with great taste and ingenuity, hit on the combination of *forward flee*—

> doth forward flee
>
> By town, and tower, and hill, and cape, and isle,
> And in the middle of the great *salt* sea
> Keeps his blue waters fresh for many a mile.

A noble wish, beautifully expressed, that he may not be confounded with the deluge of ordinary poets, but, amidst their discoloured and briny ocean, still preserve his own bright tints and sweet savour. He may be at ease on this point—he never can be mistaken for any one else. We have but too late become acquainted with him yet we assure ourselves that if a thousand anonymous specimens were presented to us, we should unerringly distinguish his by the total absence of any particle of *salt*. . . .

Next comes another class of poems,—Visions. The first is the *Palace of Art*, or a fine house, in which the poet *dreams* that he sees a very fine collection of well-known pictures. An ordinary versifier would, no doubt, have followed the old routine, and dully described himself as walking into the Louvre, or Buckingham Palace, and there seeing certain masterpieces of painting:—a true poet dreams it. We have not room to hang many of these *chefs-d'oeuvre*, but for a few we must find space.—'The Madonna'—

> The maid mother by a crucifix,
>   In yellow pastures sunny warm,
> Beneath branch work of costly sardonyx
>   Sat smiling—*babe in arm*—

The use of this latter, apparently, colloquial phrase is a deep stroke of art. The form of expression is always used to express an habitual and characteristic action. A knight is described '*lance in rest*'—a dragoon, '*sword in hand*'—so, as the idea of the Virgin is inseparably connected with her child, Mr Tennyson reverently describes her conventional position— '*babe in arm.*'

His gallery of illustrious portraits is thus admirably arranged:—The Madonna—Ganymede—St Cecilia—Europa —Deep-haired Milton—Shakspeare—Grim Dante—Michael Angelo—Luther—Lord Bacon—Cervantes—Calderon—King David—'the Halicarnassean' (*quaere*, which of them?)— Alfred, (not Alfred Tennyson, though no doubt in any other man's gallery *he* would have had a place) and finally—

> Isaiah, with fierce Ezekiel,
>   Swarth Moses by the Coptic sea,
> Plato, *Petrarca*, Livy and Raphael,
>   And eastern Confutzee!

We can hardly suspect the very original mind of Mr Tennyson to have harboured any recollection of that celebrated Doric idyll, *The Groves of Blarney*, but certainly there is a strong likeness between Mr Tennyson's list of pictures and the Blarney collection of statues—

> Statues growing that noble place in,
>   All heathen goddesses most rare,
> Homer, Plutarch, and Nebuchadnezzar,
>   All standing naked in the open air!

In this poem we first observed a stroke of art (repeated afterwards) which we think very ingenious. No one who has ever written verse but must have felt the pain of erasing some happy line, some striking stanza, which, however excellent in itself, did not exactly suit the place for which it was destined. How curiously does an author mould and remould the plastic verse in order to fit in the favourite thought; and when he finds that he cannot introduce it, as Corporal Trim says, *any how*, with what reluctance does he at last reject the intractable,

but still cherished offspring of his brain! Mr Tennyson man-
ages this delicate matter in a new and better way; he says, with
great candour and simplicity, 'If this poem were not already
too long, *I should have added* the following stanzas,' and
then he adds them,—or, 'the following lines are manifestly
superfluous, as a part of the text, but they may be allowed to
stand as a separate poem,' *which they do*;—or, 'I intended to
have added something on statuary, but I found it very difficult;'
—(he had, moreover, as we have seen, been anticipated in this
line by the Blarney poet)—'but I had finished the statues of
Elijah and *Olympias*—judge whether I have succeeded'—and
then we have these two statues. This is certainly the most
ingenious device that has ever come under our observation,
for reconciling the rigour of criticism with the indulgence of
parental partiality. It is economical too, and to the reader
profitable, as by these means

> We lose no drop of the immortal man.

The other vision is *A Dream of Fair Women*, in which the
heroines of all ages—some, indeed, that belong to the times of
'heathen goddesses most rare'—pass before his view. We have
no time to notice them all, but the second, whom we take to
be Iphigenia, touches the heart with a stroke of nature more
powerful than even the veil that the Grecian painter threw
over the head of her father.

>   —dimly I could descry
> The stern blackbearded kings with wolfish eyes,
>   Watching to see me die.
>
> The tall masts quivered as they lay afloat;
>   The temples, and the people, and the shore;
> One drew a sharp knife through my tender throat—
>   Slowly,—and *nothing more*!

What touching simplicity—what pathetic resignation—
he cut my throat—'nothing more!' One might indeed ask,
'what *more*' she would have?

The Quarterly Review 1833

CHRISTOPHER NORTH

The *Englishman's Magazine* ought not to have died; for it threatened to be a very pleasant periodical. An Essay 'on the Genius of Alfred Tennyson', sent it to the grave. The superhuman—nay, supernatural—pomposity of that one paper, incapacitated the whole work for living one day longer in this unceremonious world. The solemnity with which the critic approached the object of his adoration, and the sanctity with which he laid his offerings on the shrine, were too much for our irreligious age. The Essay 'on the genius of Alfred Tennyson', awoke a general guffaw, and it expired in convulsions. Yet the Essay was exceedingly well-written—as well as if it had been 'on the Genius of Sir Isaac Newton'. Therein lay the mistake. Sir Isaac discovered the law of gravitation; Alfred had but written some pretty verses, and mankind were not prepared to set him among the stars. But that he has genius is proved by his being at this moment alive; for had he not, he must have breathed his last under that critique. The spirit of life must indeed be strong within him; for he has outlived a narcotic dose administered to him by a crazy charlatan in the *Westminster*, and after that he may sleep in safety with a pan of charcoal.

But the Old Man must see justice done to this ingenious lad, and save him from his worst enemies, his friends. . . .

At present he has small power over the common feelings and thoughts of men. His feebleness is distressing at all times when he makes an appeal to their ordinary sympathies. And the reason is, that he fears to look such sympathies baldly in the face,—and will be—metaphysical. What all the human race see and feel, he seems to think cannot be poetical; he is not aware of the transcendent and eternal grandeur of commonplace and all-time truths, which are the staple of all poetry. . . .

Mr Tennyson's admirers say he excels wondrously in personating mermen and mermaids, fairies, *et id genus omne*, inhabiting sea-caves and forest glades, 'in still or stormy weather', the 'gay creatures of the element', be that element air, earth, fire, or water, so that the denizens thereof be but 'of imagination all compact'. We beg of you to hear, for a few sentences, the quack in the *Westminster*. . . . It is a perfect specimen of the super-hyperbolical ultra-extravagance of outrageous Cockney eulogistic foolishness, with which not even a quantity of common sense less than nothing has been suffered, for an indivisible moment of time, to mingle; the purest mere matter of moonshine ever mouthed by an idiot-lunatic, slavering in the palsied dotage of the extremest super-annuation ever inflicted on a being, long ago, perhaps, in some slight respects and low degrees human, but now sensibly and audibly reduced below the level of the Pongos. . . .

Shakspeare — Spenser — Milton — Wordsworth — Coleridge—The Ettrick Shepherd—Allan Cunninghame, and some others, have loved, and been beloved by mermaidens, sirens, sea and land fairies, and revealed to the eyes of us who live in the thick atmosphere of this 'dim spot which men call earth', all the beautiful wonders of subterranean and submarine climes—and of the climes of Nowhere, lovelier than them all. It pains us to think, that with such names we cannot yet rank that of Alfred Tennyson. We shall soon see that he possesses feeling, fancy, imagination, genius. But in the preternatural lies not the sphere in which he excels. . . .

The gentle reader who understands that sonnet [*The Kraken*], will perhaps have the goodness to interpret for us the following oracular sentence, which from childhood has been to us a great mystery.—'An old horse came in to be shaved; curse you, where's the suds? The estate was entailed to male heirs; and poor Mrs Molly lost all her apple-dumplings.'

Thin as is this volume we are now reviewing, and sparse the letterpress on its tiny pages, 'twould yet be easy to extract from it much more unmeaningness; but having shewn by gentle chastisement that we love Alfred Tennyson, let us now shew by judicious eulogy that we admire him; and, by well-chosen specimens of his fine faculties, that he is worthy of our admiration.

Odes to Memory are mostly mummeries; but not so is the *Ode to Memory* breathed by this young poet. In it, Memory and

Imagination, like two angels, lead him by the hands back to the bowers of paradise. . . .

There is fine music there; the versification would be felt delightful to all poetical ears, even if they missed the many meanings of the well-chosen and happily-obedient words; for there is the sound as of a various-voiced river rejoicing in a sudden summer shower, that swells without staining its translucent waters. But the sound is echo to the sense; and the sense is sweet as that of life's dearest emotions enjoyed in 'a dream that is not all a dream'.

Mr Tennyson, when he chooses, can say much in few words. A fine example of that is shewn in five few-syllabled four-lined stanzas on a *Deserted House*. Every word tells; and the short whole is most pathetic in its completeness—let us say perfection—like some old Scottish air sung by a maiden at her wheel—or shepherd in the wilderness. . . .

. . . He has a delicate perception of the purity of the female character. Any one of his flesh and blood maidens, walking amongst flowers of our own earth, is worth a billowy wilderness of his Sea-Fairies. Their names and their natures are delightful —sound and sight are spiritualized—and yet, as Wordsworth divinely saith, are they

> Creatures not too bright or good
> For human nature's daily food,
> For transient sorrows, simple wiles,
> Praise, blame, love, kisses, tears and smiles!

We are in love—as an old man ought to be—as a father is with his ideal daughters—with them all—with Claribel, and Lilian, and Isabel, and Mariana, and Adeline, and Hero, and Almeida, and the Sleeping Beauty, and Oriana. What different beings from King Charles's beauties! Even in bodily charms far more loveable; in spiritual, pure

> As heavenly Una with her milk-white lamb—

objects, for a moment's thought, of passion; but of affection, for ever and a day. In face, form, figure, circumstance and character, delicately distinguished from one another are all the sweet sisterhood. . . .

Our critique is near its conclusion; and in correcting it for the press, we see that its whole merit, which is great, consists in the extracts, which are 'beautiful exceedingly'. Perhaps, in the first part of our article, we may have exaggerated Mr Tennyson's not unfrequent silliness, for we are apt to be carried away by the whim of the moment, and in our humourous moods, many things wear a queer look to our aged eyes, which fill young pupils with tears; but we feel assured that in the second part we have not exaggerated his strength—that we have done no more than justice to his fine faculties— and that the millions who delight in Maga [*Blackwood's*] will, with one voice, confirm our judgment—that Alfred Tennyson is a poet.

But, though it might be a mistake of ours, where we say that he has much to learn, it can be no mistake to say that he has not a little to unlearn. . . .

. . . he must consider that all the fancies that fleet across the imagination, like shadows on the grass or the tree-tops, are not entitled to be made small separate poems of—about the length of one's little finger; that many, nay, most of them, should be suffered to pass away with a silent 'God bless ye', like butterflies, single or in shoals. . . .

Now, Mr Tennyson does not seem to know this; or if he do, he is self-willed and perverse in his sometimes infantile vanity; (and how vain are most beautiful children!) and thinks that any Thought or Feeling or Fancy that has had the honour and the happiness to pass through *his* mind, must by that very act be worthy of everlasting commemoration.

Blackwood's Magazine 1832

MILL

Towards the close of the year 1830 appeared a small volume of poems, the work of a young and unknown author, and which, with considerable faults (some of them of a bad kind), gave evidence of powers such as had not for many years been displayed by any new aspirant to the character of a poet. The first publication was followed in due time by a second, in which the faults of its predecessor were still visible, but were evidently on the point of disappearing; while the positive excellence was not only greater and more uniformly sustained, but of a higher order. The imagination of the poet and his reason had alike advanced: the one had become more teeming and vigorous, while its resources had been brought more habitually and completely under the command of the other.

The notice which these poems have hitherto received from the more widely-circulated and influential organs of criticism consists, as far as we are aware, of two articles—a review of the first publication in *Blackwood's Magazine*, and of the second, in the *Quarterly Review*. The article in *Blackwood*, along with the usual flippancy and levity of that journal, evinced one of its better characteristics—a genuine appreciation and willing recognition of genius. It was not to be expected that a writer in *Blackwood* could accomplish a criticism on a volume of poetry, without cutting capers and exhibiting himself in postures, as Drawcansir says, 'because he dare'. . . . If we can forgive this audacious sporting with his reader and his subjects, the critique is otherwise not without merit. The praise and blame, though shovelled out rather than measured, are thrown into the right places. . . .

Of Mr Tennyson's two volumes, the second was the only one which fell into the hands of the Quarterly Reviewer; and his treatment of it, compared with the notice taken by *Blackwood* of its more juvenile predecessor, forms a contrast characteristic of the two journals. Whatever may be in other respects our opinion of *Blackwood's Magazine*, it is impossible to deny to its principal writers (or writer) a certain susceptibility of sense, a geniality of temperament. Their mode of writing about works of genius is that of a person who derives much enjoyment from them and is grateful for it. Genuine powers of mind, with whatever opinions connected, seldom fail to meet with response and recognition from these writers. The *Quarterly Review*, on the other hand, both under its original and under its present management, has been no less characterised by qualities directly the reverse of these. Every new claim upon its admiration, unless forced upon it by the public voice, or recommended by some party interest, it welcomes, not with a friendly extension of the hand, but with a curl of the lip: the critic (as we figure him to ourselves) taking up the book, in trusting anticipation of pleasure not from the book, but from the contemplation of his own cleverness in making it contemptible. . . . The plan he adopts is no new one, but abundantly hacknied: he selects the few bad passages (not amounting to three pages in the whole), and such others as, by being separated from the context, may be made to look ridiculous; and in a strain of dull irony, of which all the point consists in the ill-nature, he holds forth these as a specimen of the work. A piece of criticism resembling, in all but their wit, the disgraceful articles in the early Numbers of the *Edinburgh Review*, on Wordsworth and Coleridge.

Meanwhile, these poems have been winning their way, by slow approaches, to a reputation; the exact limits and measure of which it would be hazardous at present to predict, but which, we believe, will not ultimately be inconsiderable. . . .

Of all the capacities of a poet, that which seems to have arisen earliest in Mr Tennyson, and in which he most excels, is that of scene-painting, in the higher sense of the term: not the mere power of producing that rather vapid species of composition usually termed descriptive poetry—for there is not in these volumes one passage of pure description: but the power of *creating* scenery, in keeping with some state of human feeling; so fitted to it as to be the embodied symbol of it, and to summon up the state of feeling itself, with a force not to be surpassed by anything but reality. . . .

. . . The nominal subject [of *Mariana*] excites anticipations which the poem does not even attempt to fulfil. The humblest poet, who is a poet at all, could make more than is here made of the situation of a maiden abandoned by her lover. But that was not Mr Tennyson's idea. The love-story is secondary in his mind. The words 'he cometh not' are almost the only words which allude to it at all. To place ourselves at the right point of view, we must drop the conception of Shakspeare's Mariana, and retain only that of a 'moated grange', and a solitary dweller within it, forgotten by mankind. And now see whether poetic imagery ever conveyed a more intense

I

perception of such a place, or of the feelings of such an inmate. From the very first line, the rust of age and the solitude of desertion are on the whole picture. Words surely never excited a more vivid feeling of physical and spiritual dreariness: and not dreariness alone—for that might be felt under many other circumstances of solitude—but the dreariness which speaks not merely of being far from human converse and sympathy, but of being *deserted* by it. . . .

In powers of narrative and scene-painting combined, this poem [*The Lady of Shalott*] must be ranked among the very first of its class. The delineation of outward objects, as in the greater number of Mr Tennyson's poems, is, not picturesque, but (if we may use the term) statuesque; with brilliancy of colour superadded. The forms are not, as in painting, of unequal degrees of definiteness; the tints do not melt gradually into each other, but each individual object stands out in bold relief, with a clear decided outline. This statue-like precision and distinctness few artists have been able to give to so essentially vague a language as that of words: but if once this difficulty be got over, scene-painting by words has a wider range than either painting or sculpture; for it can represent (as the reader must have seen in the foregoing poem), not only with the vividness and strength of the one, but with the clearness and definiteness of the other, objects in motion. Along with all this, there is in the poem all that power of making a few touches do the whole work, which excites our admiration in Coleridge. Every line suggests so much more than it says, that much may be left unsaid: the concentration, which is the soul of the narrative, is obtained, without the sacrifice of reality and life. Where the march of the story requires that the mind should pause, details are specified; where rapidity is necessary, they are all brought before us in a flash. Except that the versification is less exquisite, *The Lady of Shalott* is entitled to a place by the side of *The Ancient Mariner* and *Christabel*.

Mr Tennyson's two volumes contain a whole picture-gallery of lovely women. . . .

Every great poet, every poet who has extensively or per-manently influenced mankind, has been a great thinker;—

has had a philosophy, though perhaps he did not call it by that name;—has had his mind full of thoughts, derived not merely from passive sensibility, but from trains of reflection, from observation, analysis and generalization; however remote the sphere of his observation and meditation may have lain from the studies of the schools. Where the poetic temperament exists in its greatest degree, while the systematic culture of the intellect has been neglected, we may expect to find, what we do find in the best poems of Shelley—vivid representations of states of passive and dreamy emotion, fitted to give extreme pleasure to persons of similar organisation to the poet, but not likely to be sympathized in, because not understood, by any other persons; and scarcely conducing at all to the noblest end of poetry as an intellectual pursuit, that of acting upon the desires and characters of mankind through their emotions, to raise them towards the perfection of their nature. This, like every other adaptation of means to ends, is the work of cultivated reason; and the poet's success in it will be in proportion to the intrinsic value of his thoughts, and to the command which he has acquired over the materials of his imagination, for placing those thoughts in a strong light before the intellect, and impressing them on the feelings.

The poems which we have quoted from Mr Tennyson prove incontestably that he possesses, in an eminent degree, the natural endowment of a poet—the poetic temperament. And it appears clearly, not only from a comparison of the two volumes, but of different poems in the same volume, that, with him, the other element of poetic excellence—intellectual culture—is advancing both steadily and rapidly; that he is not destined, like so many others, to be remembered for what he might have done, rather than for what he did; that he will not remain a poet of mere temperament, but is ripening into a true artist. . . .

. . . Mr Tennyson seems, as he proceeded, to have raised his aims still higher—to have aspired to render his poems not only vivid representations of spiritual states, but symbolical of spiritual truths. His longest poem, *The Palace of Art*, is an attempt of this sort. As such, we do not think it wholly successful, though rich in beauties of detail; but we deem it of the

most favourable augury for Mr Tennyson's future achievements, since it proves a continually increasing endeavour
towards the highest excellence, and a constantly rising standard
of it.

We predict, that, as Mr Tennyson advances in general
spiritual culture, these higher aims will become more and
more predominant in his writings; that he will strive more and
more diligently, and even without striving, will be more and
more impelled by the natural tendencies of an expanding
character, towards what has been described as the highest
object of poetry, 'to incorporate the everlasting reason of man
in forms visible to his sense, and suitable to it'. For the fulfilment of this exalted purpose, what we have already seen of
him authorizes us to foretell with confidence, that powers
of execution will not fail him; it rests with himself to see that
his powers of thought may keep pace with them. To render
his poetic endowment the means of giving impressiveness to
important truths, he must, by continual study and meditation,
strengthen his intellect for the discrimination of such truths,
he must see that his theory of life and the world be no chimera
of the brain, but the well-grounded result of solid and mature
thinking;—he must cultivate, and with no half devotion,
philosophy as well as poetry.

The London Review 1835

FITZGERALD

What you say of Tennyson and Wordsworth is not, I think,
wholly just. I don't think that a man can turn himself so
directly to the service of morality, unless naturally inclined
I think Wordsworth's is a natural bias that way. Besides, one
must have labourers of different kinds in the vineyard of
morality, which I certainly look up to as the chief object of
our cultivation: Wordsworth is first in the craft: but Tennyson
does no little by raising and filling the brain with noble
images and thoughts, which, if they do not direct us to our
duty, purify and cleanse us from mean and vicious objects
and so prepare and fit us for the reception of the higher
philosophy. A man might forsake a drunken party to read

Byron's *Corsair*: and Byron's *Corsair* for Shelley's *Alastor*: and the *Alastor* for the *Dream of Fair Women* or the *Palace of Art*: and then I won't say that he would forsake these two last for anything of Wordsworth's, but his mind would be sufficiently refined and spiritualised to admit Wordsworth, and profit by him, and he might keep all the former imaginations as so many pictures, or pieces of music, in his mind. But I think you will see Tennyson acquire all that at present you miss: when he has *felt* life, he will not die fruitless of instruction to man as he is.

Letter to John Allen 1835

I had a note from Alfred three months ago. He was then in London: but is now in Ireland, I think, adding to his new poem, *The Princess*. Have you seen it? I am considered a great heretic for abusing it; it seems to me a wretched waste of power at a time of life when a man ought to be doing his best; and I almost feel hopeless about Alfred now. I mean, about his doing what he was born to do. . . .

Letter to Frederick Tennyson 1848

As to Alfred, I have heard of his marriage &c. from Spedding, who also saw and was much pleased with her indeed. But you know Alfred himself never writes, nor indeed cares a halfpenny about one, though he is very well satisfied to see one when one falls in his way. You will think I have a spite against him for some neglect, when I say this, and say besides that I cannot care for his *In Memoriam*. Not so, if I know myself: I always thought the same of him, and was just as well satisfied with it as now. His poem I never did greatly affect: nor can I learn to do so: it is full of finest things, but it is monotonous, and has that air of being evolved by a Poetical Machine of the highest order. So it seems to be with him now, at least to me, the Impetus, the Lyrical œstrus, is gone . . . It is the cursed inactivity (very pleasant to me who am no Hero) of this 19th century which has spoiled Alfred, I mean spoiled him for the great work he ought now to be

entering upon; the lovely and noble things he has done must
remain.

Letter to Frederick Tennyson 1850

When Tennyson was telling me of how the *Quarterly*
abused him (humourously too), and desirous of knowing why
one did not care for his later works, etc., I thought if he had
lived an active life, as Scott and Shakespeare; or even ridden,
shot, drunk, and played the Devil, as Byron, he would have
done much more, and talked about it much less. 'You know,'
said Scott to Lockhart, 'that I don't care a Curse about what
I write,' and one sees he did not. I don't believe it was far
otherwise with Shakespeare. Even old Wordsworth, wrapt up
in his Mountain mists, and proud as he was, was above all
this vain Disquietude: proud, not vain, was he: and that
a Great Man (as Dante) has some right to be—but not to care
what the Coteries say.

Letter to Fanny Kemble 1876

BROWNING

I send with this Tennyson's new vol., and, alas, the old
with it—that is, what he calls old. You will see, and groan!
The alterations are insane. *Whatever* is touched is spoiled.
There is some woeful infirmity in the man—he was months
buried in correcting the press of the last volume, and in that
time began spoiling the new poems (in proof) as hard as he
could. *Locksley Hall* is shorn of two or three couplets . . . I
have been with Moxon this morning, who tells me that he is
miserably thin-skinned, sensitive to criticism (foolish criticism), wishes to see no notices that contain the least possible
depreciatory expressions—poor fellow! But how good when
good he is—that noble *Locksley Hall*, for instance—and
St Simeon Stylites—which I think perfect. . . .

Letter to Domett 1842

LEIGH HUNT

We are compelled to say, then, in justice to the very respect
which we entertain, and the more which we desire to entertain,

for the genius of Mr Tennyson, that the above 'lettings out of the bag' of his dates and alterations, are a little too character- istic of a certain mixture of timidity and misgiving with his otherwise somewhat defying demands upon our assent to his figments and his *hyphens*, and that we have great objections to a certain air of literary dandyism, or fine-gentlemanism, or fastidiousness, or whatever he may *not* be pleased to call it, which leads him to usher in his compositions with such exordiums as those to *Morte d'Arthur* and *Godiva*; in the former of which he gives us to understand that he should have burnt his poem but for the 'request of friends'; and, in the latter, that he 'shaped' it while he was waiting 'for the train at Coventry', and hanging on the bridge 'with grooms and porters.' Really this is little better than the rhyming fine- ladyism of Miss Seward, who said that she used to translate an ode of Horace 'while her hair was curling'. And, if the 'grooms and porters' have any meaning beyond a superfluous bit of the graphic, not in keeping with his subject, it is a little worse, for why should not Mr Tennyson, in the universality of his poetry, be as content to be waiting on a bridge, among 'grooms and porters,' as with any other assortment of his fellow-men? Doubtless he would disclaim any such want of philosophy; but this kind of mixed tone of contempt and nonchalance, or, at best, of fine-life phrases with better fellowship, looks a little instructive, and is, at all events, a little perilous. There is a drawl of Bond-street in it. We suspect that these poems of *Morte d'Arthur* and *Godiva* are among those which Mr Tenny- son thinks his best, and is most anxious that others should regard as he does; and therefore it is that he would affect to make trifles of them. The reader's opinion is at once to be of great importance to him, and yet none at all. There is a boyish- ness in this which we shall be happy to see Mr Tennyson, who is no longer a boy, outgrow. . . .

He has fancy, imagination, expression, thought, knowledge, and music, too—in short, all the materials of an admirable contemplative poet, and in some instances his success has already been great, and his name, we trust, will be lasting. But at present he still shows a little too much of the spoiled child. He is indolent, over-refining, is in danger of neutralizing his earnestness altogether by the scepticism of thought not too strong, but not strong enough to lead or combine, and he runs, or rather reposes, altogether upon feelings (not to speak it offensively) too sensual. His mind lives in an atmosphere heavy with perfumes. He grows lazy by the side of his Lincolnshire water-lilies; and, with a genius of his own sufficient for original and enduring purposes (at least we hope so), subjects himself to the charge of helping it too much with the poets gone before him, from Homer to Wordsworth, and to Shelley and Keats. . . .

'Madeline' is held forth to us a lady, who 'smiling frowning evermore,' is considered 'perfect in love'. 'Delicious spites and darling angers' are here; things such as Tasso took delight in praising; and as long as they only amused him, they were very well; but when he came to take a deeper interest, adieu to the lovingness of the lady and to his own happiness. So with this ever frowning and smiling coquette of Mr Tennyson's, who fixes a smile at him if he offers to go, and then 'blushes angerly' if he offers to kiss the tips of her fingers. We confess we have no faith in the lady's knowledge of love at all, nor any vast deal in the loveability of Mr Tennyson's ladies in general. They remind us too much of the fine young ladies in souvenirs and beauty-books, with rapturous eyes, dark locks and tresses, and all that—ready made to conquer between the meretricious and the moral—between a boarding-school education, and prudential, and in truth cold contradictions to it. He has a whole seraglio of them. The list would make a song of itself. There is Mariana, Eleonora, Oriana, Fatima, Dora, Margaret, Olivia, Rose, Emilia, Claribel, Isabel, Adeline, Madeline, Lady Clara, and Lady Flora. Poets are bound to be admirers of the fair sex; but Mr Tennyson talks as if he really loved most of these ladies, while it is pretty clear that his admiration is of a very ordinary sort, and that he makes the poor creatures pegs to hang characters upon; for which we are not surprised that they seldom appear to return his passion. We think him more ingenious than happy in these portraitures. There is sometimes a good deal of observation in them, and metaphysical acuteness; but it is too ostentatiously shown, often in numbers affectedly musical;

and he makes them so very conscious, or fastidious, or stately, or in some way or other almost always puts some such unpleasant contradiction to their loveability in the midst of their exuberant airs and graces, that they end in impressing us as a sort of poetical milliners, or artificial idealisms full dressed. . . .

The *Recollections of the Arabian Nights* . . . runs too much into mere luxury and exuberance. We are oppressed as with the nook of Lincolnshire weeds. The better part of the stateliness and drapery of the East is not in it, much less the human variety of that wonderful set of stories. When Mr Tennyson's subject is spiritual, he is apt to become sensuous enough; and very beautiful he *then* is in his sensuousness. When his subject is *sensual*, it is to his detriment; for his luxury tends to rankness. . . .

The Two Voices is a summary of the argument, *pro* and *con*, about suicide, capitally well put on both sides, and ending, as they ought to do, in the victory of a cheerful wisdom befitting the beauty of the universe and the goodness of its Creator. . . . This is genuine, manly, and poetical philosophy, far better than a hundred elaborate luxuries, whether of voluptuousness or woe, and in a style more advanced than that which heaps up compound epithets and an ostentation of thoughts. There has been a reaction of late years in favour both of thought and feeling, and a very salutary reaction it is, against the unthinking commonplace that prevailed at the beginning of the century; but, with the usual tendency of revolutions, it has gone to an extreme, and young poets are in danger of exchanging one set of impertinences, that is to say irrelevancies, for another. They *think* that they must *think* at any rate, and be in an incessant state of exuberant remark and imagery, in order to show what is in them. But real abundance is not under the necessity of taking those violent measures to prove itself. . . . Now, one thing said with thorough truth, and to the purpose, is worth millions of half-apposite fancies, and similes, and collateralities . . .

Mr Tennyson is at present a kind of philosophical Keats, without the later judgment of that extraordinary genius, and of a turn of mind less naturally and thoroughly given to poetry, in its essence. But there can be no doubt that he is a genuine poet too in his degree (a sacred name—pray let him know how to value it, and be at his ease with it): and there is a class of poetry in which we think he may obtain for himself a name, perhaps as great in its way as that of the other, and one of an independent sort, and that is in a mixture of thought and feeling, more abundant in the former respect than Keats, and more pleasurable and luxuriant in the latter than Wordsworth. We have already characterized . . . his poetical merits as well as defects, and surely out of all these he might produce another volume which, if less in bulk than the two before us, would have a far greater real abundance His poems of *Mariana*, and *A Character*, and the *Merman* and *Mermaid*, and *Oriana* (in spite of its burden), and the *Miller's Daughter* and *Simeon Stylites*, and the *Two Voices*, are almost all written in a style as clear and compact as the fancy and imagination are poetical. . . .

Such is the position, in the opinion of poets and lovers of genuine poetry (the opinion of critics, and of the public, may not as yet be quite in accordance with the former), which Mr Tennyson has attained after having been before the world during ten or twelve years. With the first class his genius was at once recognized—with the critics and the public it has, as usual, been a matter of slow progress and much contest; but we think that, on the whole, he has little reason to be dissatisfied, and no reason at all, when we consider the ill treatment and tardy admission of the claims of Shelley, of Keats, and of Wordsworth.

Church of England Quarterly Review   1842

[Of this review, Browning wrote to Domett: 'Hunt's criticism is neither kind nor just, I take it—he don't understand that most of Tennyson's poems are *dramatic*—utterances coloured by an imaginary speaker's moods']

HORNE

The name of Alfred Tennyson is pressing slowly, calmly, but surely,—with certain recognition but no loud shouts of greeting,—from the lips of the discerners of poets, of whom

there remain a few, even in the cast-iron ages, along the lips
of the less informed public, 'to its own place' in the starry
house of names. That it is the name of a true poet, the drowsy
world exerts itself to acknowledge; testifying, with a heavy
lifting of the eyelid, to its consciousness of a new light in
one of the nearer sconces. This poet's public is certainly
awake to him, although you would not think so. And this
public's poet, standing upon the recognition of his own
genius, begins to feel the ground firm beneath his feet, after
no worse persecution than is comprised in those charges of
affectation, quaintness, and mannerism, which were bleated
down the ranks of the innocent 'sillie' critics as they went one
after another to water. Let the toleration be chronicled to the
honour of England. And who knows?—There may be hope
from this, and a few similar instances of misprision of the
high treason of poetry, that our country may conclude her
grand experience of a succession of poetical writers unequalled in the modern world, by learning some ages hence
to know a poet when she sees one. Certainly if we looked only
to the peculiar genius of Tennyson, with the eyes of our fore-
fathers, and some others rather nearer to our own day, we
should find it absolutely worthy of being either starved or
stoned, or as Shelley said of Keats, 'hooted into the grave'. . . .

Whatever he writes is a complete work: he holds the unity
of it as firmly in his hand as his Oenone's Paris holds the
apple—and there is nothing broken or incomplete in his two
full volumes. His few 'fragments' are entire in themselves,
and suggest the remainder. But for all this unity of every
separate poem produced by him, there is, or appears to be,
some vacillation of intention, in his poetry as a mass. To any
question upon the character of his early works, the reply rises
obviously,—they are from dream-land; and of the majority
of those which he has since produced, the same answer should
be returned. The exceptive instances are like those of one who
has not long awakened from his Dreams. But what dreams
these have been—of what loveliness of music, form, and colour,
and what thoughtfulness—our foregoing remarks have very
faintly expressed and declared. In the absence of any marked
and perceptible design in his poetical faith and purposes,

Tennyson is not singular. It would be equally difficult to
decide the same question with regard to several others; nor
perhaps is it necessary to be decided. As the matter rests in
this instance, we have the idea of a poet (his volumes in our
hands) who is not in a fixed attitude; not resolute as to means,
not determined as to end—sure of his power, sure of his
activity, but not sure of his objects. There appears to be some
want of the sanctification of a spiritual consistency; or a
liability at intervals to resign himself to *The Lotus Eaters*.
We seem to look on while a man stands in preparation for
some loftier course—while he tries the edge of his various
arms and examines the wheels of his chariots, and meditates,
full of youth and capability, down the long slope of glory.
He constantly gives us the impression of something greater
than his works. And this must be his own soul. He may do
greater things than he has yet done; but we do not expect it.
If he do no more, he has already done enough to deserve the
lasting love and admiration of posterity.

A New Spirit of the Age   1844

STERLING

What poetry might be in our time and land, if a man of the
highest powers and most complete cultivation exercised the
art among us, will be hard to say until after the fact of such a
man's existence. Waiting for this desirable event, we may at
least see that poetry, to be for us what it has sometimes been
among mankind, must wear a new form, and probably com-
prise elements hardly found in our recent writings, and impossible in former ones.

Of verse, indeed, of every sort but the excellent, there is no
want: almost all, however, so helpless in skill, so faint in
meaning, that one might almost fancy the authors wrote
metre from mere incapacity of expressing themselves at all
in prose—as boys at school can sometimes make nonsense-
verses before they can construct a rational sentence. Yet it is
plain that even our magazine stanzas, album sonnets, and
rhymes in corners of newspapers aim at the forms of emotion,
and use some of the words in which men of genius have

symbolized profound thoughts. The whole, indeed, is generally a lump of blunder and imbecility, but in the midst there is often some turn of cadence, some attempt at an epithet of more significance and beauty than perhaps a much finer mind would have hit on a hundred years ago. The crowds of stammering children are yet the offspring of an age that would fain teach them—if it knew how—a richer, clearer language than they can learn to speak.

It is hard in this state of things not to conceive that the time, among us at least, is an essentially unpoetic one—one which, whatever may be the worth of its feelings, finds no utterance for them in melodious words.

Yet our age is not asleep. Great movements, various activities, are heard and seen on all sides. In the lowest department, that of mere mechanics, consider what fifteen years have done. It was only in the autumn of 1830, following close on the French three memorable days of July, that the Duke of Wellington opened the Manchester and Liverpool Railroad. The population of the busiest region on this earth were assembled round him, whom all acknowledged as the greatest man in England, at the inauguration of a new physical power, then felt to double the swiftness and strength of human beings. While, among myriads of gravely joyous faces, the new machines travelled at a speed matching that of eagles, the life of a great statesman shot off on a darker and more distant journey, and the thrill of fear and pain at his destruction gave the last human tragic touch to an event which would at any rate have retained for ever a historic importance. The death of Mr Huskisson[1] startled the fixed bosom of the veteran soldier, and those who were near perceived a quiver of the lip, a movement of the eye, such as had hardly been caused by the most unlooked-for and dreadful chances of his mighty wars. To a calm observer, the emotion of the whole multitude, great and small, might strangely have recalled far-distant ages and the feelings with which ancient peoples held every great event as incomplete, wanting the blood of a victim—too often human—solemnly shed. In the most prosperous and peaceful

[1] President of the Board of Trade, eminent economist, run over by an inaugural engine.

of national triumphs the dark powers again claimed a share, and would not be forgotten. . . .

Or look at one of our general elections. The absurdities are plain, no doubt—has not the ocean froth and bubbles? But take the thing altogether, and observe the mixture and spread of interests and faculties brought into action—above all the open boldness with which a nation throws itself into the streets and markets, casting off, in the faith that it can reproduce, its company of rulers, and letting the fools clamour, the poor groan, the rich humble themselves, and all men bring all to judgment, without a moment's fear but that quiet will spring out from the tumult, and a government be born from the mob. . . .

On the whole, the country in which these varieties of good and evil are found mixed on such a scale can hardly be considered in a state of lifeless inertness. Its want cannot be of themes and interest, but rather of those able to seize what lies before them, and turn it to right imaginative use. For every one indeed knows that all our activities, mechanical, political, missionary, celestial or diabolical, are the immediate outgrowths of the human beings engaged in such matters, and might be found with much more inside and beneath them in the hearts and lives of the individuals. This is all the poet requires; a busy, vigorous, various existence in the matter *sine qua non* of his work. All else comes from within, and from himself alone. . . .

See how Chaucer exhibits to us all that lay around him. . . . In Shakespeare again, who never meant anything of the kind, that period, with its far deeper wants and more abundant forces, all lies softly, firmly drawn by every random jotting of his pen.

In thus pointing to the problem which poetry now holds out, and maintaining that it has been but partially solved by our most illustrious writers, there is no design of setting up an unattainable standard, and then blaming any one in particular for inevitably falling short of it. Out of an age so diversified and as yet so unshapely, he who draws forth any graceful and expressive forms is well entitled to high praise. Turning into fixed beauty any part of the shifting and mingled matter of our time, he does what in itself is very difficult, and affords valuable help to all his future fellow-labourers. If he has not given us back our age as a whole transmuted into crystalline clearness and lustre, a work accomplished only by a few of the greatest minds under the happiest circumstances for their art, yet we scarce know to whom we should be equally grateful as to him who has enriched us with any shapes of lasting loveliness 'won from the vague and formless infinite.'

Mr Tennyson has done more of this kind than almost anyone that has appeared among us during the last twenty years. And in such a task of alchemy a really successful experiment, even on a small scale, is of great worth compared with the thousands of fruitless efforts or pretences on the largest plan, which are daily clamouring for all men's admiration of their nothingness. . . .

The *Morte d'Arthur*, the first poem in the second volume, seems to us less costly jewel-work, with fewer of the broad flashes of passionate imagery, than some others, and not compensating for this inferiority by any stronger human interest. The miraculous legend of *Excalibur* does not come very near to us, and as reproduced by any modern writer must be a mere ingenious exercise of fancy. The poem, however, is full of distinct and striking description, perfectly expressed; and a tone of mild, dignified sweetness attracts, though it hardly avails to enchant us. The poet might perhaps have made the loss of the magic sword, the death of Arthur, and dissolution of the Round Table, a symbol for the departure from earth of the whole old Gothic world, with its half-pagan, all-poetic faith, and rude yet mystic blazonries. But it would be tyrannical exaction to require more philosophy in union with so fiery and productive a fancy. No one but Coleridge among us ever combined a thoroughly speculative intellect with so restless an abundance of beautiful imagery as we find in Mr Tennyson; and the younger minstrel has as much of the reflection proper to an age like ours as any living poet except Mr Wordsworth, and as any but a few deceased ones.

The gift of comprehensive thoughtfulness does not, however, show itself to advantage in *St Simeon Stylites*, a kind of monological personation of a filthy and mad ascetic. . . . How

different, how superior is *Ulysses*! There is in this work a
delightful epic tone, and a clear unimpassioned wisdom
quietly carving its sage words and graceful figures on pale but
lasting marble. Yet we know not why, except from schoolboy
recollections, a modern English poet should write of Ulysses
rather than of the great voyagers of the modern world, Columbus, Gama, or even Drake. Their feelings and aims lie far
nearer to our comprehension—reach us by a far shorter
line. . . .

In *Locksley Hall* the fancy is again at home. It is, perhaps,
the one of all these poems in which far-extended thought is
best involved in genuine and ardent imagination. A quick
and generous heart pours out through the lips of a young
man who has been deceived by the woman he loved, and who,
inflamed with disappointment, reviews at passionate speed—
far unlike the prosaic slowness of professional reviewers—
the images that the darkened world now presents to him, and
the diverse paths of action he is tempted to try. We know not
what the author means by his hero's talk of comrades and
bugle-horns; for all the rest is the direct outbirth and reflection
of our own age. . . .

The Quarterly Review 1842

BULWER-LYTTON

I seek no purfled prettiness of phrase,—
A soul in earnest scorns the tricks for praise.
If to my verse denied the Poet's fame,
This merit, rare to verse that wins, I claim;
No tawdry grace shall womanize my pen!
Ev'n in a love-song, man should write for men!
Not mine, not mine, (O Muse forbid!) the boon
Of borrowed notes, the mock-bird's modish tune,
The jingling medley of purloin'd conceits,
Outbaying Wordsworth, and outglittering Keats,
Where all the airs of patchwork-pastoral chime
To drowsy ears in Tennysonian rhyme!
Am I enthrall'd but by the sterile rule,
The formal pupil of a frigid school,

If to old laws my Spartan tastes adhere,
If the old vigorous music charms my ear,
Where sense with sound, and ease with weight combine,
In the pure silver of Pope's ringing line;
Or where the pulse of man beats loud and strong
In the frank flow of Dryden's lusty song?
Let School-Miss Alfred vent her chaste delight
On 'darling little rooms so warm and bright!'
Chaunt 'I'm aweary,' in infectious strain,
And catch her 'blue fly singing i' the pane.'
Tho' praised by Critics, tho' adored by Blues,
Tho' Peel with pudding plump the puling Muse,
Tho' Theban taste the Saxon's purse controuls,
And pensions Tennyson, while starves a Knowles,
Rather, be thou, my poor Pierian Maid,
Decent at least, in Hayley's weeds array'd,
Than patch with frippery every tinsel line,
And flaunt, admired, the Rag Fair of the Nine!

The New Timon   1846

[The reference to Peel's pudding is to the pension granted to Tennyson in 1845]

KINGSLEY

This deep simple faith in the divineness of Nature as she appears, which, in our eyes, is Mr Tennyson's differentia, is really the natural accompaniment of a quality at first sight its very opposite, and for which he is often blamed by a prosaic world; namely, his subjective and transcendental mysticism. It is the mystic, after all, who will describe Nature most simply, because he sees most in her; because he is most ready to believe that she will reveal to others the same message which she has revealed to him. Men like Behmen, Novalis, and Fourier, who can soar into the inner cloud-world of man's spirit, even though they lose their way there, dazzled by excess of wonder—men who, like Wordsworth, can give utterance to such subtle anthropologic wisdom as the *Ode on the Intimations of Immortality*, will for that very reason most humbly and patiently 'consider the lilies of the field, how they grow.' And even so it is just because Mr Tennyson is, far more than Wordsworth, mystical, and what an ignorant and money-getting generation, idolatrous of mere sensuous activity, calls 'dreamy', that he has become the greatest naturalistic poet which English has seen for several centuries. . . . No doubt there are in the earlier poems exceptions to this style—attempts to adorn nature, and dazzle with a barbaric splendour akin to that of Keats—as, for instance, in the *Recollections of the Arabian Nights.* But how cold and gaudy, in spite of individual beauties, is that poem by the side of either of the Marianas, and especially of the one in which the scenery is drawn, simply and faithfully, from those counties which the world considers the quintessence of the prosaic—the English fens. . . . Throughout all these exquisite lines occurs but one instance of what the vulgar call 'poetic diction.' All is simple description, in short and Saxon words, and yet who can deny the effect to be perfect —superior to any similar passage in Wordsworth? And why? Because the passage quoted, and indeed the whole poem, is perfect in what artists call tone—tone in the metre and in the sound of the words, as well as in the images and the feelings expressed. The weariness, the dreariness, the dark mysterious waste, exist alike within and without, in the slow monotonous pace of the metre and the words, as well as in the boundless fen, and the heart of her who, 'without hope of change, in sleep did seem to walk forlorn'. . . .

In saying that *Locksley Hall* has deservedly had so great an influence over the minds of the young, we shall, we are afraid, have offended some who are accustomed to consider the poem as Werterian and unhealthy. But, in reality, the spirit of the poem is simply anti-Werterian. It is man rising out of sickness into health—not conquered by Werterism, but conquering his selfish sorrow, and the moral and intellectual paralysis which it produces, by faith and hope—faith in the progress of science and civilisation, hope in the final triumph of good. Doubtless, that is not the highest deliverance—not a permanent deliverance at all. Faith in God and hope in Christ alone can deliver a man once and for all from Werterism, or any other moral disease; that truth was reserved for *In Memoriam*: but as far as *Locksley Hall* goes, it is a step forward—a whole moral aeon beyond Byron and Shelley; and a step, too, in the right direction, just because it is a step forward—because the path of deliverance is, as *Locksley Hall* sets forth, not backwards towards a fancied paradise of childhood—not backwards to grope after an unconsciousness which is now impossible, an implicit faith which would be unworthy of the man, but forward on the road on which God has been leading him, carrying upward with him the aspirations of childhood, and the bitter experience of youth, to help the organised and trustful labour of manhood. There are, in fact, only two deliverances from Werterism possible in the nineteenth century; one is into Popery, and the other is—

> Forward, forward, let us range;
> Let the peoples spin for ever down the ringing grooves
>   of change;
> Through the shadow of the world we sweep into the
>   younger day:
> Better fifty years of Europe than a cycle of Cathay. . . .

It has been often asked why Mr Tennyson's great and varied powers had never been concentrated on one immortal work. The epic, the lyric, the idyllic faculties, perhaps the dramatic also, seemed to be all there, and yet all sundered, scattered about in small fragmentary poems. *In Memoriam*, as we think, explains the paradox. Mr Tennyson had been employed on higher, more truly divine, and yet more truly human work than either epos or drama. Within the unseen and alone truly Real world which underlies and explains this mere time-shadow, which men miscall the Real, he has been going down into the depths, and ascending into the heights, led, like Dante of old, by the guiding of a mighty spirit. And in this volume, the record of seventeen years, we have the result of those spiritual experiences in a form calculated, as we believe, to be a priceless benefit to many an earnest seeker in this generation, and perhaps to stir up some who are priding themselves on a cold dilettantism and barren epicurism, into something like a living faith and hope. Blessed and delightful it is to find, that even in these new ages the creeds which so many fancy to be at their last gasp, are still the final and highest succour, not merely of the peasant and the outcast, but of the subtle artist and the daring speculator. Blessed it is to find the most cunning poet of our day able to combine the complicated rhythm and melody of modern times with the old truths which gave heart to martyrs at the stake; and to see in the science and the history of the nineteenth century new and living fulfilments of the words which we learnt at our mother's knee. . . .

. . . all Mr Tennyson's instinctive choice of tone, his mastery of language, which always fits the right word to the right thing, and that word always the simplest one, and the perfect ear for melody which makes it superfluous to set to music poetry which, read by the veriest schoolboy, makes music of itself. The poem [*The Princess*], we are glad to say, is so well known that it seems unnecessary to quote from it; yet there are here and there gems of sound and expression of which, however well our readers may know them, we cannot forbear reminding them again. For instance, the end of the idyl in book vii. beginning 'Come down, O maid' (the whole of which is perhaps one of the most perfect fruits of the poet's genius):

> Myriads of rivulets hurrying through the lawn,
> The moan of doves in immemorial elms,
> And murmuring of innumerable bees.

Who, after three such lines, will talk of English as a harsh and clumsy language, and seek in the effeminate and monotonous Italian for expressive melody of sound? Who cannot hear in them the rapid rippling of the water, the stately calmness of the wood-dove's note, and, in the repetition of short syllables and soft liquids in the last line, the

> Murmuring of innumerable bees?

Tennyson 1850

ANON

Tennyson is the most *modern* of poets, that is, of great poets, and in the broad and permanent aspects of what constitutes us modern. Lesser poets may represent more vividly the transient phases, the accidents of the passing time; but it is Tennyson who gives us back the true characteristics in small as well as in great matters. His *air* is modern. He dispenses with the old formalities thought necessary to poetry. He has cast the ancient costume. His dress is to the old forms what a wide-awake and easy morning coat is to a wig and claret velvet suit, or the high hat and tight pantaloons of the Regency. He has the free *insouciant* demeanour characteristic of modern society; but of English society,—never American. . . .

There is a dreamy, indolent air about Tennyson's poetry, an evident want of tonic in the system, which, again, is quite in accordance with the temper of his times. His sympathy is wide and warm, but it is that of the conviction and the conscience, rather than of the will. His poetry—take his political and social allusions, for instance—is full of the indications of noble instincts and true philosophy; but it comparatively interests itself little in right deeds. How rarely he deals with action at all! States of feeling, existing moods, quiescence; this is his natural ground. . . .

When we say Tennyson shares a vice of his age in being morbid, we use a current phrase which we suppose carries something of a common impression to us all, but which nobody dares to define very clearly. Perhaps we mean that he and all of us have a perverted tendency to take an undue interest, and exaggerate the importance of particular aspects of things which are such as lie apart from our wholesome, every-day life, the natural bent of our feelings, and the just and regular subjects of our attention. There is a trace of this in Tennyson's earlier writings here and there, and *Maud* overflows with it. If it be said that the poem is expressly devoted to the delineation of morbid character, the answer is, that a morbid tendency must have guided such a selection of a subject for art, and moreover that the treatment of it is morbid. . . .

Popular opinion is false enough in its transitory expressions; the plaudits accorded to Alexander Smith are valueless; the neglect suffered by Beddoes is inconclusive; but it can measure a man *against himself* pretty accurately. It is now pronouncing a very unmistakeable judgement on the merits of Mr Tennyson's last production. There may be some immediate exaggeration in the tone of the condemnation, yet we cannot doubt that in the main it will be confirmed by that ultimate public estimate, which is neither the voice of the loudest nor of the most numerous, but which sooner or later expresses what the men competent to think really do think,—the unbiased and deliberate judgement of a man's peers. This beats like death at every gate, and strikes with as unsparing an arrow. More credit will probably, after a little time has elapsed, be given for the beauties which *Maud* undoubtedly does contain; yet it must always stand as a heavy item on the debtor side of his reputation account. No other man could have written it at all: no one would have supposed that its author could have written it so ill. It abounds with scintillations of his genius, but the whole imaginative form is so confused and shapeless, the body of thought so valueless, and the execution on the whole so poor and degenerate, that his most earnest admirers must find it impossible to read it with pleasure. . . .

The blind raving against peace in *Maud may* be only dramatic, but it is in such a form as not to be distinguishable by any one from the approved sentiments of the author, and is a poor contribution from the great popular poet of his day, to a cause which demands the greatest strength and most persistent resolution of which England is capable, standing as she does the harassed upholder of a difficult cause, between a powerful foe and a distrusted and incompetent guidance. . . . Tennyson gives an exaggerated expression to the mere warspirit, and no prominence to the cause and principles involved, which alone can make war a duty and a blessing. In so doing he is echoing back and furthering one of the worst evils of a war—the danger that it should be loved for its own sake; an evil only less than that of passing by great duties, and sacrificing great interests, for the mere dread of the sufferings it brings, and from a cowardly and interested regard for peace. . . .

We earnestly trust that *Maud* indicates only some sudden

and passing perversion of taste and judgment; that it is the symptom of an acute seizure, not of a chronic failing; and that one to whom the English language is already so deeply indebted, has still the power and the will to add some things worthy of his genius and his fame.

The National Review 1855

ARNOLD

From the extracts I have seen from *Maud*, he seems in his old age to be coming to your manner in the Bothie and the Roman poem. That manner, as you know, I do not like: but certainly, if it is to be used, you use it with far more freedom, vigour and abundance than he does—Altogether I think this volume a lamentable production, and like so much of our literature thoroughly and intensely *provincial*, not European.

Letter to Clough 1855

... By the time you come I hope ... to be well plunged in the Middle Age. I have a strong sense of the irrationality of that period, and of the utter folly of those who take it seriously, and play at restoring it; still, it has poetically the greatest charm and refreshment possible for me. The fault I find with Tennyson in his *Idylls of the King* is that the peculiar charm and aroma of the Middle Age he does not give in them. There is something magical about it, and I will do something with it before I have done. The real truth is that Tennyson, with all his temperament and artistic skill, is deficient in intellectual power; and no modern poet can make very much of his business unless he is pre-eminently strong in this.

Letter to his sister 1860

ANON

We think that Mr Tennyson's remarkable subjection to present and external influences explains, in some degree, both his empire over some, and the indifference to his poetry of other by no means less able judges. We have seen, for instance, in *Maud*, how his political morality can be warped by a gust of war. His taste follows the fashion of the time, whether for great exhibitions or Gothic manor houses. Even the question of women's 'rights,' which we hope will have its death as well as birth in our generation, could draw from him a poem that was not, as we should have anticipated, a satire, but an elaborate adjustment of modern flirtation. His preaching, and he is fond of preaching, is tinged by the cheerful paganism of muscular divinity, while his exaltation of doubt above dogma betrays the temper of modern criticism. In short, the age governs Mr Tennyson's utterances, which are the accepted expression of its complex fashions. It is true, they gain in their passage through the refining fire of his almost perfect taste or undoubted originality—at least of form; for if Mr Tennyson be not among the chief creators, he is supreme in his command of beauty. Eminently sensitive to the ideas of his time, he reflects them to us in a magic mirror which hides the deformities and enhances the excellences of the world in which he moves. The inhabitants of that world naturally love him as their spokesman, and all who care for perfect presentation of the floating sentiment of his age and country, must praise him loudly. His rare culture pleases educated minds, the music of his verse appeals to those who love the harmonies of our Elizabethan English. His minute touches, when he describes landscape, suit modern tendencies of art. His psychological studies, though purged from superficial faults, have the same characteristics as modern romance. In the latest of his publications we find with regret the violent situations which our new school of fiction delights in, and at the same time a morbid anatomy of motive with a somewhat unreal morality. . . .

Enchanted as we were by glimpses of Arthur's court, should we have read a long epic that sang of that dim past? Mr Tennyson gratifies our *dilettanti* enthusiasm for the faith, and loyalty, and high standard of morality, which, if not adhered to, was at least not foresworn by the crusaders; but he relieves his studies of past costume by a constant return to English hearths, just as he mingles with his classic outlines of Greek forms sketches of modern manners. He is the

thorough representative of our eclectic culture in his fragmentary publications; nor does he neglect the strictly modern
production of rural poetry. He shakes hands with farmers and
labourers as warmly as any Coningsby need, though it be with
the languor of an amateur who studies the picturesqueness of
poverty and avoids the near approach of its squalor. We think
the wide range of Mr Tennyson's subjects has been unfavourable to the beauty of his poems. He gives us a congeries of
studies rather than a harmonious picture. The very completeness of details proves his accurate memory rather than
his truth of poetic vision. The central interest of his pictures is
injured sometimes by the finish of his accessories. . . .

British Quarterly Review 1864

HOPKINS

You call Tennyson 'a great outsider'; you mean, I think,
to the soul of poetry. I feel what you mean, though it grieves
me to hear him depreciated, as of late years has often been
done. Come what may he will be one of our greatest poets.
To me his poetry appears 'chryselephantine'; always of
precious mental material and each verse a work of art, no
botchy places, not only so but no half wrought or low-toned
ones, no drab, no brown-holland; but the form, though fine,
not the perfect artist's form, not equal to the material. When
the inspiration is genuine, arising from personal feeling, as in
In Memoriam, a divine work, he is at his best, or when he is
rhyming pure and simple imagination, without afterthought,
as in the *Lady of Shalott*, *Sir Galahad*, the *Dream of Fair
Women*, or *Palace of Art*. But the want of perfect form in the
imagination comes damagingly out when he undertakes
longer works of fancy, as his Idylls: they are unreal in motive
and incorrect, uncanonical so to say, in detail and keepings.
He shd. have called them *Charades from the Middle Ages*
(dedicated by permission to H.R.H. etc). The Galahad of one
of the later ones is quite a fantastic charade-playing trumpery
Galahad, merely playing the fool over Christian heroism.
Each scene is a triumph of language and of bright picturesque,
but just like a charade—where real lace and good silks and

real jewelry are used, because the actors are private persons and wealthy, but it is acting all the same and not only so but the make-up has less pretence of correct keeping than at Drury Lane. His opinions too are not original, often not independent even, and they sink into vulgarity: not only *Locksley Hall* but *Maud* is an ungentlemanly row and *Aylmer's Field* is an ungentlemanly row and the *Princess* is an ungentlemanly row. To be sure this gives him vogue, popularity, but not that sort of ascendancy Goethe had or even Burns, scoundrel as the first was, not to say the second; but then they spoke out the real human rakishness of their hearts and everybody recognised the really beating, though rascal, vein. And in his rhetorical pieces he is at his worst, as the *Lord of Burleigh* and *Lady Clare Vere de Vere* (downright haberdasher). But for all this he is a glorious poet and all he does is chryselephantine.

Letter to R. W. Dixon 1879

SWINBURNE

M. Taine's impeachment of Lord Tennyson's great monumental poem, *In Memoriam*, as the cold and correct work of a 'perfectly gentlemanlike' mourner, who never can forget to behave himself respectably and carry his grief like a gentleman conscious of spectators, may be classed for perfection of infelicity with Jeffrey's selection of the finest lines in Wordsworth's finest ode for especially contemptuous assault on the simple charge of sheer nonsense. Had he reserved his attack for the pretentiously unpretentious philosophy of the book, we might not so assuredly have felt that his hand had lost its cunning. Lord Tennyson is so ostentatious of his modesty, so unsparing in his reserve, so incessant and obstrusive in his disclaimer of all ambition to rank as a thinker or a teacher, while returning again and yet again to the charge as an ethical apostle or a sentimental theosophist, that we are almost reminded of the philosopher whose vociferous laudation of the dumb, and ear-splitting inculcation of silence, might seem to all half-deafened hearers enough to 'crack his lungs, and split his brazen pipe'—if such a thing might have been possible.

I trust it may be held allowable and compatible with loyalty
to observe that it is hardly reasonable to touch repeatedly
and with obvious earnestness on the gravest and the deepest
questions of life and death, of human affection and mortal
bereavement—to pour forth page upon page of passionate
speculation, of love and fear and hope and doubt and belief,
and then to turn round on the student to whose sympathy
the book—if there be any reason whatever for its existence or
publication—must surely be supposed to appeal, with the
surely astonishing protest that it does not pretend to grapple
with the questions on which it harps and the mysteries of which
it treats. The fitfulness of a mourner's mood will hardly be
held as a sufficient excuse to justify or to reconcile such incompatible incoherencies of meditation and profession. To say
that these effusions of natural sorrow make no pretence, and
would be worthy of contempt if they pretended, to solve or
satisfy men's doubts—and then to renew the appearance of an
incessant or even a fitful endeavour after some such satisfaction
or solution—is surely so incongruous as to sound almost
insincere. But the possession of a book so wholly noble and so
profoundly beautiful in itself is more precious than the most
coherent essay towards the solution of any less insoluble
problem.

Towards the Morte d'Albert, or Idylls of the Prince
Consort, I should almost equally regret to seem desirous of
playing the aforesaid part of devil's advocate. The most mealy-
mouthed critic or the most honey-tongued flatterer of Lord
Tennyson cannot pretend or profess a more cordial and
thankful admiration than I have always felt for the exquisite
magnificence of style, the splendid flashes of episodical
illumination, with which those poems are vivified or adorned.
But when they are presented to us as a great moral and poetic
whole, the flower at once of all epics and all ethics—

Cette promotion me laisse un peu rêveur.

I do not think much of Alfred de Musset as a shepherd of
souls or a moral philosopher: but I should feel very sincere
pity for a generation which felt itself obliged to fall back upon

the alternative ideal here proposed by Alfred Tennyson. A writer in a contemporary review dropped once an observation on this matter which struck me as so scientifically remarkable that I made a note of it for possible future service . . . that its moral tone was over highly pitched. We live and learn in this world: there never was a truer saying. But I should myself, I must needs confess, as soon have expected to hear that the *Memoirs of Casanova* or the *Adventures of Faublas* had ever been attacked on the score of too exalted a morality. Among all poems of serious pretensions in that line, it had appeared to the infirmity of my judgment that this latest epic of King Arthur took the very lowest view of virtue, set up the very poorest and most pitiful standard of duty or of heroism for woman or for man. To abstain from talking scandal or listening to it is a moral principle which I sincerely wish were more practically popular than it is: and ever since the first edition of *The Princess* . . . Lord Tennyson has missed few opportunities of announcing it with emphatic if not virulent iteration. But the lesson of abstinence from promiscuous tattle can hardly be considered by itself as 'the law and the gospel.' And whatever else there is of sound doctrine in Lord Tennyson's *Idylls* was preached more simply and not less earnestly in that grand old compilation of Sir Thomas Mallory. But, says the Laureate, it is not Mallory's King Arthur, nor yet Geoffrey's King Arthur, that I have desired to reproduce: on the contrary, it is 'scarce other than' Prince Albert. And in that case, of course, there is no more room for discussion. All I can say is that most assuredly I never heard 'these Idylls' attacked on any moral ground but this: that the tone of divine or human doctrine preached and of womanly or manly character exalted in them, directly or indirectly, was poor, mean, paltry, petty, almost base; so utterly insufficient as to be little short of ignoble: that it is anything but a sign of moral elevation to be so constantly preoccupied by speculations on possible contact with 'smut' and 'contamination from swine' (14): that Byron for one and Musset for another have been violently reviled and virtuously condemned on the charge of handling subjects very much less offensive than the stimulation and seduction of torpid and reluctant senility by the cajoleries and caresses of a lissom Vivien: that the tone of the original 'eleventh book,' once 'picked from the fire,' and now most incongruously incorporated with an incompatible mass of new matter, was incomparably higher, finer, manlier, than the Albertine ideal of later days. . . .

. . . with all due admiration for the genuine patriotism of his 'ballad of the fleet' and *Defence of Lucknow,* I must be permitted to observe that his general tone of thought and utterance on large questions of contemporary national history is such as might with admirable propriety find such expression as it finds at the close of *The Princess* from the lips, not even of 'the Tory member,' but of the Tory member's undergraduate son—supposing that young gentleman to be other for the nonce than a socialist. There is a strain, so to speak, as of beardless bluster about it, which could by no possible ingenuity have been so rendered as to suggest a more appropriate mouthpiece. It has the shrill unmistakeable accent, not of a provincial deputy, but of a provincial schoolboy. And this fact, it would seem, was revealed to Lord Tennyson himself, of all men on earth, by some freak of the same humorous if malicious fairy who disclosed to him the not less amusing truth, and induced him to publish it, with a face of unwonted gravity, to the nation and the world, that whenever he said 'King Arthur' he meant Prince Albert. No satirist could have ventured on either stroke of sarcasm. . . .

There are whole poems of Lord Tennyson's first period which are no more properly to be called metrical than the more shapeless and monstrous parts of Walt Whitman. . . . At times, of course, his song was then as sweet as ever it has sounded since; but he could never make sure of singing right for more than a few minutes or stanzas. The strenuous drill through which since then he has felt it necessary to put himself has done all that hard labour can do to rectify this congenital complaint: by dint of stocks and backboard he has taught himself a more graceful and upright carriage. . . .

But for one thing, and that a thing of great price, this hard-working poet had never any need to work hard. Whatever the early imperfection of his ear, no man was ever born with a truer and more perfect eye. During fifty years he has never given us a book without unquestionable evidence of this. Among his many claims and credentials as a poet, there is none more unimpeachable or more clear. Nor can any kind of study be more helpful or delightful to the naturally elect student of poetry than that which traces through the work of any poet the vein of colour or of sentiment derived from his earliest or deepest impressions of nature.

Tennyson and Musset 1880

ANON

If this synopsis of Lord Tennyson's new poem [*Locksley Hall Sixty Years After*] seem somewhat incoherent, the fault is not altogether ours. Sequent reasoning is no part of his method. His thought proceeds by fits and starts, or rather it swoops and circles round its subject like a strong-winged bird. The topical song-writers of the music-halls are not careful about their transitions from subject to subject; and the new *Locksley Hall* is a glorified topical song. It is not our part in this place (15) to attack or defend the views advanced— views, we repeat, which may or may not be strictly the poet's own—but whatever their intrinsic worth, novelty forms no part in it. The criticism which accepts Lord Tennyson as a great thinker or even a second-rate thinker is long ago exploded. He is not a thinker, but an utterer of thought. He neither digs nor sifts the ore, but he stamps it into clear-cut, weighty, ringing coin. From his mint come hundreds of the noblest and loveliest pieces in our intellectual currency of today; and no one can doubt that his new poem will add to the store . . . lapses are rare, while on the other hand there are many lines so perfect that they glide into the memory like things fore-ordained, for which we have been waiting from of old.

Pall Mall Gazette 1886

LESLIE STEPHEN

When Tennyson is presented to us as giving the true solution of the doubts which beset our time, we should have some positive as well as negative testimony to his merits. We cannot, it is true, expect a full solution. A gentleman is reported to have asked him whether the existence of evil was not the great difficulty. Tennyson certainly could not be expected to throw much light upon Job's difficulties, and seems to have judiciously diverted the conversation by referring to the 'charge of the heavy brigade'. No poet, and indeed no philosopher, can be asked to solve the eternal problems off-hand. What we do see, is that Tennyson, like many noble and deep thinkers, was terribly perplexed by the alternatives apparently offered: by his aversion on one side to certain orthodox dogmas, and by his dread and hatred of some tendencies which claim at least to be scientific. His ideal hero was the man who faced doubts boldly and attained clear convictions of one kind or other. On the other hand, he is always haunted by the fear of depriving your sister of her 'happy views' (a woefully feeble phrase, by the way, for Tennyson), and praises a philosopher for keeping his doubts to himself. The resulting attitude of mind may not be morbid: certainly it may fairly be called pathetic, and even those who do not sympathise with his doctrine will do well to feel for his distress. It may teach them, at least, what is in any case worth knowing: why their teaching is so repulsive to many tender and delicate minds. But I confess to share Carlyle's regret for the loss of the old heroic tone of the 'Ulysses.' Noble poetry, let us admit, may express either faith or scepticism; a conviction that we know or that we can never know; it may be openly pessimistic, or expressive of an enthusiastic faith in the future; but Tennyson, even in the *In Memoriam*, always seems to me to be like a man clinging to a spar left floating after a shipwreck, knowing that it will not support him, and yet never able to make up his mind to strike out and take his chance of sinking or swimming. That may be infinitely affecting, but it is not the attitude of the poet who can give a war-cry to his followers, or of the philosopher who really dares to 'face the spectres of the mind.'

Studies of a Biographer   1899

HENRY JAMES

[The writer had been taken by his friend, Mrs Greville, to luncheon with Lord Tennyson at Aldworth in 1878]

... it was a large and simple and almost empty occasion; yet empty without embarrassment, rather as from a certain high guardedness or defensiveness of situation, literally indeed from the material, the local sublimity, the fact of our all upliftedly hanging together over one of the grandest sweeps of view in England. Remembered passages again people, however, in their proportion, the excess of opportunity; each with that conclusive note of the outright all unadorned. What could have partaken more of this quality for instance than the question I was startled to hear launched before we had left the table by the chance of Mrs Greville's having happened to mention in some connection one of her French relatives, Mademoiselle Laure de Sade? It had fallen on my own ear— the mention at least had—with a certain effect of unconscious provocation; but this was as nothing to its effect on the ear of our host. 'De Sade?' he at once exclaimed with interest— and with the consequence, I may frankly add, of my wondering almost to ecstasy, that is to the ecstasy of curiosity, to what length he would proceed. He proceeded admirably—admirably for the triumph of simplification—to the very greatest length imaginable, as was signally promoted by the fact that clearly no one present, with a single exception, recognised the name or the nature of the scandalous, the long ignored, the at last all but unnameable author; least of all the gentle relative of Mademoiselle Laure, who listened with the blankest grace to her friend's enumeration of his titles to infamy, among which that of his most notorious work was pronounced. It was the homeliest, frankest, most domestic passage, as who should say, and most remarkable for leaving none of us save myself, by my impression, in the least embarrassed or bewildered; largely, I think, because of the failure—a failure most charmingly flat—of all measure on the part of auditors and speaker alike of what might be intended or understood, of what, in fine, the latter was talking about.

He struck me in truth as neither knowing nor communicating knowledge, and I recall how I felt this note in his own case to belong to that general intimation with which the whole air was charged of the want of proportion between the great spaces and reaches and echoes commanded, the great eminence attained, and the quantity and variety of experience supposable. So to discriminate was in a manner to put one's hand on the key, and thereby to find one's self in presence of a rare and anomalous, but still scarcely the less beautiful fact. The assured and achieved conditions, the serenity, the security, the success, to put it vulgarly, shone in the light of their easiest law—that by which they emerge early from the complication of life, the great adventure of sensibility, and find themselves determined once for all, fortunately fixed, all consecrated and consecrating. If I should speak of this impression as that of glory without history, that of the poetic character more worn than paid for, or at least more saved than spent, I should doubtless much over-emphasise; but such, or something like it, was none the less the explanation that met one's own fond fancy of the scene after one had cast about for it. For I allow myself thus to repeat that I was so moved to cast about, and perhaps at no moment more than during the friendly analysis of the reputation of M. de Sade. Was I not present at some undreamed-of demonstration of the absence of the remoter real, the real other than immediate and exquisite, other than guaranteed and enclosed, in landscape, friendship, fame, above all in consciousness of awaited and admired and self-consistent inspiration? . . .

But it was later on, when, my introductress having accompanied us, I sat upstairs with him in his study, that he might read to us some poem of his own that we should venture to propose, it was then that mystifications dropped, that everything in the least dislocated fell into place, and that image and picture stamped themselves strongly and finally, or to the point even, as I recover it, of leaving me almost too little to wonder about. He had not got a third of the way through *Locksley Hall*, which, my choice given me, I had made bold to suggest he should spout—for I had already heard him spout in Eaton Place—before I had begun to wonder that I didn't

K

wonder, didn't at least wonder more consumedly; as a very little while back I should have made sure of doing on any such prodigious occasion. I sat at one of the windows that hung over space, noting how the windy, watery autumn day, sometimes sheeting it all with rain, called up the dreary, dreary moorland or the long dun wolds; I pinched myself for the determination of my identity and hung on the reader's deep-voiced chant for the credibility of his: I asked myself in fine why, in complete deviation from everything that would have seemed from far back certain for the case, I failed to swoon away under the heaviest pressure I had doubtless ever known the romantic situation bring to bear. So lucidly all the while I considered, so detachedly I judged, so dissentingly, to tell the whole truth, I listened; pinching myself, as I say, not at all to keep from swooning, but much rather to set up some rush of sensibility. It was all interesting, it was at least all odd; but why in the name of poetic justice had one anciently heaved and flushed with one's own recital of the splendid stuff if one was now only to sigh in secret 'Oh dear, oh dear'? The author lowered the whole pitch, that of expression, that of interpretation above all; I heard him, in cool surprise, take even more out of his verse than he had put in, and so bring me back to the point I had immediately and privately made, the point that he wasn't Tennysonian. I felt him as he went on and on lose that character beyond repair, and no effect of the organ-roll, of monotonous majesty, no suggestion of the long echo, availed at all to save it. What the case came to for me, I take it—and by the case I mean the intellectual, the artistic—was that it lacked the intelligence, the play of discrimination, I should have taken for granted in it, and thereby, brooding monster that I was, born to discriminate *à tout propos*, lacked the interest.

Detached I have mentioned that I had become, and it was doubtless at such a rate high time for that; though I hasten to repeat that with the close of the incident I was happily able to feel a new sense in the whole connection established. My critical reaction hadn't in the least invalidated our great man's being a Bard—it had in fact made him and left him more a Bard than ever: it had only settled to my perception as not before what a Bard might and mightn't be. The character was just a rigid idiosyncrasy, to which everything in the man conformed, but which supplied nothing outside of itself, and which above all was not intellectually wasteful or hetero-geneous, conscious as it could only be of its intrinsic breadth and weight.

The Middle Years   1917

[This passage is followed by the comment on Browning as a reader of his own poems on p. 332]

HAROLD NICOLSON

And thus, in that 'ever-moaning battle in the mist' which was the spiritual life of Tennyson, there were sudden pene-trating moments when he would obtain:—

A glimpse of that dark world where I was born;

when, once again, the 'old mysterious glimmer' would steal into his soul, and when, in a sombre flash of vision, he would see his life:—

> all dark and red—a tract of sand,
> And someone pacing there alone,
> Who paced for ever in a glimmering land,
>   Lit with a low large moon.

To the vibration of so sad a cadence I should wish to leave him, trusting that the ultimate impression, thus attuned, will prove more poignant and more durable than any hollow reverence for what was once admired. The age of Tennyson is past; the ideals which he voiced so earnestly have fallen from esteem. The day may come, perhaps, when the conventions of that century will once again inspire the thoughtful or animate the weak. But, for the moment, it is not through these that any interest can be evoked. And thus, if we consider it reason-able and right that Tennyson should also stand among the poets, let us, for the present, forget the delicate Laureate of a cautious age; the shallow thought, the vacant compromise;

the honeyed idyll, the complacent ode; let us forget the dulled
monochrome of his middle years, forget the magnolia and the
roses, the indolent Augusts of his island-home; forget the
laurels and the rhododendrons.

Let us recall only the low booming of the North Sea upon
the dunes; the grey clouds lowering above the wold; the moan
of the night wind on the fen; the far glimmer of marsh-pools
through the reeds; the cold, the half-light, and the gloom.

Tennyson 1923

AUDEN

In no other English poet of comparable rank does the bulk
of his work seem so clearly to be inspired by some single and
probably very early experience.

Tennyson's own description of himself as

> An infant crying in the night;
> An infant crying for the light:
> And with no language but a cry

is extraordinarily acute. If Wordsworth is the great English
poet of Nature, then Tennyson is the great English poet of the
Nursery, of

> *das ungewisse Licht von Nachmittagen*
> *in denen man sich furchtete als Kind,*

i.e., his poems deal with human emotions in their most
primitive states, uncomplicated by conscious sexuality or
intellectual rationalization. (No other poetry is easier, and
less illuminating, to psycho-analyse). . . .

Two admissions of Tennyson's, that the first poetry which
excited him was his own, and that at the age of five he used to
walk about saying 'Alfred', 'Alfred', are significant, as are his
lines on science.

> Let Science prove we are, and then
> What matters Science unto men.

Two questions: Who am I? Why do I exist? and the panic
fear of their remaining unanswered—doubt is much too

intellectual and tame a term for such a vertigo of anxiety—
seem to have obsessed him all his life. Why he should have
felt them so strongly and at such an early age we cannot, of
course, know, but it seems not unlikely that his experience
was similar to one described by Kierkegaard in his *Journals*.

> The greatest danger is not that his father or his tutor should
> be a free-thinker, not even his being a hypocrite. No, the
> danger lies in his being a pious, God-fearing man, and in
> the child being convinced thereof, but that he should
> nevertheless notice that deep in his soul there lies hidden an
> unrest which, consequently, not even the fear of God and
> piety could calm. The danger is that the child in that
> situation is almost provoked to draw a conclusion about
> God, that God is not infinite love.

But whatever the initiating cause, Tennyson became
conscious in childhood of Hamlet's problem, the religious
significance of his own existence. Emotions of early childhood are hard to express except accidentally because the
original events associated with them are not remembered.
Hallam's death, a repetition of the abandonment experience,
gave Tennyson the symbolic event which mobilized what he
had already suffered and gave his fear a focus and a *raison
d'être.* . . .

In this basic anxiety about his existence Tennyson is the
brother of another and greater nineteenth-century poet,
Baudelaire, and it may not be unrewarding to compare these
two figures, superficially so dissimilar yet fundamentally so
alike, the provincial Englishman with his terror of political
and domestic disorder and the cosmopolitan satanic dandy of
Paris. (16) These lines

> And crowds that stream from yawning doors,
>   And shoals of puckered faces drive;
>   Dark hulks that tumble half alive,
> And lazy lengths on boundless shores;

>   Bitter barmaid, waning fast!
>   See the sheets are on my bed.

He seems as one whose footsteps halt,
Toiling in immeasurable sand,
And o'er a weary sultry land,
    Far beneath a burning vault,
Sown in a wrinkle of the monstrous hill,
The city sparkles like a grain of salt.

Ask me no more: thy fate and mine are seal'd;
    I strove against the stream and all in vain;
    Let the great river take me to the main.
No more, dear love, for at a touch I yield;
                    Ask me no more

are closer in spirit to

Un damné descendant sans lampe,
Au bord d'un gouffre dont l'odeur
Trahit l'humide profondeur,
D'éternels escaliers sans rampe,

Le beau valet de cœur et la dame de pique
Causent sinistrement de leurs amours défunts.

Et mon esprit, toujours du vertige hanté,
Jalouse du néant l'insensibilité.
—Ah! ne jamais sortir des Nombres et des Êtres!

than to any other English poetry.

In their verse technique, both display the same musical ear and love of 'line.' (Pope is to Tennyson what Racine is to Baudelaire.) Both felt themselves to be exiles from a lost paradise, desert dwellers (the barren rocks and desolate fens of Tennyson correspond to the gas-lit Paris of Baudelaire); both shared the same nostalgia for the Happy Isles, *le vert paradis des amours enfantines*, to be reached only after long voyages over water; both imagine Eden in the same Rousseau-istic terms; i.e., as a place of natural innocence rather than supernatural illumination. . . .

Baudelaire was right in seeing that art is beyond good and evil, and Tennyson was a fool to try to write a poetry which would teach the Ideal; but Tennyson was right in seeing that an art which is beyond good and evil is a game of secondary importance, and Baudelaire was the victim of his own pride in persuading himself that a mere game was

> *le meilleur témoignage*
> *que nous puissions donner de notre dignité.*

Thus if Tennyson embarrasses us by picturing Paradise as an exact replica of Somersby Rectory or Torquay, he has at least a conception, however naive, of a *good* place, and does not, like Baudelaire, insist that its goodness and badness are unimportant, for all that matters is its novelty, to be attained at whatever cost by a cultivation of hysteria with delight and terror.

Introduction to Tennyson, A Selection   1946

Browning

Being now within a stone's throw of laying down the awkward duties of the anthologist, perhaps I may be forgiven for indulging, by way of a last fling, in some slight expression of my own opinions. Great care has been taken to keep them out of the other introductions in this volume, and to utter nothing but the generalities of accepted opinion, or at most very lightly to underline what emerged from the array of criticism before me.

This temptation, to try my hand at the business myself, is the stronger in the case of Browning, because I cannot help being conscious of a sort of critical vacuum around him. In some thirty years spent attentively on the fringes of the literary world there has come out to me not a single whisper of Browning mattering much to anyone in those solemn inner circles which revolve ceremonially around the Graven Imagery of modern poetry. If he has been mentioned at all, it has been in passing, and generally neither for praise or blame, but incidentally to the last degree. There would seem to be no 'Browning problem', no critical issue. For a whole generation, he has been left to the romantic publicity of that Wimpole Street job, and to his readers.

Readers he certainly has. The whole body of poetry-readers nowadays is but a small one, and a relatively large part of it is to be found in the upper forms of schools, in the English departments of universities and training colleges. It is here, in this relatively large part of the absolutely minute body, that Browning has his readers, that he gives his obviously genuine pleasure. And one can see why. The moods of youth will sometimes fall in with the melancholy languors of Tennyson's most personal note; but much more often they will respond to the vigour and impetus of Browning's characteristic zest for the surface of life. And Tennyson, when his personal note is not being heard, is a

*Bardic pomposity the more ridiculous (as Henry James so deli-
cately hinted) because it tottered and titubated on such high
stilts; the young never easily stomach false dignity. Browning,
on the other hand, and again in the light of James' penetrating
description, was 'as little as possible a Bard'. The fault into
which he characteristically falls is sheer tediousness. He can be
very boring, but not embarrassingly ridiculous. It is a fault,
moreover, into which he does not always fall. The best pieces from*
Men and Women *are nearly free from it;* St Praxed's Church
is, for what it does, a pretty compressed piece of writing.

*But when we read Browning are we reading poetry? Or are
we reading him primarily because it is poetry? Those are the
really dubious points, for it must be granted at once that with
many of his young readers the real attraction is in the incident,
the character, the gusto of the monologue. And this, after all, is
an attraction by no means special or proper to poetry, for it is
one shared with prose fiction, and also with drama.*

*It is precisely because he had moved so far into the proper
territory of the novel that he still has his readers; because he was
the Victorian poet who most completely fell in with—surrendered
to, if you like—this new and overwhelming literary impetus. And
it is for the same reason that his best critics are novelists like
Henry James and his friend Percy Lubbock. Their critical
weapons, sharpened in the first serious attack in Britain on the
problems of prose fiction, enabled them to analyse Browning
with a sureness and delicacy that was quite beyond their poetically
trained colleagues. They dissect his approach to character, his
presentation of it, both in its strengths and its limitations; and
they comment no less adequately on his 'philosophy of life',
his slightly shaky 'moral and intellectual standards'. But on his
'poetry' they are naturally less convincing. James has a fine
remark about 'the world of Expression at any cost'; and Lubbock
has a good, if only half-developed, point, about the 'fringe of
values, the associated harmonics, of the spoken word'. But between them they offer nothing more.*

*Lubbock's point, taken a little further, may enable us to
define more exactly what elements or aspects of poetry Browning
did not surrender, but firmly kept with him, as he made his
incursion into the territory of prose fiction. Above all, he kept*

K*

*the weapon of metre, as a norm of rhythmical movement to be
established in order that it could be on occasion disarrayed. And
by this norm of rhythm, and the disruptions which only a norm
makes possible, he was able to approximate on paper, with
remarkable closeness, to spoken English. The problem to be
solved here is, perhaps, one peculiar to English, or at least
peculiarly acute in our language. For in our natural speech, in
the only rounded fullness of which any language is ultimately
capable, we make enormous use of intonation, inflection, variations of vocal emphasis; and not merely as means of decoration
or amusement but as the essence of the communication. The
notation of mere writing, inadequate in principle and in all
languages, is therefore specially incapable of transferring
English speech to the dead and silent page. But something, even
much, can be done if this bare notation is supplemented by the
lavish and skilful management of metre, with its norms of rhythm
and its departures from them; by this means, the intonation, the
emphasis of the internal voice of the reader, can be made to fall,
as often as not, where the writer needs it to fall. And in this kind
of management Browning was so skilful and so lavish that any
young writer, either in prose or in verse, does well to take him as
a principal object of study. It is, I take it, tolerably clear that
Henry James learned from him not a little, and exactly in this
matter of spoken rhythms, of syntax flexibly moulded to the
intonations and emphases of the sounding voice. This is not to
say, of course, that we should try to write like Browning, or
even like James; only that there is much to be learned from both,
and from their remarkable connection. Lubbock's prose offers a
good example of the happier effects of such tuition, in its style
no less than its content.*

*But when we have noted that this element of poetry, at least,
Browning took with him into the foreign territory, we have
noted all. That special and magical cultivation of the word
itself, which in recent years has come to be regarded as the
distinctive weapon of poetry, he did not possess, and so could
not take with him. He possessed it neither in its Shakespearean
or Metaphysical form, of coruscating imagery, wit, and richness
of association, nor in that other form, even less definable, of
surface plainness resting directly upon a dense compression of*

feeling and thought, of which Jonson was an early example, Wordsworth a later and richer. And it is because the whole movement that we call modern poetry has rested on one or both of these highly special forms of imaginative wording that Browning counts for so little with those who make it. Nor is there any reason to suppose that he will come to play a larger part. For poetry, once prose fiction had occupied, or usurped, so much of its ancient provinces, in narrative and the depiction of character, has perforce—and no doubt rightly—concentrated its forces upon what it, and it alone, can do. And this happens to be the one thing that Browning could not do.

It is exactly this that seems to me to make his work so much deserving of study;—that it illustrates, and so clearly comments upon, that decisive shift which took place in his day between the territories held by the two chief forms of literature, those of poetry and of prose fiction. It was the shift noted, a little hesitantly, by Trollope—who might, if he wished, have had the material of The Ring and the Book *for prose fiction, for Browning offered it to him—but he 'couldn't manage it'. In that very interesting, and characteristically unclever chapter of the* Autobiography *on 'The Art of Fiction', Trollope points the contrast between poetry, widely respected, but little read, and fiction, widely read, but little respected, and he makes this puzzled protest: 'He who sits down to write his tale in prose does not dream that the poet's honour is within his reach;—but his teaching is of the same nature, and his lessons tend to the same end . . . and that will be the greatest teacher who will spread such truth the widest.' The fact, more outrageously stated, was that in the course of the nineteenth century poetry ceased to be the greatest literary force exerted upon the imagination of Britain; and what poetry had ceased to be, prose fiction became.*

It is in the light of this crucial change that is best seen that crisis in the nature and conception of poetry which seems to me to emerge so clearly from the whole of this collection of criticism. And it is illuminated for us, not only by the ultimate untenability of Tennyson's posture of the Sage who was also the Bard, but even more by Browning's desertion, so much more tenable, into the other camp;—on to 'the novelist's side of the street,' as

Henry James put it. The provinces, so to speak, and the forms of government, both of modern poetry and of the modern novel, are by implication defined in this parting of the ways between the two great Victorians. And the essential difference is, that while modern poetry has not much use for Tennyson, the modern novel has a great deal of use for Browning, much of which has still to be made.

BROWNING

Intelligence, by itself, is scarcely the thing with respect to a new book—as Wordsworth says (a little altered) 'You must like it before it be worthy of your liking.' In spite of your intelligence and sympathy, I can have but little doubt that my writing has been, in the main, too hard for many I should have been pleased to communicate with; but I never designedly tried to puzzle people, as some of my critics have supposed. On the other hand, I never pretended to offer such literature as should be a substitute for a cigar, or a game of dominoes, to an idle man. So perhaps, on the whole, I get my deserts and something over—not a crowd, but a few I value more.

Letter to W. G. Kingsland 1868

Come, critics,—not shake hands, excuse me!
But—say have you grudged to amuse me
This once in the forty-and-over
Long years since you trampled my clover
And scared from my house-eaves each sparrow
I never once harmed by that arrow

. . . .
. . . .

I was forging and filing and finishing,
And no whit my labours diminishing
Because, though high up in a chamber
Where none of your kidney may clamber
Your hullabaloo would approach me?
Was it 'grammar' wherein you would 'coach' me—
You,—pacing in even that paddock
Of language allotted you *ad hoc*,

With a clog at your fetlocks,—you—scorners
Of me free of all its four corners?
Was it 'clearness of words which convey thought?'
Ay, if words never needed enswathe aught
But ignorance, impudence, envy
And malice—what word-swathe would then vie
With yours for a clearness of crystalline?
But had you to put in one small line
Some thought big and bouncing—as noodle
Of goose, born to cackle and waddle
And bite at man's heel as goose-wont-is
Never felt plague its puny *os frontis*—
You'd know, as you hissed, spat and spluttered,
Clear cackle is easily uttered!

Of Pacchiarotto, XXVIII   1876

FOX

These thoughts have been suggested by the work before us,
which, though evidently a hasty and imperfect sketch, has
truth and life in it, which gave us the thrill, and laid hold of
us with the power, the sensation of which has never yet
failed us as a test of genius. Whoever the anonymous author
may be, he is a poet. A pretender to science cannot always be
safely judged of by a brief publication, for the knowledge of
some facts does not imply the knowledge of other facts; but
the claimant of poetic honours may generally be appreciated
by a few pages, often by a few lines, for if they be poetry, he
is a poet. We cannot judge of the house by the brick, but we
can judge of the statue of Hercules by its foot. We felt certain
of Tennyson, before we saw the book, by a few verses which
had straggled into a newspaper; we are not less certain of the
author of *Pauline*.

The author cannot expect such a poem as this to be
popular, to make 'a hit,' to produce a 'sensation.' The public
are but slow in recognising the claims of Tennyson, whom in
some respects he resembles; and the common eye scarcely
yet discerns among the laurel-crowned, the form of Shelley,

who seems (how justly, we stop not now to discuss) to have been the god of his early idolatry. Whatever inspiration may have been upon him from that deity, the mysticism of the original oracles has been happily avoided. And whatever resemblance he may bear to Tennyson (a fellow-worshipper probably at the same shrine), he owes nothing of perhaps the inferior melody of his verse to an employment of archaisms which it is difficult to defend from the charge of affectation. But he has not given himself the chance for popularity which Tennyson did, and which it is evident that he easily might have done. His poem stands alone, with none of those slight but taking accompaniments, songs that sing themselves, sketches that every body knows, light little lyrics, floating about like humming birds, around the trunk and foliage of the poem itself; and which would attract so many eyes, and delight so many ears, that will be slow to perceive the higher beauty of that composition, and to whom a sycamore is no sycamore, unless it be 'musical with bees.' That his not having done so, is owing to no want of the picturesque faculty; the grace, the sentiment which give their charm to such minor effusions, can soon be shown by a few quotations taken as they rise in the volume.

The Monthly Repository 1833

CARLYLE

Unless I very greatly mistake, judging from these two works [*Sordello* and *Pippa Passes*], you seem to possess a rare spiritual gift, poetical, pictorial, intellectual, by whatever name we may prefer calling it; to unfold which into articulate clearness is naturally the problem of all problems for you. This noble endowment, it seems to me farther, you are *not* at present on the best way for unfolding;—and if the world had loudly called itself content with these two Poems, my surmise is, the world could have rendered you no fataller disservice than that same! Believe me I speak with sincerity; and if I had not loved you well, I would not have spoken at all.

A long battle, I could guess, lies before you, full of toil and pain, and all sorts of real *fighting*: a man attains to nothing here below without that. Is it not verily the highest prize you fight for? Fight on; that is to say, follow truly, with steadfast singleness of purpose, with valiant humbleness and openness of heart, what best light *you* can attain to; following truly, so, better and ever better light will rise on you. The light we ourselves gain, by our very errors if not otherwise, is the only precious light. Victory, what I call victory, if well fought for, is sure to you.

If your own choice happened to point that way, I for one should hail it as a good omen that your next work were written in prose! Not that I deny your poetic faculty; far, very far from that. But unless poetic faculty mean a higher-power of common understanding, I know not what it means. One must first make a *true* intellectual representation of a thing, before any poetic interest that is true will supervene. All *cartoons* are geometrical withal; and cannot be made until we have fully learnt to make mere *diagrams* well. It is this that I mean by prose;—which hint of mine, most probably inapplicable at present, may perhaps at some future day come usefully to mind.

But enough of this: why have I written all this? Because I esteem yours no common case; and think such a man is not to be treated in the common way.

And so persist in God's name, as you best see and can; and understand always that my true prayer for you is, God Speed in the name of God!

Letter to Browning 1841

Of Browning's *Balaustion*, Carlyle said 'I read it all twice through, and found out the meaning of it. Browning most ingeniously twists up the English language into riddles— 'There! there is some meaning in this—can you make it out?' I wish he had taken to prose. Browning has far more ideas than Tennyson, but is not so truthful. Tennyson means what he says, poor fellow! Browning has a meaning in his twisted sentences, but he does not really go into anything, or believe much about it. He accepts conventional values.'

William Allingham: A Diary 1871

RUSKIN

Robert Browning is unerring in every sentence he writes of the Middle Ages; always vital, right and profound; so that in the matter of art, with which we have been specially concerned, there is hardly a principle connected with the mediaeval temper, that he has not struck upon in those seemingly careless and too rugged lines of his. . . .

[Commenting on *The Bishop orders his Tomb in St. Praxed's Church*] I know no other piece of modern English prose or poetry, in which there is so much told, as in these lines, of the Renaissance spirit,—its worldliness, inconsistency, pride, hypocrisy, ignorance of itself, love of art, of Luxury, and of good Latin. It is nearly all that I have said of the central Renaissance in thirty pages of the *Stones of Venice*, put into as many lines, Browning's also being the antecedent work. The worst of it is, that this kind of concentrated writing needs so much *solution* before the reader can fairly get the good of it, that people's patience fails them, and they give the thing up as insoluble; though truly, it ought to be, to the current of common thought, like Saladin's talisman dipped in clear water, not soluble altogether, but making the element medicinal.

Modern Painters 1843

HORNE

Containing, as it does, so many passages of the finest poetry, no manner of doubt can exist but that *Sordello* has been hitherto treated with great injustice. It has been condemned in terms that would lead any one to suppose that there was nothing intelligible throughout the whole poem. We have shown its defects in detail, and we have also shown that it has some of the highest beauties. The style, the manner, the broken measure, the recondite form; these have constituted still greater difficulties than even the recondite matter of which it treats—although the latter only were quite enough to 'settle' or 'unsettle' an ordinary reader. . . .

The poem of *Sordello* is a beautiful globe, which rolling on its way to its fit place among the sister spheres, met with some accident which gave it such a jar that a multitude of things half slipped into each other's places. It is a modern hieroglyphic, and should be carved on stone for the use of schools and colleges. Professors of poetry should decipher and comment upon a few lines every morning before breakfast, and young students should be *grounded* upon it. It is a fine mental exercise, whatever may be said or thought to the contrary. Here and there may be found passages equal to the finest things that were ever written, and are not more difficult to the understanding than those same finest things. It is also full of passages apparently constructed with a view to make the general reader rage and foam, if ever a general reader should push forth his adventurous boat out of sight of the shore of the first page—and out of sight it will surely appear to him before he has doubled the storm-rejoicing cape of page four. To some it will appear to be a work addressed to the perception of a seventh sense, or of a class of faculties which we do not at present know we possess. To others it will seem to be a work written in the moon by the only sane individual of that sphere, viz. the man of that ilk; or a work written by a poet somewhere in the earth by the light of a remote sun whose rays are unrevealed to other eyes. To some the most vexatious part of it will be the countless multitude of little abrupt snatches of questions, snaps of answers, and inscrutable exclamations, chirping around from every branch of a wilderness of a jungle of glimmering mysteries. To others the continual consciousness of the reader's presence will most annoy, because it destroys the ideal life, and reminds him of something far less agreeable—himself, and his distracting problem! The flowing familiar style sometimes reminds us of Shelley's *Julian and Maddalo* with a touch of Keats's *Endymion*, broken up into numerous pitfalls, whether mines of thoughts or quirks of fancy; but there are also other occasions when it becomes a spiral, and of sustained inspiration, not unlike certain parts of the *Prometheus Unbound* put into rhyme; yet it is no imitation of any other poet. Certain portions also remind us of the suggestive, voluble, disconnected, philosphical jargon of

Shakespeare's fools, and with all the meaning which they often have for those who can find it. The poem is thick-sown throughout with suggestions and glances of history and biography, of dark plots, tapestried chambers, eyes behind arras, clapping doors, dreadful galleries, and deeds in the dark, over which there suddenly bursts a light from on high, and looking up, you find a starry shower, as from some remote rocket, descending in silent brilliancy upon the dazzled page. Each book is full of gems set in puzzles. It is like what the most romantic admirers of Goethe insist upon 'making out' that he intended in his simplest fables. It is the poetical portion of three epics, shaken together in a sack and emptied over the hand of the intoxicated reader. It is a perfect storehouse of Italian scenery and exotic fruits, plants and flowers; so much so, that by the force of contrast it brings to mind the half-dozen flowers and pastoral commonplaces in collections of 'Beauties of English Poets', till the recollections of the sing-song repetitions makes one almost shout with laughter. It is pure Italian in all its materials. There is not one drop of British ink in the whole composition. Nay, there is no ink in it, for it is all written in Tuscan grape juice, embrowned by the sun. It abounds in things addressed to a second sight, and we are often required to *see double* in order to apprehend its meaning. The poet may be considered the Columbus of an impossible discovery. It is a promised land, spotted all over with disappointments, and yet most truly a land of promise, if ever so rich and rare a chaos can be developed into form and order by revision, and its southern fullness of tumultuous heart and scattered vineyards be ever reduced to given proportion, and wrought into shape that will fit the average mental vision and harmonize with the more equable pulsations of mankind.

A New Spirit of the Age   1844

ANON

Browning's *Paracelsus* is indeed one of the most remarkable, —one of the most poetically beautiful works, that has bene added for many years to our stores of national literature. A profundity of thought is displayed in it, almost unrivalled in the poetic creations of our countrymen; whilst the imaginativeness, the picturesque fancy of the illustrative comparisons, the tenderness of loving depth of soul developed in the characters of the drama, form a whole that must at once challenge high admiration for its grandeur and nobility, and heartfelt sympathy with its gentler beauties. . . . The poetry in which the drama is embodied is of the very highest order: worthy indeed of its author, for whom we scruple not to challenge admiration and acknowledgement, as the first poet of the day.

The Theologian 1845

ANON

The higher the poetry, the fuller, deeper, its spirit, the more consummate and individual its expression, the fewer those competent to receive and welcome it, and the greater the obstacles to its reception, even among these . . . Without study, actual *bona-fide* study, his [Browning's] poetry must remain *caviare* to the most intelligent reader . . . Yet, to our mind, this is a great and original poet . . . His poetic genius is essentially recondite; and its expression could be nothing less . . . his assuredly must rank as a new manifestation of poetic art. . . . Popular or not, he must be a poet after his own fashion, if at all . . . Those very poems, such as *Sordello, Pippa Passes*, in respect to which, the loudest complaints of obscurity have been raised, are precisely those in which the fullest wealth of poetry, the highest creative power, have been realized. . . . Robert Browning is not one whom we can recommend to the readers of poetry at their ease: gentlemen who would have their hour's amusement out of their poet . . . we should doubt whether any could be competent to speak of Browning, till having given him a *second* reading; or fully to estimate him till after, at least, three readings.

Eclectic Review 1849

FREDERICK TENNYSON

. . . Though I have the highest esteem for Browning, and believe him to be a man of infinite learning, jest and bonhomie, and moreover a sterling heart that reverbs no hollow-ness, I verily believe his school of poetry to be the most grotesque conceivable. With the exception of the *Blot on the Scutcheon*, through which you may possibly grope your way without the aid of an Ariadne, the rest appear to me to be Chinese puzzles, trackless labyrinths, unapproachable nebulo-sities. Yet he has a very catholic taste in poetry, doing justice to everything good in all poets past or present, and he is one who has a profound admiration of Alfred.

Letter 1854

BAGEHOT

We are fortunate in not having to hunt out of past literature an illustrative specimen of the ornate style. Mr Tennyson has just given one admirable in itself, and most characteristic of the defects and the merits of this style. The story of *Enoch Arden*, as he has enhanced and presented it, is a rich and splendid composite of imagery and illustration. Yet how simple that story is in itself! . . . Told in the pure and simple, the unadorned and classical style, this story would not have taken three pages, but Mr Tennyson has been able to make it the principal—the largest tale in his new volume. He has done so only by giving to every event and incident in the volume an accompanying commentary.

The description of the tropical island on which the sailor is thrown, is an absolute model of adorned art. . . . A much less happy instance is the description of Enoch's life before he sailed:—

> While Enoch was abroad on wrathful seas
> Or often journeying landward; for in truth
> Enoch's white horse, and Enoch's ocean spoil
> In ocean-smelling osier, and his face,
> Rough-reddened with a thousand winter gales,
> Not only to the market-cross were known,
> Far as the portal-warding lion-whelp,
> And peacock yew-tree of the lonely Hall,
> Whose Friday fare was Enoch's ministering.

So much has not often been made of selling fish. . . .

Ornate art is to pure art what a painted statue is to an unpainted. It is impossible to deny that a touch of colour does bring out certain parts; does convey certain expressions; does heighten certain features; but it leaves on the work as a whole a want . . . of that inseparable chasteness which clings to simple sculpture. . . .

. . . Ornate art, indeed, uses undue disguises and unreal enhancements; it does not confine itself to the best types . . . but ornate art, as much as pure art, catches its subject in the best light it can, takes the most developed aspect of it which it can find, and throws upon it the most congruous colours it can use. But grotesque art does just the contrary. It takes the type, so to say, *in difficulties*. It gives a representation of it in its minimum development, amid the circumstances least favourable to it, just while it is struggling with obstacles, just where it is encumbered with incongruities. It deals, to use the language of science, not with normal types but with abnormal specimens. . . .

Of this art we possess in the present generation one prolific master. Mr Browning is an artist working by incongruity. Possibly hardly one of his considerable efforts can be found which is not great because of its odd mixture. He puts together things which no one else would have put together, and produces on our minds a result which no one else would have produced, or tried to produce. His admirers may not like all we may have to say of him. But in our way we too are among his admirers. No one ever read him without seeing not only his great ability but his great *mind*. He not only possesses superficial useable talents, but the strong something, the inner secret something, which uses them and controls them; he is great not in mere accomplishments, but in himself. He has applied a hard strong intellect to real life; he has applied the same intellect to the problems of his age. He has striven to know what *is*: he has endeavoured not to be cheated by counterfeits, not to be infatuated with illusions. His heart is in what he says. He has battered his brain against his creed till he believes it. He has accomplishments too, the more effective because they are mixed. He is at once a student of mysticism and a citizen of the world. He brings to the club-sofa distinct visions of old

creeds, intense images of strange thoughts: he takes to the
bookish student tidings of wild Bohemia, and little traces of
the *demi-monde*. He puts down what is good for the naughty,
and what is naughty for the good. Over women his easier
writings exercise that imperious power which belongs to the
writings of a great man of the world upon such matters.
He knows women, and therefore they wish to know him. If
we blame many of Browning's efforts, it is in the interest of
art, and not from a wish to hurt or degrade him.

If we wanted to illustrate the nature of grotesque art by
an exaggerated instance, we should have selected a poem
which the chance of late publication brings us in this new
volume. Mr Browning has undertaken to describe what may
be called *mind in difficulties*—mind set to make out the universe
under the worst and hardest circumstances. He takes 'Caliban',
not perhaps exactly Shakespeare's Caliban, but an analogous
and worse creature; a strong thinking power, but a nasty
creature. . . . Caliban speaks in the third person, and is of
opinion that the maker of the Universe took to making it on
account of his personal discomfort:—

> Setebos, Setebos, and Setebos!
> 'Thinketh, He dwelleth i' the cold o' the moon.
> 'Thinketh, He made thereat the sun, this isle,
> Trees and the fowls here, beast and creeping thing.
> Yon otter, sleek-wet, black, lithe as a leech;
> Yon auk, one fire-eye, in a ball of foam,
> That floats and feeds; a certain badger brown
> He hath watched hunt with that slant white-wedge eye
> By moonlight; and the pie with the long tongue
> That pricks deep into oakwarts for a worm,
> And says a plain word when she finds her prize,
> But will not eat the ants; the ants themselves
> That build a wall of seeds and settled stalks
> About their hole—He made all these and more,
> Made all we see, and us, in spite: how else?

It may seem perhaps to most readers that these lines are
very difficult, and that they are unpleasant. And so they are.
We quote them to illustrate, not the *success* of grotesque art,

but the *nature* of grotesque art. It shows the end at which this species of art aims, and if it fails it is from over-boldness in the choice of subject by the artist, or from the defects of its execution. A thinking faculty more in difficulties—a great type—an inquisitive, searching intellect under more disagreeable conditions, with worse helps, more likely to find falsehood, less likely to find truth, can scarcely be imagined. Nor is the mere description of the thought at all bad: on the contrary, if we closely examine it, it is very clever. Hardly any one could have amassed so many ideas at once nasty and suitable. But scarcely any readers—any casual readers—who are not of the sect of Mr Browning's admirers will be able to examine it enough to appreciate it. From a defect, partly of subject and partly of style, many of Mr Browning's works make a demand upon the reader's zeal and sense of duty to which the nature of most readers is unequal. They have on the turf the convenient expression 'staying power': some horses can hold on and others cannot. But hardly any reader not of especial and peculiar nature can hold on through such composition. There is not enough of 'staying power' in human nature. One of his greatest admirers once owned to us that he seldom or never began a new poem without looking on in advance, and foreseeing with caution what length of intellectual adventure he was about to commence. Whoever will work hard at such poems will find much mind in them: they are a sort of quarry of ideas, but whoever goes there will find these ideas in such a jagged, ugly, useless shape that he can hardly bear them. . . .

Mr Browning possibly, and some of the worst of Mr Browning's admirers certainly will say that these grotesque objects exist in real life, and therefore they ought to be, at least may be, described in art. But though pleasure is not the end of poetry, pleasing is a condition of poetry. An exceptional monstrosity of horrid ugliness cannot be made pleasing except it be made to suggest—to recall—the perfection, the beauty, from which it is a deviation. Perhaps in extreme cases no art is equal to this; but then such self-imposed problems should not be worked out by the artist; these out-of-the-way and detestable subjects should be let alone by him. It is rather characteristic of Mr Browning to neglect this rule. He is the most of a realist, and the least of an idealist, of any poet we know. He evidently sympathises with some part at least of Bishop Blougram's apology. . . . He must have a creed that will *take*, which wins and holds the miscellaneous world, which stout men will heed, which nice women will adore. The spare moments of solitary religion—the 'obdurate questionings', the 'high instincts', the 'first affections', the 'shadowy recollections',

> Which, be they what they may,
> Are yet the fountain-light of all our day—
> Are yet the master-light of all our seeing

—the great but vague faith—the unutterable tenets—seem to him worthless, visionary; they are not enough 'immersed in matter'; they move about 'in worlds not realised'. . . .

But although a suspicion of beauty, and a taste for ugly reality, have led Mr Browning to exaggerate the functions and to caricature the nature of grotesque art, we own, or rather we maintain, that he has given many excellent specimens of that art within its proper boundaries and limits.

Wordsworth, Tennyson, and Browning; or, Pure, Ornate, and Grotesque Art in English Poetry 1864

ANON

We had intended in this article to have attempted some account of *Dramatis Personæ*, a production of the year that deserves equally thoughtful attention, if not equal admiration, with Mr Tennyson's volume; but it would be difficult and unfair to give a hurried analysis of such poems as Mr Browning's *Child of the Time*. Even more emphatically than Mr Tennyson, his treatment of modern thought is strangely different. Some of our remarks on *Enoch Arden* and its companion poems apply, we think, with even greater appropriateness to *Dramatis Personæ*. Mr Browning's art, however, often fails where that of Mr Tennyson is most perfect. The Laureate charms us by his scholarly grace, while Mr Browning vexes us by his ungraceful scholarship. If Mr Tennyson disappoints

us by being fragmentary, he is singularly lucid in language,
and avoids difficulties which he cannot perfectly surmount.
He cares to please and pleases. Mr Browning, on the other
hand, true to the manner of some modern intellects, rushes
into all manner of discussions, and breaks down Pegasus
with a load of metaphysics and popular heresies. He affects
scorn of the world, from which, nevertheless, he filches the
very ideas which he flings back, and with reckless and sometimes vulgar colloquialism, he roughly elbows his way to
celebrity. Different, however, as he is in manner to the polished
grace of Mr Tennyson, the phantasms that rise at his bidding
from the seething cauldron of our epoch have a certain likeness to Mr Tennyson's sedater personages. Mr Sludge, the
medium, hints at a spiritualism that is a caricature of Mr
Tennyson's delicate mystery. The natural theology of Caliban
echoes the Northern Farmer's judgement of the divine nature.
Rabbi ben Ezra preaches the Gospel of Doubt, which Mr
Tennyson says is superior to half the creeds. The *Death in the
Desert* is an answer to M. Renan which we can imagine might
have been given by Mr Tennyson, though probably in a less
metaphysical form.

We do not affect to institute any close comparison between
our chief living poet and his contemporaries, but we cannot
help seeing that they are like in a common reflection of their
time. Mr Browning, Owen Meredith, Miss Proctor, and Mr
Woolner, have at least this resemblance to one another, and
we confess that our era produces among its other fabrics a
large supply of pleasant verse. But even this wonderful nineteenth century cannot manufacture a poet with power to
create, and not merely to reflect. We look to our artists for
news of man, and we get clever sketches of Mr This and Mrs
That; we long to see the image of beauty, and we find the
shadows of Mr Tennyson and Mr Browning. We are ready to
admit that one is an earnest and ingenious thinker, and the
other is a graceful versifier and high-toned artist, but they
have on the whole the same ideas of life as we have ourselves,
and they versify for us what we know to be the popular
fashions of thought. Meantime the newspapers are delighted,
and repeat that everything is poetic, and that there is poetry

everywhere, for do not our best writers make charming idylls of our daily life? Enthusiastic people begin to think in all sincerity that Kensington Exhibitions and a Prince's Marriage, People's Parks and Metropolitan Railroads, are as good materials for an epic as the Siege of Troy or the Fall of Man. . . .

Yet, be realistic as we may, the condition of intellect that sees but its own reflection in all around interferes fatally with art, and particularly with poetic art. The minute detail that our writers and painters resort to does not, after all, satisfy our craving for truth; their realism is only imitative, and leaves no sense of certainty. We may burrow into old faiths and imitate old forms; we may use the obsolete language of passion to conceal our apathy, and praise action that we never attempt; but our art fails to convince us of any reality in its utterances. We cannot, be the skill of presentation ever so great, believe in truth and beauty that is of our own manufacture—idols that we have made at leisure. We go through a farce of worship before them, but after all we know how much our fabrications are worth, and our worship is more fashionable than sincere. We 'feed on ashes.'

British Quarterly Review   1864

ANON

Everything Browningish is found here—the legal jauntiness, the knitted argumentation, the cunning prying into detail, the suppressed tenderness, the humanity,—the salt intellectual humour . . . not open and social, like that of Dickens, but with a similar tendency.

Athenaeum   1868

ANON

Mr Browning has many detractors. His faults lie on the surface, are patent, nay obtrusive; and he that runs may read and—revile. We admit the faults and deplore them, while we recognise in Mr Browning qualities which assign him eminent rank in the intellectual order of men. Indeed, the best proof of the force and authority of his genius is the fact that in spite of the obscurity of his thoughts, the subtlety of his allusions, and the habitual rudeness of his versification, he has, after thirty-five years of persevering labour, caught the ear of the public, and won the sympathy of the most cultivated portion of the younger generation. It is idle to attribute this sort of success—which is a real influence—to the caprice of fashion, or the whims of perverted taste and judgment. Even those who are insensible to Mr Browning's merits as a poet, must acknowledge that he has produced on his time some of the effects which are commonly attributed to great poets; and that perhaps the greatest of his achievements is to have caused the world to take an interest in his own works. It may be worth while to consider, while we are fresh from the laborious but not unwelcome task of studying his last production, to what cause this amount of success is due.

Like the majority of poets, he is remarkable for a highly sensitive emotional nature, and, like some of the great poets only, he is at the same time and to an equal degree distinguished by the serenity of his intellect. He knows (had he written only *The Ring and the Book* he would have shown that he profoundly knows) human nature; familiar with all its gradations, from the 'poach'd filth' of its lowest depravity to the 'white blamelessness' that crowns as with inviolate snow its moral heights. Everywhere he reveals his love of what is noble, his hatred of what is ignoble; but he never loses the balance of an even mind in adjudicating praise or blame. Through human nature he discerns clearly the problem of human nature, the enigma of man's existence and destiny, that 'painful riddle of the earth' which has overthrown the calm and vanquished the courage of so many a noble mind. Although he confronts that problem always with deep earnestness, he displays something of an eager alacrity in grappling it; and he has never yet come sad and crestfallen from the encounter. To blend a profound knowledge of human nature, and a keen perception of the awful problem of human destiny, with the conservation of a joyous, hopeful spirit—to know men and not despair of them, to battle with men's spiritual foes and not be broken by them

—is given only to the very strong. This is to be a valiant and unvanquished soldier of humanity. . . .

We will now lay aside the prism with which we have made some attempt to analyse the light of the sunbeam, in order that we may see the motes in it. They are proverbially numerous: so are Mr Browning's faults. As we do not, however, care to indite—nor, we suppose, our readers to peruse—a complete inventory of all the faults inherent or assigned to the most original of modern poets, we will deal only with what we think the most striking of his literary defects. The first of these which we notice, and it is a cardinal one, is due to a profuseness, and consequent prolixity, both of thought and language, which, while evidencing abundance of ideas and amplitude of vocabulary, indicates a lamentable deficiency in the mental faculty of concentration and in the moral quality of reticence. This double deficiency seriously interferes with Mr Browning's artistic power. It is but rarely that he gives to his work anything like finish; and while he shows his appreciation of the aesthetic value of completeness by the striking line,

Artistry's haunting curse, the Incomplete,

he seems to do his best to call the curse upon his own handiwork. Whether we regard his poems in their integrity, in separate sections, or in particular passages, we constantly find the artistic effect missed or marred by an apparent inability to discriminate the point at which sufficiency is reached.

The Edinburgh Review 1869

TENNYSON

On rare occasions my father would rally Browning playfully on his harshness of rhythm, the obscurity and length of his poems. The retort would be: 'I cannot alter myself: the people must take me as they find me.' My father would repeat his usual dictum about literary work: 'An artist should get his workmanship as good as he can, and make his work as

perfect as possible. A small vessel, built on fine lines, is likely
to float further down the stream of time than a big raft.'
They would laugh heartily together at Browning's faculty for
absurd and abstruse rhymes.

1875

'Browning', he said, 'never greatly cares about the glory
of words or beauty of form: he has told me that the world
must take him as it finds him. As for his obscurity in his great
imaginative analyses, I believe it is a mistake to explain
poetry too much, people have really a pleasure in discovering
their own interpretations. He has a mighty intellect, but sometimes I cannot read him. He seldom attempts the marriage of
sense with sound, although he shows a spontaneous felicity
in the adaptation of words to ideas and feelings. I wish I had
written his two lines:

> The little more and how much it is,
> The little less and what worlds away.

He has plenty of music in him, but he cannot get it out.'
He would cite *Rabbi Ben Ezra, Death in the Desert, Caliban
upon Setebos, The Englishman in Italy,* and *A Grammarian's
Funeral,* as poems of fine thought, and *Mr Sludge, the Medium*
as an example of exceeding ingenuity of mind. The last, however, he said to Browning, is 'two-thirds too long'.

Tennyson: A Memoir by his Son   1883

SWINBURNE

The charge of obscurity is perhaps of all charges the like-
liest to impair the fame or to imperil the success of a rising or
an established poet. It is as often misapplied by hasty or
ignorant criticism as any other on the roll of accusations;
and was never misapplied more persistently and perversely
than to an eminent writer of our own time. The difficulty
found by many in certain of Mr Browning's works arises from
a quality the very reverse of that which produces obscurity
properly so called. Obscurity is the natural product of turbid

forces and confused ideas; of a feeble and clouded or of a vigorous but unfixed and chaotic intellect. Such a poet as Lord Brooke, for example—and I take George Chapman and Fulke Greville to be of all English poets the two most genuinely obscure in style upon whose works I have ever adventured to embark in search of treasure hidden beneath the dark gulfs and crossing currents of their rocky and weedy waters, at some risk of my understanding being swept away by the ground-swell—such a poet, overcharged with overflowing thoughts, is not sufficiently possessed by any one leading idea, or attracted towards any one central point, to see with decision the proper end and use with resolution the proper instruments of his design. Now if there is any great quality more perceptible than another in Mr Browning's intellect it is his decisive and incisive faculty of thought, his sureness and intensity of perception, his rapid and trenchant resolution of aim. To charge him with obscurity is about as accurate as to call Lynceus purblind or complain of the sluggish action of the telegraphic wire. He is something too much the reverse of obscure; he is too brilliant and subtle for the ready reader of a ready writer to follow with any certainty the track of an intelligence which moves with such incessant rapidity, or even to realize with what spider-like swiftness and sagacity his building spirit leaps and lightens to and fro and backward and forward as it lives along the animated line of its labour, springs from thread to thread and darts from centre to circumference of the glittering and quivering web of living thought woven from inexhaustible stores of his perception and kindled from the inexhaustible fire of his imagination. He never thinks but at full speed; and the rate of his thought is to that of another man's as the speed of a railway to that of a waggon or the speed of a telegraph to that of a railway. It is hopeless to enjoy the charm or apprehend the gist of his writings except with a mind thoroughly alert, an attention awake at all points, a spirit open and ready to be kindled by the contact of the writer's. To do justice to any book which deserves any other sort of justice than that of the fire or the waste-paper basket, it is necessary to read it in the fit frame of mind; and the proper mood in which to study for the first time a book of Mr Browning's is the freshest, clearest, most active mood of the mind in its brightest and keenest hours of work. . . .

George Chapman 1875

. . . this work of exposition by soliloquy and apology by analysis can only be accomplished or undertaken by the genius of a great special pleader, able to fling himself with all his heart and all his brain, with all the force of his intellect and all the strength of his imagination, into the assumed part of his client; to concentrate on the cause in hand his whole power of illustration and illumination, and bring to bear upon one point at once all the rays of his thought in one focus. Apart from this gift of moral imagination, Mr Browning has in the supreme degree the qualities of a great debater or an eminent leading counsel; his finest reasoning has in its expression and development something of the ardour of personal energy and active interest which inflames the argument of a public speaker; we feel, without the reverse regret of Pope, how many a firstrate barrister or parliamentary tactician has been lost in this poet. The enjoyment that his best and most characteristic work affords us is doubtless far other than the delight we derive from the purest and highest forms of lyric and dramatic art; there is a radical difference between the analyst and the dramatist, the pleader and the prophet. It would be clearly impossible for the subtle tongue which can undertake at once the apology and the anatomy of such motives as may be assumed to impel us to support a 'Prince Hohenstiel-Schwangau' on his ways of thought and action, ever to be touched with the fire which turns to a sword or to a scourge the tongue of a poet to whom it is given to utter as from Patmos or from Sinai the word that fills all the heaven of song with the lightnings and thunders of chastisement. But in the place of lyric rapture or dramatic action we may profitably enjoy the unique and incomparable genius of analysis which gives to these special pleadings such marvellous life and interest as no other workman in that kind was ever or will ever again be able to give.

George Chapman 1875

A more significant parallel would be that between Mr
Browning and M. Leconte de Lisle. Each of those great writers
has something great which is wanting to the other: and on
certain points of no small importance they are as far asunder
as the poles; and yet it is impossible to overlook the manifold
and manifest points of absolute spiritual community between
them. One is the latest extant defender of the faith as cast into
the iron mould of creeds whom the roll of philosophic poets
can display to our admiring astonishment: the other is perhaps
the fiercest anti-Christian and anti-Jehovist on all the list of
poetic rebels, excepting neither Shelley nor Leopardi; his
glorious masterpiece of *Cain*, faultless and sublime throughout
the whole long length of its lofty flight as the race of an eagle
with the storm-wind, might seem to a devout spirit to have been
dictated by actual theophobia (not by any means that kind of
fear which has been defined as the beginning of wisdom). And
yet, if he were an English Christian, we cannot but think how
much liker Mr Browning he would be than any other poet;
and how much liker him than any other Mr Browning would
be, if only he were a French antitheist. Both are more unmistakably studious, in a deeper and higher than the usual
sense, than any living poet of equal rank; both have a turn—
though the Englishman has far more than the Frenchman—
for strange byways of tragic and grotesque action or passion,
occult eccentricities of history and great grim freaks of nature,
made worse or better by circumstance and time: no third
hand would have written *Un Acte de Charité* or *The Heretic's
Tragedy*. Mr Browning is by far the greater thinker, the
keener analyst, the deeper student and the higher master of
human science; but M. Leconte de Lisle, at his very highest,
is as much the more poetic poet, the more inspired voice, the
more lyrical and ardent genius. Much as he knows, he knows
much less, no doubt, than Mr Browning; but unquestionably
he can sing much better at his best. On the other hand, though
the poet of Hypatia has all requisite command of august and
manly pathos no less than of spiritual dignity, he has not a
touch of the piercing and overpowering tenderness which
glorifies the poet of Pompilia. Setting aside all irrelevant and
impertinent questions of personal agreement or sympathy

with the spirit or doctrine of either, I should venture to assign
the palm to Mr Browning for depth of pathos and subtlety
of knowledge, to M. Leconte de Lisle for height of spirit and
sublimity of song. Indeed, after Victor Hugo, he is as much
the sublimest as till the appearance of Lord Tennyson's
Rizpah Mr Browning was, also of course after Victor Hugo,
the most pathetic of contemporary poets.

Tennyson and Musset   1880

ANON

The great poets who present the most difficulty are loved by
their students with a passion often in proportion to the
difficulty with which they are approached; and those students
can never for a moment believe that the more popular poet
is worthy to stand beside their own chosen one. Aeschylus and
Euripides, Dante and Tasso, Wordsworth and Scott, Browning
and Tennyson, are instances of the contrast we mean: the first
of each pair is incomparably the higher poet; but the multitude
who read for relaxation and not for study, for facile delight
and not for wise counsel, for titillation of fancy and not for
the calm satisfaction of intellect, will never believe it, nor are
they able to understand or apprehend it. . . .

Mr Tennyson . . . is in no sense dramatic. His great rival,
Mr Browning, has a marvellous power of placing himself
in the position of his heroes . . . It is true they all express
themselves in the words of Browning, and that those words
have a marked idiosyncrasy, but the characters are defined;
there is no confusion of persons, nor do we think for a
moment that in any of his creations the poet is reproducing
himself.

British Quarterly Review   1880

HOPKINS

I will give a glaring example from Browning of false perspective in an image. In his *Instans Tyrannus* he makes the tyrant
say that he found the just man his victim on a sudden shielded
from him by the vault of the sky spreading itself like a great

L

targe over him, 'with the sun's disk for visible boss'. This is monstrous. The vault of heaven is a vault, hollow, concave towards us, convex upwards; it therefore could only defend man on earth against enemies above it, an angry Olympus for instance. And the tyrant himself is inside it, under it, just as much as his victim. The boss is seen from behind, like the small stud of a sleevelink. This comes of frigid fancy with no imagination.

Letter to R. W. Dixon   1881

R. W. DIXON

With what you say of 'false perspective' in Browning, I am inclined to agree—certainly in the instance you give: & I fancy it is a thing not unusual in him. But I sd. hardly accuse him of frigid imagination; or rather, as you have it, 'frigid fancy with no imagination': but perhaps you do not mean this as a general judgment on him. . . .

The Ring and Book seemed to me to shew a failure in Browning's power, which is confirmed by his subsequent productions: & manifests itself in these ways. 1. Loss of form, with every kind of monstrosity. 2. The impotent remarking of particulars: as when he observes that the names of Wiseman, Newman, and Manning all contain the word man. 3. Preaching instead of teaching. Whole pages of the Bk and Ring preach, and there is nothing to be learned out of it. Even in Browning's best work I always had an indefinable feeling that he was not thoroughly educated; i.e. that he had not taken poetry at the highest point at which it had been left by others, and so was, as it were, off the track.

Letter to G. M. Hopkins   1881

HOPKINS

In speaking of 'frigid fancy' I referred to the particular passage only. But Browning has, I think, many frigidities. Any untruth to nature, to human nature, is frigid. Now he has got a great deal of what came in with Kingsley and the Broad

Church school, a way of talking (and making his people talk) with the air and spirit of a man bouncing up from the table with his mouth full of bread and cheese and saying that he meant to stand no blasted nonsense. There is a whole volume of Kingsley's essays which is all a kind of munch and not standing of any blasted nonsense from cover to cover. Do you know what I mean? (17) The *Flight of the Duchess*, with the repetition of 'My friend', is in this vein. Now this is *one* mood or vein of human nature, but they would have it all and look at all human nature through it. And Tennyson in his later works has been 'carried away with their dissimulation.' The effect of this style is a frigid bluster. A true humanity of spirit, neither mawkish on the one hand, nor blustering on the other, is the most precious of all qualities in style, and this I prize in your poems, as I do in Bridges'. After all it is the breadth of his human nature that we admire in Shakespeare.

I read some, not much, of *The Ring and the Book*, but as the tale was not edifying and one of our people, who had been reviewing it, said that further on it was coarser, I did not see, without a particular object, sufficient reason for going on with it. So far as I read I was greatly struck with the skill in which he displayed the facts from different points of view: this is masterly, and to do it through three volumes more shews a great body of genius. I remember a good case of 'the impotent collection of particulars' of which you speak in the description of the market place at Florence where he found the book of the trail: it is a pointless photograph of still life, such as I remember in Balzac, minute upholstery description; only that in Balzac, who besides is writing prose, all tells and is given with a reserve and simplicity of style which Browning has not got. Indeed I hold with the oldfashioned criticism that Browning is not really a poet, that he has all the gifts but the one needful and the pearls without the string; rather one should say nuggets and rough diamonds. I suppose him to resemble Ben Jonson, only that Ben Jonson had more real poetry.

Letters to R. W. Dixon 1881

THE BROWNING SOCIETY

This Society is founded to gather together some, at least, of the many admirers of Robert Browning, for the study and discussion of his works and the publication of Papers on them, and extracts from his works illustrating them. The Society will also encourage the formation of Browning Reading-Clubs, the acting of Browning's dramas by amateur companies, the writing of a Browning Primer, the compilation of a Browning Concordance or Lexicon, and generally the extension of the study and influence of the poet.

Without entering on the vexed question of who is the greatest living poet, Mr Browning's admirers are content to accept the general verdict that he is both one of the greatest, and *the* most thought-full.

Browning Society Papers   1881

As Wilkes was no Wilkeite, I am quite other than a Browningite. But I cannot wish harm to a society of, with a few exceptions, names unknown to me, who are busied about my books so disinterestedly. . . . That there is a grotesque side to the thing is certain; but I have been surprised and touched by what cannot but have been well-intentioned, I think.

Browning, on the Browning Society. Letter to Edmund Yates
1882

PATER

The individual, the personal, the concrete, as distinguished from, yet revealing in its fulness, the general, the universal—that is Mr Browning's chosen subject-matter:—'Every man is for him an epitome of the universe, a centre of creation.' It is always the particular soul, the particular act or episode, as the flower of the particular soul—the act or episode by which its quality comes to the test—in which he interests us. With him it is always 'a drama of the interior, a tragedy or comedy of the soul, to see thereby how each soul becomes conscious of itself.' In the Preface to the later edition of *Sordello*, Mr Browning himself told us that to him little else seems worth study except the development of a soul, the incidents, the story, of that. And in fact, the intellectual public generally agrees with him. It is because he has ministered with such marvellous vigour, and variety, and fine skill to interest, that he is the most modern, to modern people the most important, of poets.

Browning 1887

THE TIMES

It has been Mr Browning's fate to divide the reading world into two hostile camps. There are no lukewarm friends on his side; and from those who have never acquired a taste for the strong wine of his muse it is sometimes difficult to extort recognition of the vigour, the insight, the tenderness, and the variety of intellectual sympathy which characterize the man even if we make abstraction of the poet . . . Those who love the poets of prettiness, of artificial measures, and dainty trifles have at the present day an almost embarrassing wealth of choice. But Mr Browning in his own sphere had no rival and no imitator. No other so boldly faces the problems of life and death, no other like him braces the reader as with the breath of a breeze from the hills, and no other gives like him the assurance that we have to do with a man. His last public words are the fit description of his strenuous attitude through all his literary work:—

'Strive and thrive!' cry 'Speed—fight on, fare ever
There as here!'

Obituary   December 13 1889

SANTAYANA

It is obvious that we are in the presence of a great writer, of a great imaginative force, of a master in the expression of emotion. What is perhaps not so obvious, but no less true, is that we are in the presence of a barbaric genius, of a truncated imagination, of a thought and art inchoate and ill-digested, of a volcanic eruption that tosses itself blindly and ineffectually into the sky. . . .

Browning, who had not had the education traditional in his own country, used to say that Italy had been his university. But it was a school for which he was ill prepared, and he did not sit under its best teachers. For the superficial ferment, the worldly passions, and the crimes of the Italian Renaissance he had a keen interest and intelligence. But Italy has been always a civilized country, and beneath the trappings and suits of civilization which at that particular time it flaunted so gaily, it preserved a civilized heart to which Browning's insight could never penetrate. . . .

For him the crude experience is the only end, the endless struggle the only ideal, and the perturbed 'Soul' the only organ of truth. The arrest of his intelligence at this point, before it has envisaged any rational object, explains the arrest of his dramatic art at soliloquy. His immersion in the forms of self-consciousness prevents him from dramatizing the real relations of men and their thinkings to one another, to Nature, and to destiny. For in order to do so he would have had to view his characters from above (as Cervantes did, for instance), and to see them not merely as they appeared to themselves, but as they appear to reason. This higher attitude, however, was not only beyond Browning's scope, it was positively contrary to his inspiration. . . .

We thus see that Browning's sphere, though more subtle and complex than Whitman's, was still elementary. It lay far below the spheres of social and historical reality in which Shakespeare moved; far below the comprehensive and cosmic sphere of every great epic poet. Browning did not even reach the intellectual plane of such contemporary poets as Tennyson and Matthew Arnold, who, whatever may be thought of their powers, did not study consciousness for itself, but for the sake of its meaning and of the objects which it revealed.

Interpretation of Poetry and Religion 1900

HENRY JAMES

How difficult to banish the idea that Robert Browning would have enjoyed prefiguring and playing with the mystifications, the reservations, even perhaps the slight buzz of scandal, in the Poets' Corner, to which his own obsequies might give rise! Would not his great relish, in so characteristic an interview with his crucible, have been his perception of the bewildering modernness, to much of the society, of the new candidate for a niche? That is the interest and the fascination, from what may be termed the inside point of view, of Mr Browning's having received, in this direction of becoming a classic, the only official assistance that is ever conferred upon English writers.

It is as classics on one ground and another—some members of it perhaps on that of not being anything else—that the numerous assembly in the Abbey holds together, and it is as a tremendous and incomparable modern that the author of *Men and Women* takes his place in it. He introduces to his predecessors a kind of contemporary individualism which surely for many a year they had not been reminded of with any such force. The tradition of the poetic character as something high, detached and simple, which may be assumed to have prevailed among them for a good while, is one that Browning has broken at every turn; so that we can imagine his new associates to stand about him, till they have got used to him, with rather a sense of failing measures. A good many oddities and a good many great writers have been entombed in the Abbey; but none of the odd ones have been so great and none of the great ones so odd. There are plenty of poets whose right to the title may be contested, but there is no poetic head of equal power—crowned and recrowned by almost importunate hands—from which so many people would withhold the distinctive wreath. All this will give the marble phantoms at the base of the great pillars and the definite personalities of the honorary slabs something to puzzle out until, by the quick operation of time, the mere fact of his lying there among the classified and protected makes even Robert

Browning lose a portion of the bristling surface of his actuality.

For the rest, judging from the outside and with his contemporaries, we of the public can only feel that his very modernness—by which we mean the all-touching, all-trying spirit of his work, permeated with accumulations and playing with knowledge—achieves a kind of conquest, or at least of extension, of the rigid pale. We cannot enter here upon any account either of that or of any other element of his genius, though surely no literary figure of our day seems to sit more unconsciously for the painter. The very imperfections of this original are fascinating, for they never present themselves as weaknesses; they are boldnesses and overgrowths, rich roughnesses and humours, and the patient critic need not despair of digging to the primary soil from which so many disparities and contradictions spring. He may finally even put his finger on some explanation of the great mystery, the imperfect conquest of the poetic form by a genius in which the poetic passion had such volume and range. He may successfully say how it was that a poet without a lyre—for that is practically Browning's deficiency: he had the scroll, but not often the sounding strings—was nevertheless, in his best hours, wonderfully rich in the magic of his art, a magnificent master of poetic emotion.

... Just as his great sign to those who knew him was that he was a force of health, of temperament, of tone, so what he takes into the Abbey is an immense expression of life—of life rendered with large liberty and free experiment, with an unprejudiced intellectual eagerness to put himself in other people's place, to participate in complications and consequences; a restlessness of psychological research that might well alarm any pale company for their formal orthodoxies.

But the illustrious whom he rejoins may be reassured, as they will not fail to discover: in so far as they are representative it will clear itself up that, in spite of a surface unsuggestive of marble and a reckless individualism of form, he is quite as representative as any of them. For the great value of Browning is that at bottom, in all the deep spiritual and human essentials, he is unmistakably in the great tradition—is, with all his Italianisms and cosmopolitanisms, all his victimisation by societies organised to talk about him, a magnificent example of the best and least dilettantish English spirit. That constitutes indeed the main chance for his eventual critic, who will have to solve the refreshing problem of how, if subtleties be not what the English spirit most delights in, the author of, for instance, *Any Wife to any Husband* made them his perpetual pasture, and yet remained typically of his race. He was indeed a wonderful mixture of the universal and the alembicated. But he played with the curious and the special, they never submerged him, and it was a sign of his robustness that he could play to the end. His voice sounds loudest, and also clearest, for the things that, as a race, we like best—the fascination of faith, the acceptance of life, the respect for its mysteries, the endurance of its charges, the vitality of the will, the validity of character, the beauty of action, the seriousness, above all, of the great human passion. If Browning had spoken for us in no other way, he ought to have been made sure of, tamed and chained as a classic, on account of the extraordinary beauty of his treatment of the special relation between man and woman. It is a complete and splendid picture of the matter, which somehow places it at the same time in the region of conduct and responsibility. But when we talk of Robert Browning's speaking 'for us' we go to the end of our privilege, we say all. With a sense of security, perhaps even a certain complacency, we leave our sophisticated modern conscience, and perhaps even our heterogeneous vocabulary, in his charge among the illustrious. There will possibly be moments in which these things will seem to us to have widened the allowance, made the high abode more comfortable, for some of those who are yet to enter it.

Browning in Westminster Abbey 1890

Another force pushes its way through the waste and rules the scene, making wrong things right and right things a hundred times more so—that breath of Browning's own particular matchless Italy, which takes us full in the face and remains from the first the felt, rich, coloured air in which we live. The quantity of that atmosphere that he had to give out is like nothing else in English poetry, any more than in English prose, that I recall . . . This straight saturation of our author's, this prime assimilation of the elements for which the name of Italy stands, is a single splendid case, however; I can think of no second one that is not below it—if we take it as supremely expressed in those of his lyrics and shorter dramatic mono- logues that it has most helped to inspire. The Rome and Tuscany of the early 'fifties had become for him so at once a medium, a bath of the senses and perceptions, into which he could sink, in which he could unlimitedly soak, that wherever he might be touched afterwards he gave out some effect of that immersion. This places him to my mind quite apart, makes the rest of our poetic record of a similar experience comparatively pale and abstract. Shelley and Swinburne—to name only his compeers—are, I know, a part of the record; but the author of *Men and Women*, of *Pippa Passes*, of certain of the *Dramatic Lyrics* and other scattered felicities, not only expresses and reflects the matter; he fairly, he heatedly, if I may use such a term, exudes and perspires it. Shelley, let us say in the connexion, is a light, and Swinburne, let us say, a sound; Browning alone of them is a temperature. We feel it, we are in it at a plunge, with the very first pages of the thing before us; to which, I confess, we surrender with a momentum drawn from fifty of their predecessors, pages not less sovereign, elsewhere. . . .

To express his inner self—his outward was a different affair! —and to express it utterly, even if no matter how, was clearly, for his own measure and consciousness of that inner self, to *be* poetic; and the solution of all the deviations and disparities or, speaking critically, monstrosities, in the mingled tissue of this work, is the fact that whether or no by such convulsions of soul and sense life got delivered for him, the garment of life (which for him was poetry and poetry alone) got disposed in its due and adequate multitudinous folds. We move with him but in images and references and vast and far corres- pondences; we eat but of strange compounds and drink but of rare distillations; and very soon, after a course of this, we

feel ourselves, however much or however little to our advantage
we may on occasion pronounce it, in the world of Expression
at any cost. That, essentially, *is* the world of poetry—which
in the cases known to our experience where it seems to us to
differ from Browning's world does so but through this latter's
having been, by the vigour and violence, the bold familiarity,
of his grasp and pull at it, moved several degrees nearer us, so
to speak, than any other of the same general sort with which
we are acquainted; so that, intellectually, we back away from
it a little, back down before it, again and again, as we try to
get off from a picture or a group or a view which is too much
upon us and thereby out of focus. Browning is 'upon' us,
straighter upon us always, somehow, than anyone else of his
race; and we thus recoil, we push our chair back, from the
table he so tremendously spreads, just to see a little better
what is on it. This makes a relation with him that is difficult
to express; as if he came up against us, each time, on the
same side of the street and not on the other side, across the
way, where we mostly see the poets elegantly walk, and where
we greet them without danger of concussion. It is on this
same side, as I call it, on *our* side, on the other hand, that
I rather see our encounter with the novelists taking place;
we being, as it were, more mixed with them, or they at least,
by their desire and necessity, more mixed with us, and our
brush with them, in their minor frenzy, a comparatively muffled
encounter.

The Novel in The Ring and the Book   1912

[Of Browning's relation with the novel, and of James' comment on it here, this incident is illustrative: it is recorded in
Allingham's *Diary* for May 26 1868:

'Lunch at Browning's. Talk runs chiefly on his forthcoming new Poem in many thousand lines. He takes me
into his study, and shows me the original Book, a small
brown quarto, printed account of the trial of Count
Guido, with some original MS. letters, stitched in at the
end pleading for his respite. B. bought it off a stall in

Florence for a few pence. He has told the story over and
over again to various friends; offered it to A. Trollope to
turn into a novel, but T. couldn't manage it; then R.B.
thought, "why not take it myself?" ']

On two or three occasions of the aftertime I was to hear
Browning read out certain of his finest pages, and this exactly
with all the exhibition of point and authority, the expressive
particularisation, so to speak, that I had missed on the part of
the Laureate; an observation through which the author of
Men and Women appeared, in spite of the beauty and force of
his demonstration, as little as possible a Bard. He particularised
if ever a man did, was heterogeneous and profane, composed
of pieces and patches that betrayed some creak of joints, and
addicted to the excursions from which these were brought
home; so that he had to *prove* himself a poet, almost against
all presumptions, and with all the assurance and all the
character he could use. Was not this last in especial, the
character, so close to the surface, with which Browning fairly
bristled, what was most to come out of his personal delivery
of the fruit of his genius? It came out almost to harshness;
but the result was that what he read showed extraordinary
life. During that audition at Aldworth the question seemed on
the contrary not of life at all—save, that is, of one's own;
which was exactly not the question. With all the resonance of
the chant, the whole thing was yet *still*, with all the long swing
of its motion it yet remained where it was—heaving doubtless
grandly enough up and down and beautiful to watch as
through the superposed veils of its long self-consciousness.
By all of which I don't mean to say that I was not, on that day
at Aldworth, thoroughly reconciled to learning what a Bard
consisted of; for that came as soon as I had swallowed my own
mistake of having supposed Tennyson something subtly other
than one.

The Middle Years   1917

[This passage follows directly on the description of Tennyson's
reading of *Locksley Hall*, given on pp. 288-91 above]

And yet, for all that, one needs only to re-read his work, only to feel its matchless energy, its various power, its swift and sudden beauty, close in upon the mind and call out with undiminished keenness the old responses; no less unmistake-able, in the end, than its power and virtue is the sense that it has not in fact developed in harmony with itself. There was an undertow the effect of which can be discerned here and there throughout his work, and which finally mastered and re-directed the conflicting impulse that was surely more thoroughly and originally his own. Browning had little to fear from any confessed hostility of fate; but fate had planned a more ingenious device than an open attack. This prodigal, restless, inquisitive mind, passionately awake, instantly appre-ciative of the gifts of life, was thrown into a time when appre-ciation, curiosity, creative energy, could indeed find as ample material and as free a play as at any moment in history, but always on a condition liable in the circumstances to be very dangerous to them, The condition was that they should justify themselves to the age's rather vulgar conception of moral and material usefulness—a condition, as it is not now the mode to question, entirely rational in itself, but which presupposes a more disciplined self-criticism than was abroad at that remarkable moment.

Browning, while it would have been impossible for open pressure to have deflected him from what he proposed to do, was by the very nature of his endowment particularly exposed to the invisible pressure of the moral atmosphere in which he might find himself. All his affinities brought him out into the open. Far from taking shelter from life, he had not even his back to the wall; he stood forward with life all round him. He flung his mind wide to it and absorbed it, delighted with its staring colours, fascinated by its grotesque shapes and con-trasts. These he could deal with, we know how consummately; but with the rest he appropriated moral and intellectual standards which needed a different treatment, one which it was not in him to give. He could not criticise them; that is why we are able to say that the first impulse we distinguished, the impulse to fasten, in an ecstasy of perception, on things seen, and to represent them in all their sharpness, was more truly characteristic. When he became a moralist he could only bring to the task the same energy; and all his acuteness in disentangling the moods of men and women, all his quickness in seizure and presentation, availed nothing beside the fact that, though he could dramatise their application, he could not really criticise the standards themselves which were offered to him. Anarchy in the ideal world troubled him as little (or rather pleased him as much) as the fantastic jumble of objects displayed in the market-place . . . So in the world of ideas his delight was in the process itself, in the mercurial dance of thought, till thought will accept no other fulfilment than to go dancing on for ever. Thus Browning could be satisfied with the self-stultifying conclusion that energy was its own end and conflict its own eternal reward. He could celebrate the antagonism between good and evil without caring for the implication that, if it is the fight itself which is the one essential, the names of the antagonists could be exchanged without spoiling the moral. . . .

. . . the age to which he was born was certainly not an age of exhausted vitality or starved refinements. . . . At any rate it amassed its abundance of impressions and ideas with the stout appetite of heroes. But it was not an adventurous time, and it strikes us rather as jovially or heavily feasting on the profusion spread out before it, than as dashing irrepressibly forth to discover and explore. We feel that in the Elizabethan consciousness, for example, there was a temper, nervous and robust at the same time, which is not to be found either in the robust self-satisfactions or in the nervous self-denunciations of the middle decades of the nineteenth century. Genius was lavished upon those decades as it has only been at the most magnificent moments in the history of art; and if, in the curious loss of the sense of formal beauty, it could be little trained in habits of discipline, that again could be matched at such moments. It is not the pervading want of discipline, but the pervading want of enterprise, which is of importance when we consider the effects of his time on Browning. It was not in his nature to sit still while good things were set before him. He would be out, rummaging, ransacking, probing, long before the board was spread. But he finds himself, as he turns over the glittering heaps, in a world which, in imposing the demand that things should be useful, gets itself into a false position by adding that they must be definitely and patently useful, and that too this very minute; in other words, the moral of any artistic transaction must be immediately definable and applicable, it being oddly assumed that this aspect of the case, the one demanding for true judgment the widest knowledge and synthetic power, was just that which anybody could ban or bless offhand. . . .

. . . his lightning power of assimilation, doubled with his power of doing without any keenly intimate life of his own, could not help him to the judging and appraising of values, if he should wish to proceed beyond the mere representation of them. And here comes in that unsuspected pressure of the atmosphere in which he lived. I am not, of course, alluding to any direct demand from imperious auditors, for we are still at the time when 'he who praised and read and wrote Was apt to find himself the self-same me'; but to the diffused spirit which was just the one thing he could not see, and which, therefore, had him at discretion. It is as though the injunction to moralise as well as dramatise, to reason as well as represent, were conveyed to him in his sleep, so that he woke up thinking it was his own idea; where, if it had been offered him openly, he would simply have seized and dramatised the demand itself. Add to this that the spirit, as we have said, was decidedly unenterprising, easily satisfied, and as easily bullied; and it will be seen that it was no happy influence for a dramatist. As it was, Browning led it a pretty dance, and made it some-what breathlessly recognise that at any rate all its first judg-ments were wrong. But he was in the position of his own Blougram, offering arguments good enough for his critic, and lacking the stimulus of a capable opponent, who would not be bewildered by being caught out on separate points, and who might have demanded a more embracing synthesis. . . .

That which surely, whether consciously or no, turned him from the set-play form to the dramatic monologue with which he had started, was his lack of power to grasp a character, as opposed to his immense and varied power to grasp a mood. It is not for nothing that in most of his plays unity of time is so closely observed, the connection being often practically continuous, or at most contained within a limited number of hours. This device does not, of course, in true drama, meet the difficulty of the writer who sees his personages only in the light of the particular situation, but it disguises it. Character is character and mood is mood, however short or long the exposure; and tragic drama absolutely demands the figure in the round, even though we may immediately be concerned with but one aspect of it . . . Just as, speaking generally, we find him perceiving like an angel and rationalising like the very human Briton he was; so, on that side of character-drawing which is analysis, he cannot be surpassed for certainty and swiftness of touch, while, when it comes to the synthetic grasp of the myriad fragments, he fails us . . . if again and again we feel that what the action lacks is not beauty or order, but simply weight—if we enjoy watching these spiritual intrigues disentangled and forget all about the human beings who are doing it—that is because Browning himself has seen the innumerable ways in which they would act and react upon each other so much more clearly than he has seen their own substance. . . .

Not the evasion of life, which somehow claims us again soon enough, but the translation of the whole of it to the level of passion—that was Browning's achievement, and it has almost been his alone. No one else, not Shakespeare himself, has written poetry of this order in an atmosphere where life— life which, whatever happens, has to be lived from day to day —can be sustained and continued. Nothing in the necessities of ordinary existence is contradicted by these poems at their greatest intensity. . . . Browning's grave and searching realism evades no difficulties here, and never condescends to the idea that beauty is exquisite or pleasure rare if either is thought of as separable from the sum of life.

Thus it is, then, that he is able to linger among the emotional refinements and ingenuities which he so loves to explore, without forfeiting in their minuteness the ardour and glow of passionate beauty. His passion is living and enduring because it has understood that nothing can endure—however brilliant its moment of climax—which is discontinuous with all else. There are features in his work, obvious enough, which have suggested to some an affinity between his treatment of these themes and that which is to be seen in the lyrical poems of Donne; and indeed, if we must have an antetype in literature to Browning's lyric, it is there if anywhere that we shall find it. But Donne, precisely, bringing the same fire to the same intricacies of experience, shows only too often how easily the simplicity of true passion may be damaged in the quest for an ever closer notation of the labyrinth. Browning, with a brain far inferior, indeed, for keenness and force, could yet indulge to all lengths its subtlety of perception, without losing his relation to reality, because he had once for all achieved simplicity first. And if it was this that gave him his control over complexity, it is to this, and to nothing less, that is due the entirely unique savour of his style. Browning's handling of words, in the best of his lyric poetry, becomes more and more of a wonder, the deeper they fix themselves in the mind; and we end—where we do not perhaps begin—by discovering, under their appearance of informality, how instantly sensitive they prove themselves to his touch. Their response is so quick that the movement by which they slip into their places escapes us; they do not make the gesture, of one sort or another, that in other writers enables us to watch the process of expression. It is an artless judgment which concludes that with Browning there was no process, that language was an obstacle to his bursting thought, which he broke down unscrupulously, careless so long as his thought got through. Language, rather, obeyed the candour of his passion, and answered by yielding him effects of beauty which, when we look at the extreme simplicity of the means, it seems impossible to analyse. . . .

. . . The poems that last, the poems that we never exhaust, seem mysteriously to have caught a note of style for which no precept can be laid down, but which can be described by saying that it possesses the fringe of values, the associated harmonics, of the *spoken* word. Between writing and speaking (by which, it should possibly be noted, I do not at all mean

oratory or recitation) there lies a chasm which tempts an
effort to sound and measure it. Mere differences between the
formal and the informal, the plain and the coloured, are
negligible when it comes to the discrimination between the
moral and emotional values of a word picked up from a
written page, and those which it bears when a voice utters it as
the immediate symbol proposed by the brain. These values
Browning incessantly captures for the written word; if a
quotation is desired it might be any of a hundred, and may be
this:

> But he looked upon the city, every side,
>   Far and wide,
> All the mountains topped with temples, all the glades'
>   Colonnades,
> All the causeys, bridges, aqueducts—and then,
>   All the men!

'All the men!' It is not a line in a written poem; it is a
remark, suddenly dropped to us by an urgent and present
imagination, to which the listener reacts as instinctively as to
an unexpected voice.

                                        Robert Browning 1912

Appendix

1. (*p. 20*) Young's *Night Thoughts*, illustrated by Blake.

2. (*p. 21*) It is doubtful whether this is quite what Wordsworth said. The *Diary*, in which Crabb Robinson recorded the conversation at the time, gives this version:

> I read Wordsworth some of Blake's poems; he was pleased with some of them, and considered Blake as having the elements of poetry a thousand times more than either Byron or Scott. (*Diary*, 1812)

In the same conversation, Wordsworth had suggested that Byron, not Blake, was rather mad, like so many aristocrats, hereditarily.

3. (*p. 21*) 'Deserts' instead of 'forests' in this line is not found in any of the versions of the poem from Blake's own hand. It seems to have been invented by Lamb, who was no doubt quoting from memory.

4. (*p. 113*) It is remarkable that Crabb Robinson, a very intelligent and sensitive reader, should have picked out precisely the two poems which struck Herzen as specially Byronic forty years later, see pp. 130–2

5. (*p. 138*) See Arnold's essay, *The Function of Criticism at the Present Time*.

6. (*p. 143*) In 1820, Byron wrote in a letter to Murray: 'The styles of the day are *all bombastic* (I don't except my *own*—no one has done more through negligence to corrupt the language).'

7. (*p. 170*) For the metaphysical reason of this, as, indeed, furnishing the key to all Shelley's poetry, see an article called 'Two Kinds of Poetry', in the *Monthly Repository* for 1833 (vol. vii, p. 714), one of the most luminous and profound specimens of philosophical criticism we have yet met with, and which should be consulted for its own sake.

8. (*p. 170*) The same with Dante's allusion to the west, '*la dove*

339

'*l sol tace*.' We may admit that there where the sun is silent he is reposing, and he reposes in the west, but it is too remote.

9. (*p. 202*) Easy to make fun of. See Congreve, *Way of the World* III, iii. 'Smoke the boots, the boots.'

10. (*p. 215*) Readers to whom this objection may seem fanciful should remember that it is precisely in matters such as this that contemporary opinion is always liable to be sounder than the opinion of later centuries; so much turns on the immediate climate of opinion, and on the evanescent flavour of words. They might also remind themselves of Bernard Shaw's one contribution to the criticism of Keats:

'. . . Keats achieved the very curious feat of writing one poem of which it may be said that if Karl Marx can be imagined as writing a poem instead of a treatise on Capital, he would have written *Isabella*. The immense indictment of the profiteers and exploiters with which Marx has shaken capitalistic civilization to its foundations, even to its overthrow in Russia, is epitomized in . . . [Here follow the three stanzas to which the above review refers.] Everything that the Bolshevik means and feels when he uses the fatal epithet 'bourgeois' is expressed forcibly, completely and beautifully in those three stanzas, written half a century before the huge tide of middle-class optimism and complacency began to ebb in the wake of the planet Marx. Nothing could well be more literary than the wording: it is positively euphuistic. But it contains all the Factory Commission Reports that Marx read, and that Keats did not read, because they were not written in his time. And so Keats is among the prophets with Shelley and, had he lived, would no doubt have come down from *Hyperions* and *Endymions* to tin tacks as a very full-blooded revolutionary.'

The John Keats Memorial Volume 1921

11. (*p. 219*) It is interesting to note that Horne was quoting from memory. 'Immortals' in this line should be 'eternals'. Perhaps he had not perceived how much Shelley might have preferred the second word to the first.

12. (*p. 231*) Intoning these lines became a regular Victorian ritual. Burne-Jones, for example, once said of poetry: 'What I most love are little things, not many lines long, that make me tingle every time I say them—whereof the crown and ensample are those piercing ones, "Magic casements etc."' (*Memorials*, 1895.) And Theodore Watts-Dunton was described, in old age, thus: 'His body had aged, his voice had shrunk; but once launched into the

subject of literature . . . he seemed immediately to become a young man. When quoting his favourite passage from Keats, his voice would falter with emotion "Charm'd magic casements etc." These lines he regarded as the finest in English poetry.'

13. (*p. 248*) The lumbering irony perhaps needs the help of two comments by Keats' publisher, John Taylor. In 1822, he wrote to Clare: 'of Keats' *Poems* there have never yet been five hundred sold.' And in 1833—the year in which this review was written—he told a friend: 'I should like to print a complete Edition of Keats' *Poems*, with several of his *Letters*, but the world cares nothing for him. I fear that 200 copies would not sell.'

14. (*p. 284*) The dislike between Swinburne and Tennyson was nothing if not reciprocal, and perhaps it is only fair to mention a curiously apposite comment of Tennyson's, made to Allingham when the gentlemen had retired for their smoke after dinner at Faringford: 'T.'s den at top of house; smoking,—Public Schools, Charterhouse, etc., effect of a few bad boys on the rest—Tupper—Swinburne.'*Diary*, London 1907, p. 117.

15. (*p. 286*) In another place, in the first leader on the front page, the same journal had strongly protested against the pessimism of the poem, and had urged that its view of England was not justified by the facts. Mr Gladstone agreed, and a month later published in *The Nineteenth Century* an obliquely worded, very statesmanlike protest to the same effect. It surveyed the achievements of Whig legislation, and ended thus: 'the minutes spent upon this roughly drawn paper will possibly not have been wasted, if it shall have helped to show that the country is still young as well as old, and that in these latest days it has not been unworthy of itself. Justice does not require, nay rather she forbids, that the Jubilee of the Queen be marred by tragic tones.' Tennyson had drawn blood—but it was one of the very few occasions when he did so.

16. (*p. 293*) 'Tennyson read Baudelaire's *Fleurs du Mal*, and thought him "a kind of moralist," though his subjects, he allowed, are shocking. I could not agree (and had, I think, studied Baudelaire more closely); he seems to me to take pleasure in seeing evil committed, and also in seeing evil-doing punished—a devil rather than a moralist.' *Diary*, W. Allingham.

17. (*p.323*) If the reader cares to glance at the passages from Kingsley's critical essays on pp. 132-4 and pp. 172-4, he will probably have no difficulty in seeing what Hopkins meant.

Index of Poets
(Volumes 1 and 2)

Index of Critics
(Volumes 1 and 2)